Additional praise for *Investigator and Fraud Fighter Guidebook: Operation War Stories*

"This guidebook is a game changer! Readers will learn to conduct investigations like never before. Charles Piper's decades of real-life investigative war stories provide insight all investigators and future investigators will appreciate."
—**Scott Baldwin, Licensed Private Investigator and Owner of Advanced Investigative & Screening Solutions, Houston, Texas**

"I sure hope the bad guys don't ever get hold of this. Charles Piper has written the book on fraud—and how to expose it. A tough, thorough investigator, Piper details how to peel back layers of financial schemes. His informal style is engaging. Each chapter includes personal anecdotes that provide rich context for cases that don't always go right. It should be required reading for law enforcement and financial-crimes examiners."
—**Robert Anglen, Investigative Reporter, *The Arizona Republic*, 12 News (KPNX)**

"[*Investigator and Fraud Fighter Guidebook: Operation War Stories*] by Mr. Piper is very informative and will add great insight to fraud investigators. His stories and how he worked through problems that all fraud fighters will encounter will give both newcomers and old time investigators encouragement and are thought provoking. An excellent book."
—**Durand Ferguson, CFE, Senior Audit Advisor, Memphis, Tennessee**

"A good investigator is always learning. A great investigator uses his experience to help others learn. In this book, Charles E. Piper, CFE, shares a lifetime of experience to provide a critical framework for approaching investigative work and understanding the managerial environment. Whether new on the job or a veteran of many years of service, this is a book that every investigator must read."
—**Gilbert R. Jimenez, Licensed Private Investigator; Principal, Insight Investigation Services of Chicago, IL; Attorney; Former Deputy Inspector General, Illinois**

Investigator and Fraud Fighter Guidebook

Investigator and Fraud Fighter Guidebook

Operation War Stories

Charles E. Piper, CFE

WILEY

Library of Congress Cataloging-in-Publication Data:

Piper, Charles E., 1957–
    Investigator and fraud fighter guidebook: operation war stories / Charles E. Piper.
       pages cm
    Includes index.
    ISBN 978-1-118-87117-1 (hardback)—ISBN 978-1-118-87847-7 (ebk)—
ISBN 978-1-118-87850-7 (ebk)   1. Criminal investigation.   2. Investigations.   I. Title.
    HV8073.P565 2014
    363.25—dc23

                                                                          2013046820

Printed in the United States of America

10 9 8 7 6 5 4 3 2 1

Contents

Preface

Growing up on the South Side of Chicago in the early 1960s through mid-1970s was a lot of fun. Actually, I don't think I ever really grew up. Having worked in the field of law enforcement and investigations for approximately 35 years (spanning from the late 1970s through current day), I've been able to combine two of my favorite things (and even got/get paid for it): having fun (while being daring) and catching bad guys.

I'm not quite sure if my career choice was more influenced by reading superhero comic books in the local barber shop as a kid or just by having a general dislike for bullies and people who harm others. Even as a youngster riding around on my bike with baseball cards held with clothespins flapping through the tire spokes, I had great admiration for law enforcement officers: specifically the patrol officers of the Chicago Police Department. Back then there were two large burly cops in every squad car and only one blue light on the roof. There were no cell phones in those days; but police call boxes with telephones inside were located on select street corners. Over the years many changes have been made in police work, but the ability to conduct thorough and complete investigations has always been an important part of preventing, stopping, and solving criminal activity.

After joining the profession myself and since becoming a private investigator, I've successfully completed investigations from coast to coast and even a few in Europe. After all these years, and having worked in so many different geographical locations, some say that I have more stories than Sears Tower. (Yeah, I know they renamed it; but it's still Sears Tower to me.)

The stories accumulated while on the job are usually referred to as war stories, and when told in the right environment, at the right time, those stories have often helped other cops, investigators, and fraud fighters become more effective in their profession. Sometimes they've also resulted in a lot of laughs.

The intent of this book is to provide current and future investigators, as well as fraud fighters, with my personal professional insight and descriptions of investigative practices, methodologies, techniques, and approaches utilized to conduct thorough and complete investigations. The method of communication will include the telling of many war stories.

I've been extremely fortunate during most of my life because most often I've been able to do whatever I wanted to do. The only exceptions were when I was in grade school and in high school; but even then I often did what I wanted (much to the dismay of my parents and teachers).

I got my start in law enforcement in the U.S. Army's Military Police (MP) Corps progressing through the ranks and serving as an MP officer, a squad leader, and an MP investigator. I also worked on the U.S. Army's Criminal Investigation Command's Drug Suppression Team. After seven years in the Army, I became a uniformed city police officer and then a supervisory detective while also going to college full time. After earning my bachelor's degree in criminology, I served for over 20 years as a federal special agent—criminal investigator. My office assignments included Memphis, Tennessee; Orlando, Florida; and Las Vegas, Nevada. During my career I've conducted investigations from coast to coast (from Los Angeles, California, to Washington, DC, and from North Dakota to Texas). At the time of this writing, I am a licensed private investigator, consultant, trainer, and a Certified Fraud Examiner.

Because of my childhood background, training, experience, use of appropriate tools and resources, and sometimes a little luck, I've often solved cases that many thought were unsolvable. I have frequently linked criminal activity that was officially reported, not reported, and sometimes not even previously known to have occurred. Over the years, I've also implemented measures and made recommendations to deter and prevent future occurrences of wrongdoing and criminal activity. I've been fortunate to have led federal investigative task forces and worked jointly with some of the finest and best trained investigators in the United States, including those from the Federal Bureau of Investigation (FBI); the Bureau of Alcohol, Tobacco, Firearms and Explosives (ATF); U.S. Immigration and Customs Enforcement (ICE); U.S. Postal Inspection Service; numerous federal Offices of Inspector General (OIG); the U.S. military investigative agencies; and many others. While in Germany, serving as a U.S. Army MP officer, I also had the opportunity to work a few times with the German polizei (police), who are some of the best-trained police officers in the world.

Over the years, I have provided formal and informal training to numerous law enforcement officers and investigators. My teaching objectives are for those individuals to become as effective as possible in their professions. I also want them to have fun when doing their jobs and to be able to go home at the end of their shifts unharmed (give or take a few scrapes and bruises).

Some of the best training received is not in a classroom; it's through work completed in the field. Sometimes investigative successes are preceded by making mistakes—sometimes huge ones! In fact, over the years, I think I have become a self-educated expert at knowing what not to do! Therefore, when training others (as in this book), I make it a point not only to teach how to do things correctly but also how *not* to do things.

It is usually wiser to learn from others' trial-and-error experiences than trying to learn everything for yourself. I hope this book serves as a reference guide for many investigators and fraud fighters across the globe to conduct more thorough and complete investigations.

Many different approaches, methods, and steps can be utilized when conducting investigations, and they are usually left to the discretion of the investigator (unless their boss is a micromanager). This book provides investigators and fraud fighters with personal insight not collectively provided in other books, manuals, or training classes. I hope it helps new investigators and fraud fighters get off to good starts and helps seasoned investigators become even better at their jobs.

CAUTION: *Readers should be aware that this book contains war stories and other information that is sometimes humorous and enlightening and may include more than a touch of sarcasm.*

I hope that readers don't consider the stories offensive (don't worry—the language is clean). This book also occasionally ridicules past and present investigative and supervisory strategies, methodologies, and practices often utilized by others. In my opinion, some of the best investigative successes and war stories come from rocking the boat, traveling the path less traveled, following instincts, and occasionally being a bit of a maverick.

In an effort to avoid any finger pointing at any particular federal investigative agencies, most often I refer to investigative agencies generically, as federal investigative agencies. However, occasionally I mention the actual agencies or organizations—especially when praise is warranted. When referring to supervisory personnel in this writing I will often use male pronouns but I am not necessarily referring to either sex.

Large investigative agencies often call proactive investigative activity an, "Operation" when the effort is directed at specific targets/causes with specific objectives. Usually those operations are conducted covertly or semicovertly (at least in the early stages). Investigative operations typically have (somewhat related) catchy-sounding names or phrases that the investigative agency usually enjoys flaunting to the media at or near the conclusion of the investigations.

Sometimes those well-intended operations become more of an embarrassment, not only to the participating investigative agencies but to the entire U.S. Government. For example: Between 2006 and 2011, the ATF ran an undercover operation named Operation Fast and Furious. This was a gunwalking sting operation in Arizona in which the ATF purposely allowed weapons to be illegally sold, hoping the guns could be tracked to Mexican drug cartel leaders. The intent of the operation was to stop or slow the flow of firearms into Mexico. It's been reported that during the operation, about 2,000 firearms were sold but less than half that amount were recovered. Many ATF field agents and others questioned the tactics used during operation. Reportedly some of the guns tracked by the ATF were later found at crime scenes on both sides of the border and where a U.S. Border Patrol Agent was killed. Mexican authorities have said that some of these guns were found at crime scenes where numerous Mexican civilians were killed or maimed.

On a more positive note, a press release described a 2012 FBI undercover operation called Operation Card Shop, which resulted in 24 arrests in 13 countries. The operation targeted "carding" crimes in which crooks used the Internet to exploit or traffic in bank account and personal identification of victims as well as stolen credit card information.

Police officers, investigators, and fraud fighters across the globe who conduct extremely thorough and complete investigations end up with lots of their own war stories. It is my hope that this book will assist investigators in accomplishing their objectives.

NOTE: Investigators and fraud fighters should consult legal counsel and/or agency policies and procedures before considering or implementing any investigative activity. Always follow all applicable international, federal, state, and other laws, and rules before considering or conducting any investigative activities.

Acknowledgments

T his book would never have been possible if the U.S. Army had not given me an opportunity to enlist in August 1976. Thanks to a few high-ranking Army leaders (Chief Warrant Officer "Chief" Moore, First Sergeant "Top" Chester Baker, and a few others), I was given an opportunity to pursue my law enforcement and investigative dreams and started accumulating many of the war stories shared in this book. None of us knew at the time that I'd later serve over 30 years in law enforcement and investigations. I am grateful to those and other leaders who gave me the chance to serve in law enforcement.

I learned from, worked with, and teamed with countless superb military police officers, investigators, city cops, detectives, federal agents, and fraud fighters as we accomplished our mutual goals of catching bad guys and stopping criminal activity.

I was fortunate to have served under many outstanding law enforcement supervisors including but not limited to: Randy Cook, Tom Bonnar, and the late Don Mancuso. By far the very best and most effective law enforcement and investigative supervisor I ever worked for was Mr. Richard Messersmith. He served the United States of

America well for over 40 years and it was always a pleasure working for and with him. He always led by example. Under his leadership, I pursued and accomplished goals even I did not think were possible.

I'm grateful for having the opportunities to have worked closely with some of the finest federal prosecutors across the country including: Blaine Welsh, Roger Wenthe, Paul Padda, Crane Pomerantz, Nancy Jones, Wendy Goggin, Bonnie Glober, Doug Chavis, Whitney Schmidt, Tony Peluso, Jay Hoffer, Adelaide Few, Sid Alexander, and many others.

Some Chicago cops with whom I interacted before joining the Army deserve my gratitude. Sometimes just shooting the bull with them made a difference. Though they didn't know it at the time, they undoubtedly inspired me and many others to join the law enforcement/investigative profession.

Officer Frank Serpico, an honest cop from the New York City Police Department, became an idol of mine before I even entered the law enforcement–investigative profession. In 1973, I saw a movie made about his law enforcement career titled *Serpico*, starring Al Pacino. I watched the movie again about 34 years later when I was fighting internal obstructions and hindrances and trying to conduct an honest investigation that the alleged good guys did not want completed. Much to their dismay, I completed the investigation anyway.

The street smarts I learned and applied to my investigative approaches were mostly acquired by hanging out with some good (and not always good) guys and gals on the South Side of Chicago before joining the Army. Somehow we survived our crazy escapades and went on to live productive lives.

I'm grateful to Ted Williams, the late Major League Baseball Hall of Famer (and last Major Leaguer to hit over .400), for his support and encouragement during one of my first professional writings.

Special thanks to the Association of Certified Fraud Examiners (ACFE) and its fine staff of professionals (particularly: Dr. Joseph Wells, CFE, CPA; James Ratley, CFE; Dick Carozza, CFE; Laura Hymes, CFE; and Cora Bullock). The ACFE gave me my first opportunities to write about my fraud-fighting and investigative approaches in the ACFE's *Fraud Magazine* and in another anti-fraud book. The positive feedback received from readers convinced me to write this book.

The new professionals I've begun working with since starting my own company also deserve a special thanks. They include attorneys, paralegals, administrative personnel, business owners, executives and others, and my fellow private investigators. There was a big learning curve going from serving as a federal criminal investigator to a serving as a civilian private investigator and consultant.

Many family members inspired me to join the law enforcement–investigative profession. One of my grandfathers was a persistent and detail-oriented investigative auditor for the state of Illinois. My other grandfather was a brave and daring Chicago fireman who left behind a couple of fireman's badges after he died (which as a kid I pretended were detective badges). One of my uncles (Cal) proudly served during World War II and later became a metropolitan cop. My older brother (Ed) enlisted during the Vietnam War, became a city cop, earned his master's degree, and has headed security of large organizations. Once I saw how my older brother made it, I just kind of followed his personal and professional growth road map. Ed has always encouraged me and others to pursue our dreams and goals. He's a patriotic professional and genuine good guy.

My wife and daughters had to put up with a lot of the hardships that went along with serving in my chosen profession, which included a few moves. (But there are worse places to get transferred to than Orlando, Florida, and Las Vegas, Nevada.) They also had to bear with the transition of my going from being a senior federal agent to starting a new business in West Tennessee as a private investigator, consultant, and trainer. None of that was easy, and I'm sure they have some war stories of their own. My wife, who is also my best friend, has always encouraged me and supported my personal and professional decisions.

Of course, this book would just be words on my laptop computer if not for the great assistance of Sheck Cho, executive editor of this book's publisher, John Wiley & Sons. His work ethic and professionalism are second to none. Special thanks to Mr. Cho, John Wiley & Sons, and their professional staff including Helen Cho and Natasha Andrews-Noel.

Last and by no means least, I'd like to thank the readers of this book. I hope my shared experiences will benefit you and others for many years to come.

Chapter 1

The Successful Investigator

"Some investigators have 20 years of experience; others have one year of experience 20 times."

–Senior federal agent

War Story 1.1

During the later years of my federal law enforcement career (2006–2008), I was investigating several high-ranking U.S. military generals and other military officers for allegedly applying undue influence on lower-ranking government contracting officials to circumvent the contract award process. As a result of their influence, many government contracts worth several millions of dollars were awarded to favored contractors (including retired

1

military officers' companies) sometimes at highly inflated prices, and often they were awarded without required competition.

The assigned federal prosecutor was also an officer in the military reserves. During the investigation, the prosecutor surprisingly ordered me to stop conducting interviews, stop writing reports, and stop analyzing other improperly awarded government contracts. My own supervisor, who was also an officer in the military reserves, took things a step further and ordered me to completely close the investigation!

As implied in the preface of this book, I'm a bit of a maverick—especially when it allows for the opportunity for good to triumph over evil. So despite my instructions, I just kept right on investigating, conducting interviews, writing reports, and examining other government contracts. In the end, I obtained evidence indicating that some of the highest-ranking U.S. military generals and other high-profile officers should have been considered for courts martial (military criminal trials). My final draft investigative report, approximately 275 pages, provided clear and detailed descriptions of the investigative results including a required evidence section.

So what happened? My final draft report was altered. (Some might call it "edited," but there's a big difference.) Before my report was finalized, critical information was completely removed, including the entire evidence section. The final version of my report was reduced to approximately 250 pages and made to look as if the highest senior military officers (four-star generals) had done nothing that warranted consideration for criminal prosecution. That was in complete contrast to what the evidence indicated and in complete contrast to what I wrote in my draft report!

In addition, in my final draft report I stated that the investigation was not yet complete because more interviews and re-interviews needed to be conducted. That statement was completely removed before the report was finalized. Consequently, the final "approved" report gave the false impression that the investigation was 100 percent complete.

NOTE: Yes, I did notify senior government officials about what transpired, but they failed or refused to respond. As a result, I learned firsthand the meaning of the term "good ole boys' network."

The moral of the story is that even the best investigators in the world cannot control the outcome of every investigation. In all probability, most other investigators will never encounter the obstacles, hindrances, and roadblocks imposed on my efforts during and after that investigation. But if conducting investigations is your chosen profession, you'd better be prepared for some occasional shenanigans by others (including the "good guys") that you will not be able to control. What others do before, during, and after you complete your investigation may very well affect the outcome of the investigation.

The Basics

Before embarking on this unique voyage to learn how to become a more successful investigator, it is important to have a basic understanding of the meaning of those two words and how they relate to each other. Sounds pretty simple, right? I can just about guarantee you that many investigators who have received less-than-perfect scores on their annual job performance ratings would opine that their own definitions of the word "success" often differs greatly from their superiors' definitions. This chapter elaborates on the meanings of these words: investigator, investigation, and success.

Investigators

Investigators, like other professionals, must have certain characteristics, traits, and skills to be successful at their chosen profession. An investigator must:

- Possess integrity (be honest).
- Have certain job skills (acquired through training and/or experience).

- Have knowledge of many aspects of law (e.g., knowledge of others' right to privacy, the rules of evidence, and the elements of criminal offenses, etc.).
- Be dedicated to the job (willing to go beyond the call of duty).
- Be persistent (not willing to give up just because the going gets tough).
- Be self-motivated (don't need someone else telling them what to do or when to do it).
- Be resourceful (maximize the use of resources and be cost conscious where possible).

Investigators should also have other skills, including good planning, organizational, and communications skills (oral and written). It also helps to be creative and clever. Many of the skill sets needed to be an effective investigator are obtainable in a classroom or in the field; however, a few of these characteristics (e.g., integrity, dedication, and persistence) often are instilled in some people early in their lives; in others, never at all. I don't mind saying that the U.S. Army taught me the importance of persistence. The military teaches troops to never give up, no matter what. A persistent investigator is a very valuable commodity.

Having passion for your work is critical to enjoying the job. No matter what your profession, if you enjoy your work, the job really isn't about the paycheck; it's about the pursuit and accomplishment of the goal(s). Having passion for catching bad guys, righting wrongs, pursuing justice, and helping others can make it fun to go to work every day. That's why I say I've been lucky; I've always gotten to do what I wanted.

I once asked a professional baseball scout what he looked for when evaluating young prospects to be considered for baseball contracts. He replied, "What we look for is speed. We can teach players everything else, but we can't teach them speed."

If You Have the PIG, You Have It Made

Along the baseball scout's lines, in my opinion the three most important characteristics, skills, attributes, or traits that a good investigator (or any other professional) can have include: passion, integrity, and grit

(PIG). Grit might be described as the willingness to persevere while pursuing long-term goals despite unfavorable odds, despite the naysayers, and despite obstacles and hindrances. *"Passion, integrity, and grit—if you have the PIG, you have it made."*

Obviously a listing of useful characteristics, skills, or traits of a good investigator (especially a fraud investigator) could take several pages to complete. "Street smarts" are invaluable in the investigative field but not usually a requirement to become an investigator (sometimes I think they should be). A fraud investigator's skill sets should also include being computer literate, logical, and analytical. He or she also needs to be pretty good at math. Perhaps every investigator should possess a strong sense of curiosity. But an investigator does not necessarily have to be good at everything to be effective. Knowing your own limitations as well as having a willingness to learn and improve makes all the difference.

War Story 1.2

When I was a rookie federal agent, my agency required that a few other agents and I take aptitude tests to determine if we would be good candidates to become technical equipment agents for our offices. The tech equipment we'd use would include hidden electronic audio recorders and cameras and other covert and overt gadgets. One of the questions on the examination was: "Are you the type who likes to disassemble a watch to determine how it works?" I truthfully answered, "No!" because I knew I'd never get the watch put back together if I did take it apart. Most of the other questions on the test were similar in nature, and it became obvious to me that I had no business trying to become a tech agent.

I later learned that my answers to the exam questions were irrelevant because the federal investigative agency that I worked for was going to force me to attend the four-week tech training regardless of my final score.

During the first week of tech training at the Federal Academy in Brunswick, Georgia, the instructor explained to our class how electricity worked (think of a scientist wearing a long white coat.) Perhaps some of the other agents in the classroom actually comprehended the material, but I sure didn't. Later the instructor brought us to a laboratory and instructed us to assemble our own tiny covert microphones using a solder gun and other tiny pieces of electronic stuff. All I made was a mess!

However, I later learned quite a bit in the field when we used brand-new already assembled equipment. As part of our training, we went into a hotel room, installed pinhole cameras, and wired up the room and then monitored everything from the adjacent room. (Yes, we rented the two rooms for training purposes, and no, there were no unsuspecting people in the room we wired up and monitored.) Understanding how the equipment worked or why it worked was beyond my comprehension. (The same is true with the remote control for my television.)

After completing the training and receiving my diploma, I returned to my home office in Memphis and practiced on the job with the available tech equipment. I continued my self-training and use of such equipment in my next office assignments in Orlando and later in Las Vegas. With the additional hands-on experience, I was able to utilize the tech equipment in the field during several undercover operations. That knowledge and expanded use assists me today as a private investigator.

In short, everyone can learn new skills. But there are some jobs that are better suited for others. Once you have a basic understanding of what other professionals in your field do and have done to accomplish their professional objectives, you can become more effective (assuming the others are willing to assist and share information).

I've worked with certified public accountants, auditors, and analysts who've provided invaluable assistance during fraud investigations. Forensic computer experts and fingerprint and handwriting experts have also made huge contributions in my investigations. Quite honestly, I could never do what those professionals do (and wouldn't want to if I could). To be a successful investigator, you often will need assistance and/or input from other professionals to help you do your job—or to do your job more efficiently.

Another characteristic needed to become an effective investigator is "concern." Investigators who have a genuine concern for the victims, complainants, harmed organizations, and their own employers' or clients' interests typically will be more motivated to accomplish their investigative objectives. Many of us have seen investigators who carry a case file in their hand but just don't seem to care whether they solve the case or not. Others seem to investigate with a sense of urgency like there is no tomorrow. The latter investigators normally have the respect of their peers and others and regularly accomplish more.

While conducting investigations, an investigator must also keep an open mind and remain objective. A tragic mistake is to have fixed or preconceived notions (which often results in faulty conclusions) about the results of the investigation before it's been completed. (It's okay to have hunches.) Over the years, I've seen some investigators set out to obtain only that information and evidence that fits their original hypotheses, objectives, or agenda. Some investigators go so far as to document only information that meets their objectives. Two causes of reaching faulty conclusions are confirmation biases and availability heuristics.

Confirmation Bias

Confirmation bias occurs when people assign more value to information that goes along with their own belief or hypotheses. When an investigator or fraud fighter consciously or subconsciously has this bias, the consequences can be many including: wrongly charged individuals, actual criminals not being charged, complaints being wrongly dismissed, and so on.

Availability Heuristic

An availability heuristic occurs when somone consciously or subconsciously overvalues information that is right in front of them. An example might be when an investigator makes a conclusion about a suspect based on information one person "reported," and the investigator assumes it "must" be true. Failing to thoroughly investigate based on this mental shortcut could cause the wrong conclusion to be made.

I have seen reputable investigators whose agencies are well known and well respected intentionally omit factual information from reports simply because the information did not fit what they wanted to prove. In my opinion, that's how innocent people end up in prison! Over the years, I came to my own conclusion that some of these one-sided investigators were trained to conduct investigations in that manner because that's what was/is expected of them. In the real world, some "professionals" are more concerned about putting points on their own personal scoreboard, getting notches on their belts, or getting promoted than pursuing justice and/or establishing the truth.

War Story 1.3

As a private investigator and consultant, I was once asked to review a police department's voluminous policies and procedures and then review the details of an incident that resulted in an arrest and a civilian's being injured. The injured party had a long history of previous arrests. My natural instinct was to lean toward taking the police officers' side, but I refrained from taking that position during my review. What I found were (in my opinion) clear violations of the police department's policies and procedures as well as critical omissions in official police reports. In short, from my viewpoint, it looked like a cover-up.

Next I reviewed the reported internal affairs inquiry into the complaint and found that all of the potential witnesses were not interviewed and that those interviews that were conducted were completed in such a way as to favor the police officers. Some of the questions asked actually included suggested answers; no logical follow-up questions were asked; and way too many closed-end (yes or no) questions were asked. In short, if you are going to conduct an investigation, it should be conducted objectively, thoroughly, and completely.

Many organizations and agencies have their own written codes of conduct, codes of ethics, and/or core values. The ones I have seen have always been well thought out and well written. Some are longer than the Ten Commandments, and some are as short as a campaign slogan.

The advantage of having lengthy codes is that they can cover just about everything. The disadvantage is nobody can remember them. The advantage of having a short code is that people will remember it; the disadvantage is that it probably won't cover everything. In my opinion, if investigators just try to do what honest people expect of them (or just do what's right), things will usually take care of themselves.

Investigation

Most of the sources I checked to obtain a definition for the word "investigation" utilize some of the same words or phrases, including: detailed, systematic examination; fact-finding; truth searching and/or carefully looking for something hidden or previously unknown.

All of the words combined would seem to adequately describe what an investigation means. However, it's probably worth noting that in addition to sometimes attempting to find evidence that supports the allegation/hypothesis that a wrong did occur or that a particular person(s) or suspect(s) committed the wrong, it just as important attempt to search for evidence that supports that perhaps the "wrong" never occurred or that a particular person (the suspect) did not commit the wrong.

An objective investigation should strive to learn all the facts, not just the ones that support a preconceived notion. An exception, of course, would be an investigation on behalf of a defendant where the sole purpose might be to disprove the prosecutor's or plaintiff's case. A thorough, complete, and well-documented investigation usually (maybe I should say often) will overwhelmingly prove if wrongdoing did or did not occur and who did it or who did not do it.

War Story 1.4

When I was a senior federal agent, a high-ranking federal prosecutor once told me, "The more you write in your reports, the more you have to defend in court." The prosecutor wanted me to write short and generic reports to describe my investigative activity. Another prosecutor once instructed me to stop taking notes during our meetings out of concern that the defense counsel would be able to obtain my notes during discovery. For those attorneys (who coincidentally worked in the same office with each other), it was all about winning (or not losing) in court. Other attorneys, from that very same prosecutors' office, were later chastised by judges and the media for wrongfully withholding case information from defense attorneys on other cases.

TIP: Be careful you don't fall into ethical traps set by others that could cause you to swallow your integrity. You'll sleep better if you do the right thing.

Success

Everyone has their own definition of the word "success." Various sources might describe success as obtaining a favorable or desired outcome. Most would probably agree that the opposite of success means "failure."

Here are two questions to ponder:

1. Is a "successful" investigator one that does not fail?
2. If so, what does "failure" mean in an investigation?

Before reading further, I suggest that you take a few moments and consider how you think the words "success" and "failure" pertain to an investigator and to an investigation.

War Story 1.5
After serving seven years in the U.S. Army, I became a candidate to be hired as a police officer by a metropolitan police department. As part of the selection process, I was interviewed by a panel of senior police officers (sergeants and lieutenants). An older lieutenant asked me a question, but he spoke as if he had marbles in his mouth and I couldn't understand him. I asked the lieutenant to repeat himself three times before figuring out what he was asking. His question was "How does fear play a role in police work?"

Based on my prior military police experience, I provided a response with confidence and ensured I made eye contact with all the members of the panel while speaking. I also ended my response with a half smile and added, "I'm not sure that completely answers your question, but I hope it does."

The lieutenant snarled, leaned forward, and stared at me in silence. Then he said something I wasn't expecting. He repeated the question, "How does fear play a role in police work?"

Because he repeated the same question, I assumed that he did not like my first answer. But since my initial response was what I believed, I just reiterated my earlier comments. (I later learned that part of the evaluators' critiques included determining whether the candidates stood by their responses when challenged.)

Later in my career, I realized that the lieutenant's question was probably the most important one that could ever be asked of a law enforcement officer. And the officer's response is even more important. If you can't overcome fear, you cannot become an effective law enforcement officer—period! The same is true of investigators or fraud fighters (even if they do not put their lives on the line).

An investigator's job is to learn the truth and report the truth. Sometimes the truth is not what some people want to hear. As far as I'm concerned, that's their problem. As an investigator, sometimes you will have to make moral decisions as to how you will conduct your investigation and how you will report facts. I mention this because it's better to think about what you would do *before* you are put into a potentially compromising situation.

By the way, I did get selected to be a police officer for that metropolitan police department. After graduating from the two-month police academy, I reported for my first midnight shift and saw that same snarling lieutenant standing in the front of the briefing room at the podium for roll call. One of the veteran patrol officers walked up behind me and whispered, "The lieutenant at the podium is our shift commander. Whatever you do, don't ask him to repeat himself; it really ticks him off." (Oops!) I later learned firsthand that particular lieutenant was one of the most effective patrol supervisors a city could ask for. He took crime fighting seriously and he made sure we did too.

After reading the preceding material, it should be obvious that much thought needs to be given to how an investigator (and an investigator's supervisor) determines if an investigator is successful. If investigators overlook some things that they should not have, that certainly would not be a good thing. If investigators unintentionally made vital reporting errors or forgot to interview key witnesses, those are indicators of poor-quality work. But investigators who do their jobs to the best of their ability, seek assistance when needed, report facts, and never omit critical information have generally done all that most can expect of them.

Often the outcome of an investigation depends on who receives the information (the decision maker). For example, an investigator can prove wrongdoing of an employee, but the business owner might give the employee a slap on the hand or a verbal warning. A prosecuting attorney might receive an airtight case and then blow it when presenting the facts at trial (that does not happen very often). Worse yet, the investigator might provide a solid case and the prosecutor, for one reason or another, may decline to accept the case for prosecution. A judge or jury might determine that the evidence presented does not prove the case. Those types of outcomes usually cannot be controlled by an investigator.

A few other things can affect the outcome of an investigation. Factually, sometimes victims, complainants, and witnesses lie or are mistaken. In those cases, the matters being investigated may not have ever happened or didn't happen as reported. Also, for some cases, there just isn't enough information to complete the investigation. With limited resources, investigators and their supervisors have to prioritize how investigators spend their time. Case overload sometimes causes investigators to almost work like a MASH unit and do the best they can as quickly as they can. Realistically, every single case cannot be solved. In short, when investigations do not result in convictions, that does not necessarily mean the investigators did not do their jobs as well as they could.

Based on this information, a successful investigator might be described as a well-trained, persistent, and ethical person who conducts honest, objective, detailed, systematic examinations, inquiries, and investigations (as permitted by law); obtains assistance where needed while striving to identify and report facts and the truth. The investigator should perform those actions to the best of his or her ability while maximizing the use of available resources and minimizing time and other expenditures. At the same time, the investigator still should do his or her best to serve the overall objectives of the employer or client and/or the well-being of those sworn to protect.

So if proving that bad guys committed some violations is a good thing, wouldn't it be even better to identify what other violations those same individuals perpetrated? And wouldn't it be even better to identify others who completed similar acts of wrongdoing? Before I demonstrate how to do that, the next chapter touches on the case initiation decision process.

Chapter 2

Case Initiation

"I will not prosecute that individual because the dollar loss is not high enough."

—Government prosecutor

After a preliminary (short-term) inquiry/investigation is completed, a decision must be made to open or not to open an official (longer-term) investigation. Sometimes matters can be referred to other investigative agencies/officials for their own joint or sole consideration. In large organizations, the chief of investigations (or similar title) or subordinates often make case initiation decisions. Usually, but not always, those decision makers were selected to serve in those positions because they previously demonstrated their success on the job over an extended period of time. Often those individuals have served within the same or similar organization for several years. However, it has been proven all too often that some of those decision makers really don't belong in those positions.

War Story 2.1

During my 30-plus years in law enforcement, I worked for some of the best and most dedicated supervisors on the planet. I also worked for some of the worst and most pathetic supervisors, some of whom in my opinion couldn't find feces in a diarrhea factory.

The good supervisors had some common characteristics: They knew their jobs and the investigators' jobs very well; knew how to manage caseloads, time, and resources; were good planners; cared about the welfare of their subordinates; disciplined employees as needed and rewarded employees' good work; understood the importance of teamwork and morale; and were dedicated to the cause.

Although some of the bad supervisors I worked for had their own unique quirks, many shared common characteristics. For example, they:

- Possessed none or few of the characteristics just described.
- Seemed to care more about their next performance evaluation or promotion than anything else.
- Didn't want to work any harder than they had to.
- Watched the clock to ensure lower-ranking employees always showed up on time (even if the employee worked 18 hours the previous day) and ensured the employees didn't take extended lunch breaks or leave work early (even when employees worked excess amounts of uncompensated overtime).
- Seldom gave recognition for outstanding performance but always pointed out where mistakes were made.
- Used red ink pens to make corrections on paper reports (on electronic reports they over utilized Microsoft Office's "Tracking" and "Comments").
- Religiously measured the side margins of hard-copy reports and counted the number of spaces between periods in sentences.
- Seldom (if ever) provided any useful suggestions to improve investigative progress.
- Frequently inspected vehicles for cleanliness.

- Were anal about ensuring that time sheets, vehicle mileage logs, and administrative reports were turned in early or first thing in the morning at the beginning of each month.
- Were physically unfit.
- Were extremely well polished in their appearance.
- Kissed the rears of senior officials from other organizations and anyone who outranked them.
- Never argued or disagreed with their superiors.
- Failed to support their employees when the going got tough.

Having served in the public and private sector as a supervisor, senior investigator, and low man on the totem pole, I understand that many factors have to be considered before decisions are made to initiate official investigations. Some of those factors are:

- Jurisdiction, venue, and purview
- Believability, reliability, or credibility of the source of the information or complaint
- Amount of the dollar loss
- Seriousness of the matter (harm done)
- Current case inventory size
- Availability of investigative resources (internal and external)
- Funding/finances
- Investigators' desires to conduct the investigation(s)
- Organization's investigative priorities
- Projected remedy or outcome (criminal, civil, or administrative)
- Prosecutor's prerogative (track record of accepting/declining certain types of cases)
- Media or public's interests (or pressures)
- Political interests (or pressures)

Jurisdiction, Venue, and Purview

The term "jurisdiction" refers to the geographical area where a specific law enforcement organization has power and authority to enforce laws.

For example, an Illinois State Trooper would be out of her jurisdiction if she set up a speed trap in Indiana.

"Venue" refers to the location where a court case might get heard. For example, a single murder committed in Texas ordinarily is not tried in New Mexico or some other state.

"Purview" refers to what and where an agency, organization, or section is responsible for handling or investigating certain matters. For example, the Federal Bureau of Investigation (FBI) has purview on kidnapping and bank robbery cases. No matter where those cases occur in the United States, the FBI investigates. But other investigators and/or law enforcement officers often assist (with some restrictions) the FBI in those (and other) investigations.

Most crimes on a military installation are investigated by members of the military organizations' own investigative agencies—the U.S. Army Criminal Investigation Command's Criminal Investigations Division (CID), Air Force Office of Special Investigations (AFOSI), or Naval Criminal Investigative Service (NCIS)—or their subordinate investigative agencies, Military Police Investigations (MPI) or Air Force Security Forces. Sometimes investigations can be conducted jointly with other agencies or organizations. Corporate internal investigations often are conducted by the entity's own internal investigators. Sometimes private investigators (PIs) are called in to conduct independent investigations.

Before initiating an investigation, consideration must be given to where the offense occurred and where the alleged wrongdoer resides (or where a suspect company is physically located). This is important because in a federal case, if the wrongdoing occurred in the same area where the suspect lives, the investigative results often (but not always) will need to be referred to the prosecuting office in the same geographical area where the suspect lives or where the suspect company is physically located.

For example, if a hospital in Nevada allegedly submitted false insurance claims to an insurance company in Tennessee, odds are a federal investigation eventually would have to be presented to a prosecutor(s) in Nevada. Therefore, under this scenario, it would be more practical and economical for the case to be assigned to an investigator(s) in Nevada. Also, most (but not all) of the witnesses to be interviewed and individual suspects likely would be located in Nevada. Therefore, most often the investigation would be conducted most efficiently by investigator(s) in the same area where the suspect resides—if that's where the offense took place. In the above example, if the agency did not have an office in Nevada, the office that covers that state would investigate.

War Story 2.2

When I was a federal agent working Las Vegas, Nevada, I was notified about a man from Los Angeles, California, who was arrested by the local police in a small town in Georgia (near Atlanta) for possessing and utilizing a fake California driver's license and four counterfeit credit cards—including one counterfeit credit card issued for business purposes to a member of my organization. The same fake name was printed on all the counterfeit credit cards and fake driver's license.

The following day, I was notified about the arrest of another man from Los Angeles, but this one was arrested by the local police in Las Vegas, for possessing and utilizing a fake California driver's license and four counterfeit credit cards—including one counterfeit credit card issued to another member of my organization for business purposes. The same fake name was used on all the credit cards and driver's license (but it was different name than the fake name used in Georgia).

The two cases fell within my purview because two of the credit card numbers were issued (for business purposes) by my organization. Because I was a federal agent and could conduct investigations throughout the United States, the two cases were within my jurisdiction. Venue for the case could be within either the state or appropriate county court in Georgia for one suspect and the state or appropriate county court in Nevada for the other.

Venue could also be in federal court. One suspect could be considered for prosecution in the Northern (Federal) District of Georgia and the other in the Federal District of Nevada (Nevada has only one district). I suspected that if I could prove there was a conspiracy between the two suspects to utilize counterfeit credit cards, they could both potentially be considered for prosecution in federal court in Nevada because one of the overt acts occurred in Nevada.

I examined copies of the eight counterfeit credit cards and two fake California driver's licenses and saw some similarities: Both fake driver's licenses listed the driver's address in the same city in California; the design of the fake driver's licenses were similar; and both suspects used the same fake first name: Robert. Although the counterfeit credit cards were printed and made on different color plastic with different bank names, all eight cards started with the same 12 (of 16) digits and a few had the same first 14 (of 16) numbers.

I also learned that both suspects utilized the counterfeit credit cards to purchase gift cards at or near shopping malls. Both suspects were black, in their early 20s, and lived in Los Angeles. Both had previously been separately arrested and tried in state courts around the United States (including Alabama and California) for the use of less than five counterfeit credit cards. The original credit card issuing financial institutions were different on a few of the cards, which meant that several banks were affected. And I learned that eight separate individuals (victims) unknowingly had their credit card numbers compromised. The victims lived at different locations throughout the United States.

I met with a federal agent from another federal investigative agency (FIA) in Las Vegas, briefed him on the two cases, and showed him the evidence. That particular FIA had investigative purview on the use, possession, and production of counterfeit credit cards. After the briefing, the agent told me he was not interested in working the case with me because the FIA only investigated cases involving five or more counterfeit credit cards. I responded, "Well, the suspects obviously know that because they only carry four at a time. If they each counterfeited four credit cards, they probably also counterfeited 40 and if they counterfeited 40, they might have made 400."

The FIA agent stuck to his agency's policy, and I left his office knowing I had to investigate the case alone. (I had never before investigated a counterfeit credit card case.) I next briefed a federal criminal prosecutor in Las Vegas on the two cases. I emphasized that it was my suspicion that the two suspects knew each other and that further investigation would identify the use of numerous other counterfeit credit cards by these and other related individuals across the United States.

The first question the prosecutor asked was where the suspects resided. I said they lived in Los Angeles. He next asked if the suspects also used counterfeit credit cards in Los Angeles and/or California. I answered that they probably did.

The federal prosecutor said that based on that information, any consideration for federal prosecution of the two suspects would be in California, where the two suspects lived, since they probably committed similar crimes in their home state.

This presented a dilemma for me because my office's assigned area of responsibility was only in Nevada, not California. Although I was legally permitted to conduct investigations anywhere in the United States, my agency drew its own turf lines as to which of its offices would work cases in designated areas.

After briefing my supervisor, I was told to transfer the case to our Los Angeles office. I shipped the case file and a summary report to our California office, and the newly assigned Los Angeles investigator asked me to continue assisting on the case. So for the next several months, we worked the case jointly. (He was considered the lead agent and I was secondary.)

The Los Angeles investigator and I created various Excel spreadsheets and link analyses while conducting the investigation. We checked the suspects' previous arrests and obtained the corresponding police reports, which also identified the names of other people the suspects were with when arrested, the fake names used when committing the credit card fraud, and of course what cities and states they were in on the dates of their arrests. Then we ran criminal history checks on the associates who accompanied the suspects when they were arrested earlier.

Using logic, we had reason to believe the suspects were in the cities on the day(s) before their arrests and most probably used the same fake names that they were caught using when arrested. (Our theory was if they used the fictitious name Robert Crookmaster on January 17 when arrested in Orlando, Florida, they probably also used the name Robert Crookmaster with counterfeit credit cards in or around Orlando on January 17, 16, 15, and/or 14, before they got arrested.)

Based on that theory, we contacted merchants in those areas where we knew the suspects historically made purchases of gift cards and contacted car rental companies. We asked if anyone using the known fake names (e.g., Robert Crookmaster) made any purchases/rentals during our specified time periods (January 17, 16, 15, and 14). Sometimes I initiated conversations with car rental companies by saying "I think you may have rented a car to Robert Crookmaster, which was subsequently stolen." Sometimes the response was "How did you know?"

In the end, the federal agent from Los Angeles and I identified about a dozen additional suspects who were affiliated with the original two suspects. We also found evidence indicating that they all knew each other and had been utilizing thousands of counterfeit credit cards across the United States. Purchasing gift cards from department stores and national chain stores with counterfeit credit cards was a favorite crime.

The suspects also rented late-model cars and paid for the rentals using counterfeit credit cards. But then they stole the cars by never returning them. So what appeared on paper to be a few counterfeit credit card transactions for a couple hundred dollars each, paying for car rentals frequently also resulted in the theft of several $30,000 vehicles! This was a big-time operation.

War Story 2.3
When I was a junior federal agent in Memphis, Tennessee, I investigated allegations that a company in Memphis submitted false claims to a government facility in Philadelphia, Pennsylvania.

It was alleged that the Memphis company had submitted invoices and received payment for goods that actually never were shipped to the government. During the investigation, I also uncovered evidence that the Memphis company's owner paid bribes to a government contracting officer to get awarded government contracts.

As soon as my agency's Philadelphia office learned that I had a bribery case with a subject located in their area of responsibility, they wanted to take control of the investigation. Factually, venue for prosecuting this bribery case could have been considered either Memphis (where the company owner lived/worked) or Philadelphia (where the contracting officer lived/worked).

At the time of the investigation, my agency and the Department of Justice (DoJ) had an existing memorandum of understanding (MOU) with each other reflecting that the FBI needed to be notified on any public corruption cases. (Keep in mind that the FBI is part of DoJ.)

But the word on the street was that if the FBI was notified, I'd probably lose control of my investigation. (This is kind of an example of how law enforcement turf wars can get started.) Factually, because I was a rookie agent, I didn't even know anything about the MOU; obviously my bosses didn't know about it either. Everyone likes to work corruption cases because they are high profile and draw media interest; plus, it's always fun to take out corrupt government officials. In short, the FBI was never notified about my case, and quite frankly, it was not needed.

When discussing my case with agents from our own Philadelphia office, I downplayed the possibility of the bribes until after a federal prosecutor in Memphis accepted my case for prosecution consideration. (Apparently the prosecutor who worked for the DoJ didn't know about the MOU either.) I knew that after the case was officially open in Memphis for a while, it would be very unlikely that my case would be reassigned to our Philadelphia office.

In the end, I uncovered evidence of the full scheme (including the *quid pro quo*—Latin meaning "this for that"). I identified over $80,000 in bribery payments from the Memphis company owner to the government contracting officer in Philadelphia. I proved that the contracting officer circumvented the contract award process so that the Memphis company would be awarded government contracts—often without required competition. I also proved the Memphis company shipped invoices and received payment for goods it never delivered. In total, two companies and three individuals were criminally charged with wrongdoing resulting in prison sentences and fines.

During my investigation, I shared my analytical investigative case knowledge with a special agent from our Philadelphia office. He went on to complete his own investigations resulting in the arrests for bribery of several additional government contracting officials at the same contracting facility.

The point of this story is that sometimes agencies and investigators in other areas will argue about who gets to work a case. Other times a case may get tossed around like a hot potato because nobody wants to work it. Usually there are laws, policies, and/or MOUs that establish which agencies and which locations are supposed to conduct certain types of investigations.

Believable, Reliable, or Credible Source of Information

Over the years, I learned that sometimes victims, complainants, and witnesses lie or provide inaccurate information. Early in the investigative process, a decision needs to be made as to whether the information received is most probably believable, reliable, and/or credible. Cases cannot (should not) be quickly dismissed just because the complaints might appear to lack these characteristics. The repercussions for not investigating something that should have been investigated might be immense—especially if the media learns of it. So before a determination can be made that a complaint/allegation is not worth pursuing, decision makers must ensure they can support their conclusion.

War Story 2.4

As a young Army investigator, I often investigated property crimes that occurred on the U.S. Army bases where I was assigned. Some "victims" reported that they had valuable items stolen from their "secured" vehicles, barrack rooms, or homes. Most victims knew that if it was discovered that the property had been left unsecured, they would not be reimbursed by the government for the thefts. Based on that knowledge, many victims falsely reported that their lockers, rooms, homes, or cars were secured and that someone unlawfully entered to commit the thefts.

However, as an investigator, I was trained to search for signs of forced entry at crime scenes, and often I could not find any. The lack of signs of forced entry did not necessarily mean the complainants lied, but sometimes the victims were incorrect about the security of their items. I also learned that some people inflate the amount or items reported stolen for the sole purpose of getting higher insurance reimbursements.

In short, you cannot always assume that the initial information provided by a victim/complainant is complete and/or accurate. Some effort should be made early on to determine if the information is believable, reliable, and/or credible.

Dollar Loss

Many investigative organizations utilize an established dollar threshold to determine if they will initiate an investigation. For some agencies, the loss of $1 might be enough to justify opening a case. For some others, a loss of a higher dollar amount (perhaps as much as $100,000) might be required (especially on a fraud case). A small town with a low crime rate probably will treat any reported crime as serious; a large metropolitan police department might not investigate any crimes unless the dollar loss or harm is significant. In larger organizations, established policies for opening cases normally are already in existence.

War Story 2.5

When I served in the U.S. Army's Military Police Investigations (MPI) Section in the early 1980s, we only investigated property crimes with values of less than $500. The Army's CID agents investigated the more serious offenses, including thefts of property of $500 and over. It seemed like some CID agents routinely found ways not to investigate many theft cases when the reported value of the missing items was in excess of $500, but not too much over.

Some CID agents I worked with depreciated the value of the reportedly missing property, which frequently resulted in determinations that the stolen property was worth less than what was reported missing—even when the victims had their original purchase receipts showing the actual value exceeded $500. One CID agent told me that he determined the value of items based on what a pawnshop would sell them for (which is not necessarily the fair market value). That agent often said something like, "Oh, that item is a year old. It's not worth what the victim paid for it anymore." In short, MPI investigated the majority of the thefts of property on base, not CID.

Ironically, if it was later determined that the stolen property had been secured and there were signs of forced entry, the government reimbursed the victims for the "replacement costs" for the items stolen. The replacement costs often were even higher dollar amounts than the original purchase amounts. (Obviously this was another broken system within the federal government because those CID agents who used the depreciation method should have been using the replacement value method to base their decisions as to whether cases fell under their purview.) The policies may have changed since then.

Seriousness/Harm

Most readers probably will agree that the next few examples are serious matters that warrant detailed investigations:

- Abuse of the elderly
- Capital offenses

- Defective electric cable (especially when used on nuclear aircraft carriers and submarines)
- Defective medical implants
- Espionage
- Felony offenses
- Intentional harm or neglect of children
- Terroristic actions and threats

But there are incidents that sometimes are considered serious by one investigator but not considered serious by another. (In War Story 2.2, the federal investigator, or his agency, did not think the use of four counterfeit credit cards was serious enough to warrant his spending time on the case.) Serious matters and/or matters where there is (or could potentially be) severe harm should be given high priority when deciding whether to open investigations.

War Story 2.6

While serving as a metropolitan police officer, I responded to a complaint of shots fired. Upon my arrival, a woman showed me evidence that someone had repeatedly shot a rifle at her third-floor apartment window. The bullet fragments were still stuck in the brick wall directly under her windowsill. The woman suspected her ex-husband was trying to kill her. I thought this was serious enough to call the detectives and figured they might want to come out and collect the bullet fragments as evidence. But after I informed the detectives on the radio, they just told me to write a report and said they were not coming out to the scene. So I did what I was told. Truthfully, I do not know if the woman was later killed.

Caseload

An investigative section that is overwhelmed with too much work understands it cannot investigate everything. If they try to investigate everything, more serious investigative matters will suffer. At some point, decisions need to be made to prioritize which cases will be worked and when they will be worked. With many investigative agencies and organizations cutting back on resources due to budgetary constraints, investigators and others often are tasked to do more with less. In War Story 2.6, the detectives simply did not have time to investigate the matter because they were busy investigating actual murders. But the investigative section still needs to utilize tools and resources that will allow it to connect criminal activity whenever possible.

War Story 2.7

Recently, at the end of the calendar year, one city's news media reported an increase in crime statistics. It was also highlighted that the police department's case clearance (solve) rate decreased. One of the senior leaders within that police department claimed that the clearance rate decreased because of the increase in the number of reports of crimes that the police responded to.

That law enforcement "leader" in effect waved the white flag by essentially saying if there is more crime, the criminals are less likely to get caught. In my opinion, making use of the information about known criminal activity (as is outlined in subsequent chapters) could result in an increased clearance rate even if the cops responded to more calls! The more crimes that occur, the more information that is available. When investigators connect the dots, often they will find that many of the crimes are related and were committed by the same persons.

Ironically, in November 2013, the same police department reported it had over 12,000 rape kits that could contain DNA evidence that were never even tested! Some of the untested kits were dated from as far back as the 1980s. Obviously failing to examine evidence doesn't do much to increase a police department's solve rate. Many of those rapists undoubtedly committed other crimes too.

Resources

Resources and caseload often go hand in hand. Sometimes investigators or their organizations simply don't have the knowledge, experience, equipment, or personnel to conduct the type of investigations that are necessary. Some business entities or small organizations may not have the expertise to conduct investigations of highly complex white-collar offenses. If they do not have investigators experienced at conducting fraud investigations, they might elect just to close those cases from the onset. If you need an auditor, do not have one, and can't afford to hire one, odds are some losses will never get investigated. Even some larger investigative agencies focus their investigative efforts on quick-hit–type cases and kick white-collar cases to the curb.

War Story 2.8

When serving as a senior federal agent, I often worked jointly with one particular FIA. Over the years, I observed that that agency concentrated its investigative activity on the sale of illegal drugs and crimes against persons and property. That agency also had responsibilities for providing executive protection whenever high-ranking officials from their agency came to town. Even though the organization spent millions of dollars in contract awards and other purchases, the agency had only one part-time investigator assigned to work fraud cases. That same investigator was also tasked to investigate all the other types of cases and provide executive protection.

My own assessment of their investigative office personnel was this: Most young law enforcement investigators would rather investigate exciting stuff and not get bogged down investigating complex fraud cases. The supervisors were evaluated on how many cases the office solved and with keeping the area's crimes stats low. It was commonly known that many white-collar investigations often took years to complete, and before an investigator completed a fraud case, the supervisor might get transferred. In many supervisors' minds, the statistics (and thus their own performance evaluations) would probably look better if their office arrested 20 dopers and 5 burglars in a month than having nothing to report for the fraud investigator's efforts for two or more years.

Funding/Finances

In the public sector, having the necessary funding to conduct investigations is essential. Often due to employee shortages, additional work hours must be paid at double time or time and a half. The reasons there are employee shortages in the first place is another story.

Understandably, these extra paid overtime hours can drain financial resources. An example might occur when a city wants to implement (or continue) concentrated anti-crime efforts in high-crime areas in addition to its customary patrol functions. If the city doesn't have or approve the funding, the cops can't perform the extra mission. Often investigative resources are scarce because of budgetary concerns. But sometimes resources are scarce only because of the way they are managed and utilized.

On the private investigative side, it has been my experience that some potential clients have no idea of the number of hours needed to complete what they want done. People have called and asked me to perform surveillance of their spouses, whom they believed were cheating on them. Some callers think the surveillance takes about as long as a television show and give no thought to how long it takes to download and review photographs, write summary investigative reports, and log and secure evidence. Conducting a reconnaissance before actually initiating the surveillance is seldom budgeted for. Good investigators know that the evidence might later have to be presented in court and that they should not compromise the quality of their work.

I've also had a couple of attorneys ask me to conduct interviews of former employees of companies when the attorneys planned on suing the companies. Yet even those high-priced lawyers didn't know if they wanted the employees interviewed in person or by telephone or if they wanted the interviews electronically recorded. And they never even thought about getting written statements from the people interviewed. The attorneys also seemed to have given absolutely no thought to how long it would take to identify the former employees, their home addresses, and the amount of time needed to prepare for the interviews. A peer suggested that those attorneys had champagne tastes but beer budgets.

When some potential clients are told the approximate number of investigative hours needed to perform their requests, they often look and sound shocked. (They look even more shocked when they get the dollar estimate.) As most consumers know, there is a big difference between quantity and quality.

Conducting private investigative work often takes just as long, and sometimes even longer, than public sector investigations. It could take longer because PIs do not have the same legal authority as law enforcement investigators. A law enforcement investigator can walk into a building, flash a badge, and start asking people questions. Odds are most people will stop what they are doing and accommodate the law enforcement official. The same is not usually true when a PI comes to the door.

War Story 2.9

As a PI, I once served a subpoena on a business owner. After showing him my state PI identification card and handing him the subpoena, he actually said to me, "Get out!" I cracked a smile because in the 30 years I had served in law enforcement, no business owner ever talked to me like that or with that tone when I served a subpoena. Just the same, my mission was accomplished. But I still felt like giving the business owner a piece of my mind.

It might sound corny or egotistical, but when I first retired from law enforcement, I described the feeling as comparable to a superhero losing his power. After spending 30 years in law enforcement, it sure felt funny to all of a sudden just be a regular civilian.

After earning my PI's license and obtaining my civilian gun permit, it felt like I regained some of what I lost (but I still had no "power"). However, make no mistake about it: PIs often can assist people in a lot of different ways. Helping people in need is really what it's always been about anyway.

It's probably worth mentioning that one of the advantages of working as a federal agent is that the turf is much bigger. Federal agents can try to connect criminal activity on a much larger scale and have access to resources in larger areas.

But there is one big advantage to being a PI as compared to being a cop: As a PI, I never get calls to go arrest some nut who is twice as big as me and doesn't want to be taken into custody. As a PI, and owner of my own company, I also can elect not to accept a case for assignment.

TIP: Prior to accepting a case, a PI may want to ensure that each potential client has the ability (and intent) to pay for the requested services. To ensure that they don't come out on the short end, most PIs collect a retainer from clients prior to performing any investigative work. When the retainer runs low, clients usually are asked to replenish it before any further work is performed. Retainers are not needed for all clients, but PIs need to be careful not to perform a lot of work for which they may not get paid. Some PIs also have clients sign contracts before any work is initiated.

Investigators' Desire

Investigators who enjoy their jobs often voluntarily assume responsibility for extraordinary amounts of work because they love catching bad guys. These types of investigators are not uncommon. As a supervisory detective, I often had to tell some investigators on my team that they could not work some cases they wanted to because they had too many existing cases. Some of those investigators routinely worked 70 to 90 hours per week. (And the divorce rate in the section was through the roof!)

As a supervisor, I usually allowed eager investigators work any new cases they wanted (in addition to the cases already assigned to them). During our monthly case reviews, I made decisions concerning the future direction of each case based on my experience along with the investigator's input. Maximizing the use of investigative labor hours is critical to the overall success of the investigative organization. But the last thing I ever wanted to do is slow down the enthusiasm of productive investigators. (War Story 2.10 provides an example of investigators' desire.)

Investigative Priorities

Organizational leaders often change their investigative priorities. Frankly, it's good to evaluate and assess investigative needs at least once annually. But investigative priorities certainly should not be changed just for the sake of change. There was a time in the 1990s when investigating healthcare fraud was a top priority for the DoJ. After the September 11, 2001, terrorist attacks on America, the War on Terror and crackdowns on illegal immigration became the top investigative priorities. About 10 years later, investigating healthcare fraud again became a high DoJ priority. One supervisor used to call the investigative priority changes "the flavor of the month."

War Story 2.10

After serving as federal agent for about 15 years, I had conducted a wide variety of different types of investigations including healthcare fraud. Those investigations resulted in the criminal and civil prosecution of doctors and others in the medical field. The cases also resulted in the criminal convictions, civil fines, and the recovery of millions of dollars.

At the beginning of 2003, my agency's leadership decided that investigating healthcare fraud would no longer be an investigative priority. In fact, our leaders immediately started making pie chart graphs of the types of open cases in each office. A few months later, based on those pie charts, superiors made separate determinations as to whether each office was complying with the newly imposed priorities. Offices that complied were considered "good"; offices that did not were considered "bad."

Perhaps those "leaders" did not understand that major fraud investigations often take years to complete. You can't close out good cases just because they make the pie slices too big on the charts. Not only were we told to close existing cases, we were also told to not open any new cases that did not fall under the new priorities!

During this time frame I was conducting an investigation of a pharmacist who was stealing prescription drugs (painkillers) from his employer's pharmacy and selling the drugs on the street. On my off-duty time, I conducted some additional research and learned that the abuse of controlled prescription drugs was fast becoming one of America's biggest problems.

Based on my experience, I drafted a proposed investigative project that would likely identify numerous prescription drug schemes

and other fraud involving physicians, pharmacists, insurance beneficiaries, dopers, and others. To maximize the investigative effort,
I met with numerous other federal and state investigative agencies
and discussed my proposal. Some of their investigators agreed to
participate in the project. I briefed a federal criminal prosecutor,
and he supported the proactive investigative effort.

I then typed the request to open the investigative project and
included a detailed step-by-step investigative process/plan to be utilized to identify wrongdoers. I forwarded the request to my supervisor. But the request just sat in my supervisor's in-box for months.
After repeatedly pestering my supervisor for a response, I was
informed that my one-agent office had too many healthcare fraud
cases already open and I could not open the investigative project.

The investigative steps I outlined in the draft plan would serve
as a blueprint to conduct the proactive investigation. Following
the outlined steps would make it relatively simple to identify
fraudsters and other schemers, and the effort would require few
extra work hours. In my opinion, conducting this investigation
would have been like shooting fish in a barrel. In an appeal for a
change of decision, I suggested to my boss that I could just work
the investigation as a side project when there was some down-
time. My request was still denied. (The pie charts dictated what
we investigated.)

Because of my strong belief for the need of the investigative
effort, I prepared an information report (IR) detailing the needs
for the investigation and outlining the steps for other investigators in my own agency to conduct their own investigative efforts
regarding the abuse of prescription drugs in their areas of responsibility (other states). I requested that copies of the proposed project be provided to each of our offices in the United States. I hated
giving up this investigative project, but I hated even more the
thought that the work would never get done anywhere else and
the crooks would keep getting away with their schemes.

After reading the IR, my boss became infuriated. But he had
no choice but to forward my recommendation to our headquarters.

What probably infuriated him even more was that I later received an award from our headquarters for my recommendation. Not only was the report's information provided to every office in my agency, it was also sent to many other investigative agencies around the country.

Sometimes an investigator's hands get tied for a variety of reasons. As I stated earlier, dedication and persistence can go a long way to becoming a successful investigator.

Projected Remedy

Depending on the mission of the investigative organization, decisions to initiate investigations may be made based on the projected likelihood that the investigative effort will result in criminal and/or civil prosecution(s). Some law enforcement and/or investigative agencies, organizations, sections, or units only conduct "criminal" investigations. Some work only "civil" investigations. Some work only "administrative" investigations. Some work both criminal and civil at the same time (called parallel proceedings). Some might work the criminal case and upon completion work the civil case. And some actually conduct criminal, civil, and administrative investigations simultaneously.

An example of allegations of a wrong being handled first criminally and then civilly involved former football star O. J. Simpson's alleged involvement in the deaths of his ex-wife, Nicole Brown Simpson, and her friend Ronald Lyle Goldman. In 1995, O. J. Simpson was acquitted (found not guilty) on two counts of the criminal charge(s) of murder. In criminal court, the prosecution had the burden of proving the case beyond a reasonable doubt.

However, in 1997, the Goldman and Brown families sued Simpson in a civil court for damages. The jury unanimously found (based on the preponderance of evidence) that O. J. Simpson was liable for damages in the wrongful death of Ronald Goldman and for battery of Nicole Brown Simpson.

Some organizations investigate internal matters only, while others might investigate internal and external matters. Knowing whether a matter being considered for investigation might be a criminal violation, civil violation, both, or just an administrative violation is important when trying to make a decision to open, refer, or close a case. The only way to know the difference between criminal and civil wrongs is to be knowledgeable of the laws and statutes and/or to seek the advice of legal counsel. As demonstrated in the O. J. Simpson case, just because someone is acquitted in criminal court does not mean the person cannot be found liable in civil court.

Here are basic (but not legal) descriptions:

- A *criminal investigation* could result in prison time and/or fines for the suspect if convicted. Knowingly and intentionally violating a criminal statute might fall into this category. The burden of proof is beyond a reasonable doubt.
- A *civil investigation* will not result in the suspect's being sent to prison but could result in financial judgments against the suspect. Unintentionally providing a defective product might fall into this category. The burden of proof is by the preponderance of the evidence.
- An *administrative investigation* ordinarily will not even end up in court, and the investigative results ordinarily will be used internally to rectify or address internal problems. Employee misconduct might fall into this category. Administrative investigations often include the investigation of waste and abuse within an organization. People usually don't go to jail for being stupid and wasting or abusing taxpayers' or an organization's money. If they did, the prisons would be even more overcrowded.

Prosecutor's Prerogative

Prosecutors (criminal and civil) often have to abide by their own organizations' priorities and therefore might only accept cases for prosecution consideration that fall under those priorities. Like the pie-charting fanatics described earlier, offices and individuals who deviate from the guidance may face professional repercussions.

For many years, prosecutors seemingly avoided fraud investigations, perhaps because some of those cases were considered too complex for a potential jury to understand. Also, simpler cases could be adjudicated much faster, resulting in more statistical accomplishments to put up on the scoreboard. (Some might say, "It's better to get 10 convictions on easy-to-prove dope pusher and prostitute cases then to get only one conviction on a complex fraud case.") This mentality might also explain why so many minorities are in prison as compared to non-minorities. But at the time of this writing, many prosecuting offices have been adding more white-collar crime prosecutors to their staffs.

It's probably worth noting that some head prosecutors at the state and local levels are elected officials—meaning people must vote them into office. Most individual state attorneys general (head prosecutors) are elected officials, but a few are appointed by their own state's governor. And a couple of state attorneys general are appointed by other means.

Street gang–related crimes, illegal drugs, murders, and such tend to get a lot more media attention than nonviolent crimes. Reducing violent or street crime is not only a good thing; it makes for good publicity (and helps win reelections).

At the federal level, the U.S. Attorney General, who is in charge of the DoJ, is nominated by the President of the United States and confirmed by the U.S. Senate. U.S. attorneys around the United States, who prosecute federal cases in their individual state districts, are also appointed by the president (subject to confirmation by the U.S. Senate), and they work for the U.S. Attorney General. U.S. attorneys are subject to removal by the President of the United States. Therefore, it would seem logical to conclude that perhaps if a President of the United States had a certain agenda of prosecuting certain types of cases (e.g., terrorism or healthcare fraud), it could very well be carried out nationwide. In 2013, the Internal Revenue Services gained national media attention when it was learned that it had targeted for investigation certain conservative groups. Does anyone think that the prioritizations of investigative efforts are not influenced by politics?

Investigators typically can't fight city hall (although I've been known to try). If the prosecutors won't accept the type of cases you bring in, you'll have to make some adjustments. A term to become familiar with is "concurrent jurisdiction," which essentially means that some criminal and civil cases can be considered by two or more courts systems (federal or state; state or county; or two different states, etc.) In other words, sometimes cases can be shopped around to determine which court system might give the more favorable result (accept versus not accept).

So, keep in mind that a case declined for federal criminal prosecution could be presented to a civil federal prosecutor (and vice versa). Cases declined by federal prosecutors in general could be presented to state prosecutors for consideration. Investigations of white-collar criminal offenses involving active-duty military personnel as suspects could be presented to either federal prosecutors and/or the military prosecutors of the military organization to which the subject(s) belongs. Consideration can also be given to transferring the case to another office or agency that also has jurisdiction over the matter. In the bribery case example mentioned earlier, the suspects could be federally prosecuted in either Memphis or Philadelphia. If you have a good strong case that for one reason or another is not accepted for prosecution consideration in one geographical location, you can consider searching around to see if your case can be presented elsewhere.

NOTE: Chapter 11 describes how investigators can make their cases more appealing to prosecutors in order to increase the likelihood cases will be accepted for prosecution and improve investigators' ability to communicate case facts.

Media or Public Interest

It took me a long time to realize it but, very often, investigations and inquiries don't get initiated unless the news media applies pressure. If not for the media, many government incidents and scandals would have been whitewashed and/or swept under the rug and would never have been exposed. (The *Washington Post*'s investigation of President Nixon's Watergate scandal is the classic example.)

Many law enforcement agencies have been rightfully criticized after one or more of their officers utilized excessive force to effect an arrest and the incidents were filmed by public citizens. (The 1992 Rodney King police beating case in Los Angeles is an example.) The media's continued coverage of the event(s) sometimes forces agencies to investigate those incidents and to evaluate their own training needs, policies and procedures, and approaches.

Law enforcement officers valiantly attempt to prevent wrongdoing every single day. Many law enforcement supervisory officials are very conscious that frequent publicity about recurring criminal wrongdoings will eventually cause public outcry. (Sniper shootings on highways and school shootings are perfect examples.) Also, high crime in cities can affect the reelection chances of city mayors. (Gang shootings in major cities receive much national publicity, causing negative publicity for mayors of those cities.)

Investigative reporting television shows often educate viewers on issues of which they might not otherwise have become aware. Some of those shows actually help police capture wanted criminals when viewers telephone in tips.

On the other side of the coin, most law enforcement agencies also understand that media coverage of their investigative successes can generate positive publicity for their agencies. That positive publicity is usually well deserved. But many officials also know that the more positive public recognition they receive, the more likely their annual budgets will be increased. And the more their budgets are increased, the larger the agency can become, and pay raises can be justified. So those press releases and news conferences sometimes serve the dual purpose of keeping the public informed while also generating favorable impressions of agencies or organizations (which often affects operating budgets).

NOTE: Law enforcement internal affairs investigations are extremely important for many reasons. The results can build or destroy the public's trust. In cases involving allegations of the use of excessive force or other civil rights violations, internal investigators should try their best to learn and document all of the facts. However, positive findings on the use of excessive force or civil rights violations can result in the use of that same evidence in potential civil suits against those officers, their supervisors, the law enforcement agency, and/or the government for which the officers were employed. Contractors and corporations that engage in self-policing and/or conduct their own internal investigations often face the same dilemmas involving defective products, accidents, corruption (kickbacks), and the like. Negative publicity can also affect suspect company's stock prices.

Investigators or fraud fighters examining a previously conducted internal investigation should keep in mind that the original investigators and/or their supervisor(s) may have (intentionally or unintentionally) protected their entity's own internal interests rather than conducting thorough and complete investigations.

War Story 2.11

One company received annual contractual bonuses from the government for not having any workplace accidents on site. The company even had signs posted around the workplace listing the number of consecutive days without an accident. Further investigation found the company had several workplace accidents that were never reported. Instead, the injured employees were compensated adequately, received medical care, and were allowed to stay home until they recovered. The bonuses the company received from the government for not having any reported injuries more than paid for the employees' care and time off from work.

War Story 2.12

In the early 1990s, I was part of an investigative task force that investigated numerous military officers—mostly aviators—for committing sexual assaults on females. The incidents occurred in the evening hours during a three-day convention held at a hotel in Las Vegas in 1991. After training sessions, some military officers got drunk and congregated on the third floor of the hotel, where they continued drinking. This became somewhat of an after-hours annual tradition at these conventions.

Also part of the tradition was for the aviators to whistle loudly and make other cat-call type remarks when women walked past them down the hallway. Over the years, the after-hours activity resulted in an increasing number of women complaining about being sexually assaulted and groped by aviators.

By 1991, the behavior had gotten completely out of hand and again numerous females reported being sexually assaulted—including female military officers. The military branch's own investigators went through the motions of conducting an investigation. It appeared to many (including the media) that the military branch's own investigation was incomplete and self-serving.

Because the senior military leaders failed to adequately remedy or investigate complaints, a large-scale independent investigation ensued by an outside government agency. The second investigation's objectives included determining what occurred, who the victims were, who committed the assaults, and also who (if anyone) was responsible for the failures in military leadership that allowed the activity to continue year after year. The investigation was covered and reported by the news media from coast to coast.

Some politicians voiced their outrage over the officers' conduct and leadership failures, which fueled the national media coverage about the facts uncovered during the more detailed investigation. In the end, many senior military officers resigned (and collected their pensions), and improvements were made in sexual harassment policies throughout the U.S. military. In fact, sexual harassment training became mandatory.

NOTE: One of the unintended consequences of the investigation was that promotions for many uninvolved military officers were delayed while the investigation occurred.

In response to that investigation, at least one branch of the U.S. military service also made significant changes to its investigative organizational, reporting, and accountability structure. It changed from having a military investigative chain of command to a civilian investigative chain of command.

Not all military branches changed their investigative leadership structure, however. (Some people/organizations just don't want to give up their power or control.) It is no coincidence that one of the branches that did not enact any investigative structure changes later experienced increased incidents of sexual harassment and assaults. In the early 2000s through 2013, this led to more scandals being exposed—particularly within the branch of military that had made no investigative structural changes.

Due in large part to the news media's continuous reporting of the increased number of sexual harassment incidents and assaults in the military, in mid-2013, all four branches of the U.S. military began making some changes in an effort to curb the number of sexual assaults and sexual harassment. Those changes reportedly included:

- New rules
- Curfews
- Alcohol bans at some basic training facilities
- The appointment of a two-star female general to oversee sexual assault prevention and assault responses
- Night patrols
- Stiffened penalties for military service members who violate the sexual harassment policies
- In-your-face sexual harassment training

But what's changed in the investigative arenas?

TIP: Auditors and truth seekers should focus on two statistics if they want to identify red flags of a corrupted or incomplete investigative and/or investigative reporting process:

1. The number of complaints received
2. The number of those investigations in which the complaints were determined to be not substantiated, not sustained, unfounded, or dismissed

These statistics should be focused on not just for incidents involving sexual harassment and sexual assaults in the military but also when investigating any and all incidents involving allegation of wrongdoing by U.S. military commissioned officers (in which the not-substantiated or not-sustained rate historically is extremely high). The same is true regarding police internal affairs investigations.

Many people, including me, have often have asked:

- Can members of the U.S. military effectively investigate themselves?

- Can members of police organizations effectively investigate themselves?
- Should members of the U.S. military, reserves, or military retirees be allowed to investigate incidents involving the U.S. military or military personnel?
- Should any federal law enforcement investigators/agents or prosecutors be permitted to serve in the military reserves or National Guard? (What purpose does that serve except give those employees an extra paycheck and pension and subtract from the overall critical mission they already serve? Those individuals are already in positions to serve their country and they are already well paid.)
- Should civilian prosecutors who are in the U.S. military reserves or retired from military service be permitted to make final decisions as to whether military officers should be prosecuted or considered for prosecution in federal or state court systems?

The point in raising these questions and concerns is to emphasize that an investigation's outcome can be greatly influenced by the investigators, the investigators' supervisors, and decision makers in the investigator's chain of command as well as those who make decisions about prosecution.

NOTE: All too often, investigators and investigative organizations report that full investigations will be or have been conducted when that may not be the case. Usually no one ever knows the difference because most people put their faith in the system, and the investigations are never reviewed for accuracy, thoroughness, and completeness by outside independent third parties who know how to conduct thorough investigations. As this book describes, there is a big difference between conducting investigations and conducting thorough and complete investigations. In the author's opinion, based on personal experiences and observations, people have a right to be skeptical.

Political Interests

As mentioned, elected officials potentially can influence which investigations and/or the types of investigations that will be initiated in the public sector. They can do so by telling or implying to the (sometimes appointed) decision makers what they want. On the local level, people with power sometimes can influence decision makers to conduct or not conduct certain types of investigations.

War Story 2.13

While serving as a senior federal agent, I was conducting an investigation into allegations that some senior military officials at the Pentagon violated the law. The investigation involved four-star generals, lower-ranking military officers, and some civilians. One of the suspects was a two-star general who was up for a promotion to get his third star. (In my walks through the Pentagon, I noticed that two-star generals are a dime a dozen but there are far fewer four-star generals.)

In the early stages of the investigation, my superiors informed me that it was imperative that I quickly determine if the two-star general was going to be charged with any criminal offenses because a high-ranking leader wanted to promote and assign him to a certain position at the Pentagon.

I informed my superiors that the investigation would take several months to complete and emphasized that the four-star generals' involvement in the alleged wrongdoing appeared much more serious than the two-star general's.

However, my superiors ordered me to stop investigating the four-star generals and to focus solely on the two-star general's involvement because the high-ranking leader wanted to know whether that general could get his third star.

I suggested that they promote the two-star general because people are innocent until proven guilty. But my suggestion was dismissed as quickly as it was offered. I also explained that it would be almost impossible to separate the two-star general's

---

involvement from that of the four-star generals because they were intertwined, and it appeared that they might all be involved in a criminal conspiracy. My superiors still instructed me to investigate only the two-star general's involvement!

I sometimes wondered if the suspect four-star generals were instigating these pressures to limit the investigation because they would know that pressing for a speedy investigation of the two-star general would likely cause the investigation to fail. If the investigation of the two-star general failed, that would likely cause the cases against the four-star generals to fade away.

One of the keys to proving the four-star generals' criminal involvement would be getting the two-star general to tell the truth. And I knew the only way I could get him to tell the truth was to prove the entire case and show him he had no way out.

Because I was ordered to stop investigating before the investigation was completed in order to write a summary report, the evidence against each suspect was not as conclusive as it probably could have been. In the end, the two-star general received a "bad boy" letter in his official military personnel file so he wasn't able to get his third star. By the time everyone got done dragging their feet, the four-star generals were retired and collecting their pensions.

War Story 2.14

The national news media, including television, regularly reported on an extremely high-profile investigation in which a U.S. military service member was killed while deployed in a combat zone in 2004. There was suspicion that a high-ranking presidential appointee had knowledge of investigative facts that the soldier was killed by friendly fire. But it was suspected that the presidential appointee might have ignored this information in favor of providing the public and the deceased soldier's family members with the originally reported (incorrect) information, which allowed for and awarding of the Silver Star, Purple Heart, and a posthumous promotion. In other words, it appeared that high-ranking government officials—possibly including the presidential appointee—knew the soldier was killed by his own men, but they led everyone to believe he was killed by the enemy.

During later questioning by a congressional committee in April 2007 (televised nationally on C-Span), the investigative agency's leader was asked if the presidential appointee was ever interviewed during the investigation. (The key questions to be answered when interviewed would be: "What did the presidential appointee know, and when did he know it?")

The investigative agency's leader replied that the appointee was never interviewed during the investigation; instead, he was provided with a written list of questions to which the appointee provided "a negative response." (The committee did not ask what he meant by a "negative response.") When asked, the investigative agency's leader said that a sworn statement was not requested of the presidential appointee.

The first thing that went through my mind upon witnessing that leader's reply was that even if it was not a cover-up, it looked like a cover-up. Guess who the immediate boss of that investigative agency's leader was? Yes, that's right; his boss was that presidential appointee! (Gee, you think it would have been too difficult to find the time to conduct an in-person interview of your own boss?)

NOTE: Remember the question asked of me during my police recruit screening: "How does fear play a role in police work?" In my opinion, no one can ensure the objectiveness, thoroughness, or completeness of an investigation if the investigators, the investigative supervisors, and/or the deciding officials have any stake whatsoever in the outcome of the investigation. When such investigations are investigated internally, those investigations should be subject to external audits, examinations and reviews by objective and experienced third party professional investigators. At some point in the investigative process, or at least at its conclusion, there *must* be transparency!

War Story 2.15

After retiring from federal service, I wrote several members of the Senate Armed Services Committee regarding some of my concerns about previously closed military related investigations. The committee was established after World War II and has legislative oversight of the nation's military. Most of the senators' offices never replied. At least one replied that he could not answer me because I did not live in his home state. (And people wonder why many Americans have lost faith in their government!)

In the 30-plus years I conducted investigations in the public sector, I experienced political interference on only a few occasions. Odds are that most investigators may never experience such obstacles. But don't think for a minute that it can't happen to you if serving as an investigator or fraud fighter. When those with power start circling the wagons and/or start pushing their rank or authority around, they can make life pretty tough for even the most honest and dedicated investigators and fraud fighters.

The next chapter provides tips on how investigators (who are permitted to do their jobs) can become more productive and successful in their efforts by conducting thorough investigations.

Chapter 3

Conducting Thorough Investigations

"Follow the money."

—Money-laundering detection instructor

A ny investigator who has ever solved what was once considered an unsolvable case knows the feeling of accomplishment that normally stems only from painstaking work (and sometimes a little luck). Many cases are solved because of the investigator's planning and organizational skills, case knowledge, identification of witnesses (and getting them to voluntarily cooperate), interviewing skills, the collection of evidence, and the timely utilization of appropriate investigative techniques, tools and resources, and so on.

During my professional career, I've received training from experts in the field in formal and informal settings as well as through my own studies. However, there's no substitute for experience. Some of the best investigative skills (especially interviewing skills) usually are progressively developed in the field. And those skills often are developed by learning what *not* to do. It is just as important to learn from your mistakes as your successes. And it's even smarter to learn from other investigators' successes and mistakes!

NOTE: I prefer to use the words "mistakes" or "shortcomings" rather than "failures" because I don't believe in failure. As long as you learn when things don't work out, those are just lessons learned. Most lessons learned usually provide greater dividends down the road. When training young patrol officers and investigators, in addition to teaching them how to do things correctly, I also teach them what not to do. Those lessons are often based on my own trial-and-error investigative efforts.

War Story 3.1

When I was relatively new in the Military Police (MP) Corps, I checked an abandoned vehicle located on a public street in a residential neighborhood. The vehicle had no license plate. As part of the preliminary investigation, I called on the police radio and asked the dispatcher to run the vehicle identification number (VIN). The vehicle came back stolen. So I had the vehicle impounded and wrote a report.

The next night I got a royal butt-chewing from my supervisor. As it turned out, I mixed up a couple of the digits when I wrote down the VIN number and the vehicle actually was not stolen. (Anyone want to guess who always triple-checks VINs, license plate numbers, serial numbers, account numbers, case numbers, and anything else that has more than one digit?) Every officer and investigator I've ever trained has heard that story (probably more than once) and I hope never made the same mistake I did.

War Story 3.2

As a brand-new plainclothes investigator in the U.S. Army, I was tasked to interview and interrogate (I&I) a low-ranking enlisted man regarding the theft of an unsecured radio from a barracks room. After obtaining background information from the suspect, I read him his legal rights for "Larceny of Private Property." (**NOTE:** U.S. military personnel who are suspects of criminal offenses must be read their legal rights before questioning even if they are not in custody.) The suspect waived his rights and I asked him to describe his activity on the date of the theft. Early in the interview process he confessed. But he didn't confess to taking a radio; he confessed to stealing a television!

Thinking quickly, I told the suspect I already knew he stole the television but needed to know about the radio. (**NOTE:** I learned early on that the art of interviewing not only requires knowledge of the case facts but also the ability to act like you know more than you actually do.) The suspect never admitted to taking the radio so at some point I said, "Okay, although I already know you took the television, why don't you tell me about that?"

The suspect went on to tell me all about the theft of a television that I didn't even know had been stolen. He also showed me where the television was, and I secured it as evidence. Since then I have completed hundreds of hours of I&I training and conducted thousands of interviews. But the experience gained from that one interview served me well for the next several decades.

War Story 3.3

On a more humorous note, while a rookie investigator and wearing a brand-new three-piece (department store) suit, I responded to a report of burglary at a residence and rang the front doorbell. When a woman answered the door, I reached into my inside suit jacket pocket to remove and show her my MP investigator credentials and badge. As soon as I pulled out the credential case from my pocket, about a dozen small white pieces of paper (about the size of Chinese fortune cookie papers) followed and slowly fell toward my feet on the front porch.

Both the woman and I watched the papers as they fell seemingly in slow motion. I think she may have been wondering if she won the Publishers Clearing House prize with all the confetti flying around! I quickly bent down and grabbed all the pieces of paper off the porch and found that they read "Inspected by Number 82." Although I tried to pretend the incident didn't happen, we both burst out laughing.

War Story 3.4
I told the last story to a fellow investigator who didn't have much more experience than I did. After he laughed, he told me had a similar embarrassing moment. The investigator said that after arriving in a chief executive officer's office to conduct an interview, the investigator reached into his own inside suit jacket pocket to grab a pen. Then he dropped the pen and had to reach down to get it. The investigator was only slightly embarrassed at that point until he accidentally kicked the pen under the CEO's desk. Feeling more embarrassed, the investigator quickly bent further to get the pen and then bumped his head hard and loud under the CEO's desk. The investigator added, "I don't think that guy had much confidence in me after that."

War Story 3.5
While in Middle Tennessee, I told a young FBI agent one of those stories and emphasized how dumb stuff seems to happen when agents are new. The FBI agent then told me his

embarrassing story. He said on his first day at work at the FBI, he was one of the last agents to leave the office at the end of the day. After locking the door behind him, he walked to the nearby elevator to make his way home. But then he dropped his keys. Somehow his office key fell through a tiny slot between where the elevator door opened and the building floor. The FBI office door key then fell all the way down the elevator shaft. Because of the obvious importance of the key, the agent had no choice but to call his supervisor and tell him what happened and then they had to call for an elevator service provider to retrieve the door key.

As investigators gain experience, they develop their own confident (less clumsy) investigative style. Characters on detective television shows usually have some unique habits, quirks, and/or personality traits that work very well for them. But what works well for one investigator may not work well for another. In baseball, players all basically do the same thing when playing the game—but they all do it a little differently. Those small differences sometimes make the difference between being an average ballplayer and a superstar. Of course talent also has a lot to do with their success.

Questions to Answer

Investigative academy instructors emphasize the importance of an investigator gaining information that will answer some basic questions.

(**NOTE:** Senior investigators, bear with me: Everything will all come together after reading this and the chapters that follow.)

The instructors will undoubtedly also emphasize the importance of later documenting the answers to those questions in investigative reports. That said, most investigators are trained to seek answers to the Five Ws, which are listed next. In addition, based on my own experience, I've learned that the answers to the Two Hs are also very important.

Seven Questions: Five Ws and Two Hs

Investigators must strive to obtain answers to these questions and must include the answers in their investigative reports:

1. Who?
2. What?
3. When?
4. Where?
5. Why?
6. How?
7. How Much?

Before, During, and After

These same seven questions can be repeated to learn about three separate time periods: before, during, and after the event/matter in question. Very often, people rehearse what they will say when questioned by investigative personnel about the time of the event/matter under investigation. But they fail to rehearse the small things they did (or would/should have done) before and after the event/matter. Obtaining extreme details, being thorough, and being persistent are the keys to finding flaws, inconsistencies, and clues and to solving and proving cases.

War Story 3.6
I once interviewed a witness (Willie Witness) who was supposed to be an alibi for another man (Danny Doper). Danny Doper sported a thick dark mustache and was believed to have sold illegal drugs (a pound of marijuana) to an undercover drug officer at about noon on a Friday afternoon. Immediately after the drug sale transaction, the undercover cop tried to arrest Danny Doper. But Danny assaulted the undercover cop and fled the scene.

An informant later provided a tip that Danny was the man who sold the drugs to the undercover cop and committed the assault.

The informant added that Danny had recently shaved off his thick dark mustache to change his appearance and avoid police suspicion/detection for the offense.

During a police line-up, the undercover cop could not identify Danny Doper as the person who sold him the dope. But other investigators interviewed Danny anyway. When questioned, Danny said he wasn't even in town on the day of the drug deal. His alibi was Willie Witness, who was Danny Doper's supervisor.

Danny said Willie Witness gave him a ride to a bus station on that Friday morning and that Danny took a bus out of state that day. A check of the bus ticket records showed Danny did indeed purchase a bus ticket for that trip. Willie Witness told investigators that he did give Danny a ride to the bus station that morning.

Based on this information, the senior investigator said he was going to close the case. The investigator said there was not enough evidence to charge Danny Doper. Because I have strong feelings about those who assault police officers, I asked to be assigned the case.

The first thing I did was reinterview Willie Witness. I asked him to provide the details about giving Danny a ride to the bus station. Along with other questions, I asked *when* Danny asked him to give him a ride to the bus station, *how long* it took to travel to the bus station, and *where* Danny was traveling to after he got on the bus. Willie provided answers to all my questions. But then I decided to ask some extremely detailed questions.

I asked Willie *how many* suitcases Danny had when he went on the trip and *what color* the suitcases were. Willie had to think long and hard about those questions but responded that Danny had two suitcases and they were both black. I then asked *where* the suitcases were placed inside the vehicle when they departed and headed to the bus station. Willie said the suitcases were put in the trunk.

I then flipped through my case file and said, "Well, that's pretty interesting. What if told you that Danny told us he only had one suitcase and it was placed in the backseat?

There was a long pause and Danny stared down at his feet. I then added, "You know, this case is not going away. There was an assault on a police officer. It seems to me the only real question is how many people are going to get charged in this case: one or two? You got a wife and kids at home. You are a good boss who looks out for his employees. But I'm not sure it's worth throwing everything away for somebody who sells dope and assaults cops. I wonder what your wife and kids would say about all this."

Willie didn't need to think long. He admitted that Danny Doper previously came to him and said that he sold dope to an undercover cop and assaulted the cop when trying to flee. Willie told me that Danny asked him to act as an alibi. Willie added that he suggested that Danny shave off his mustache so he wouldn't be recognized. In short, Willie Witness said that he never gave Danny a ride to the bus station.

When Danny Doper was later reinterviewed, he continued to lie about any involvement. But I took his fingerprints and sent them to the lab along with the bag of marijuana for fingerprint comparison. Besides Danny's alibi falling apart, he couldn't explain why his fingerprints were on the outer wrappings of the drugs sold to a cop. (Checkmate!)

Contrary to the methods many investigators are taught, usually several additional questions need to be answered in each of the seven categories. Next I provide some descriptions of the seven questions to seek answers to in any investigation. The lists are by no means inclusive.

Who?

Who is/are the victim(s), complainant(s), witness(es), suspect(s), subject(s) co-subject(s) and other(s)?

NOTE: "Others" are people who don't necessarily fall into any of the other categories, but their information may be useful for future reference. Unfortunately, most investigative and law enforcement agencies use the default label of "witness" to describe "others" who actually never witnessed anything!

Examples of those who might fit into the "other" category could include: parents or guardians of a juvenile, quality assurance representatives at a manufacturing plant, and employees who just got laid off and weren't very happy about it. These types of individuals might never have witnessed anything, but they often possess insight and/or useful information.

Sometimes people who were at key locations at specific times of interest may report that a certain person was at or not at the scene. Being able to tell who was not there might prove valuable later. Plus, getting such a statement (especially in writing or recorded) prevents individuals from later recanting their statements or later providing contradictory information.

What?

"What" normally refers to an object(s). "What" might include a listing of items stolen (including make, model, serial numbers, markings, etc.). "What" could refer to evidence left at a scene and/or recovered. In a missing person case, "what" might include a description of the clothing the missing person was last seen wearing, the person's physical characteristics (including scars, tattoos, birthmarks, etc.), the type of vehicle driven and license plate number, credit/debit cards possessed, cell phone number and provider of service, social media sites utilized, and so on.

If conducting an investigation into contract fraud or corrupt procurements, the answer to the "what" question ordinarily warrants an elaborate response because there are different types of contracts. Is it a government contract (which branch?) or private? Is it a firm-fixed price, cost-plus, or other type(s) of contracts? What is the contract for? What is the contract number? What is the matter being investigated: Defective products? Shortages? Cost mischarging? Bid rigging? Bribery or kickbacks? What documents or other potential evidence exists?

Another "what" often overlooked by investigators is "What was said?" People often say things that might seem unimportant at the time (especially to the noninvestigator) but could be of great value. So it might be important to know what was said (and by whom), when it was said, how it was said, and where it was said.

War Story 3.7

When I was actively investigating a theft of a stereo from a home shared by friends, one of the tenants stepped into the room I was in and immediately started walking away after he saw me spreading fingerprint powder around the top of a dresser. In a loud tone I asked, "Who are you?" The man stepped back, told me his name and said he lived in the house.

He was holding a paper cup with a plastic lid and straw. The cup had a logo of a national hamburger chain on the side. I asked, "Where have you been?" He said he just came back from eating at a Chinese restaurant. It seemed unlikely to me that a person would go out to eat at a Chinese restaurant and then stop on the way home at a burger place to get a soda. To make a long story short, I later proved that the cup-holding tenant stole the stereo. He pawned it at a pawnshop next door to the burger place.

When?

The answer to the "when" question might include the time and date someone became aware of something or did something. In a theft case, an investigator would ask when the victim last saw the missing item(s) and when he or she noticed the item(s) missing.

NOTE: In a fraud investigation, the answer to the "when" question might actually be a time period of several years. For example:

Q: When did the suspect commit the fraud?
A: From 2008 to 2013.

"When" might include the date an item was purchased or inventoried. "When" could also include the time and date others were in the area. For example, if investigating the theft of cash from an unsecured office safe, the time(s) that others entered and departed the area obviously would be important. Security and time recorded surveillance videotapes as well as coded security entry devices often provide good evidence that answers the "when" question.

It's a good idea to also think about the before, during, and after questions that surround the time in question. For example: "Where were you before the incident? Where did you go after the incident?"

Few people expect to be asked those questions because the questions seem (and sometimes are) irrelevant. And hardly anyone expects an investigator to investigate things that don't seem to tie directly into the matter being investigated. But as explained earlier, sometimes detailed investigations into the before-and-after show that people provided inaccurate or false information. If they did, it might be an indication that they provided inaccurate or false information about the matter being investigated.

War Story 3.8

During the investigation of the 1991 military aviators' sexual assaults on females, approximately 3,000 interviews were conducted. Many of the aviators interviewed denied ever being on the third floor where the sexual assaults occurred. But during almost every interview, aviators were asked who they were with at various times on the evenings of the assaults.

During an interview of Peter Pilot in Virginia, he said he was on the third floor with Joey Jet drinking beers and they saw some girls getting "groped" but didn't recognize anyone in the area.

NOTE: All of our interview reports were put on a computer system so we (the investigators) could run queries on individual names to prepare for each individual interview. We could pull every report in which the person's name was mentioned. Because of this resource, we were fairly well prepared for each interview.

When Joey Jet was later interviewed in Texas, he didn't know if Peter Pilot had been interviewed and certainly didn't know what Peter Pilot might have told investigators. When Joey Jet was asked if he was ever on the third floor on the night in question, he denied it. In addition, when specifically asked if he recalled being with Peter Pilot on the third floor when girls were groped, he denied it again. It wasn't until we showed him photographs of himself partying on the third floor that he finally admitted being there. But he still wasn't willing to provide us with any additional information. Joey Jet had no intentions of ever telling us anything. Both he and Peter Pilot were put on the reinterview list.

Where?

"Where" is obviously a location. In a simple assault investigation, you'd want to know where on the body a person was struck and where the incident occurred. If a weapon or other item was used to commit an aggravated assault, you'd want to know where the "weapon" is at that time and whether it was collected as evidence. You'd also want to know where the item came from and how it came to be used in the assault. For example, if a suspect shot a victim, you'd want to know if the suspect was armed long before the incident and how the weapon was obtained just prior to the incident. (Knowing the answer to this could assist in determining if there was premeditation.) Where the shooter reportedly held the gun and pulled the trigger, in relationship to the victim's body, can sometimes conflict with the physical evidence (e.g., gunpowder residue and blood splatter patterns).

"Where" is an important question to ask (along with "when") when trying to corroborate or refute a person's statement. Examples might be: Where were you before? Where were you during? Where were you after?

Throw in a bunch of the other questions like the next ones and you'll get even more responses: Where were you before? Who were you there with? What were you doing? What was said? How long were you there? What did you do after that?

TIP: Keep in mind that thorough interviews take longer to complete than less thorough interviews. Therefore, plan your schedule accordingly. Don't call someone in to be interviewed at 11:00 A.M. for a planned three-hour interview unless you plan on taking a lunch break in the middle of the interview. And ask people if they need to use the restroom before starting the long interview.

TIP: One of the most useful techniques to deploy when conducting interviews of suspects is to obtain answers to all seven questions and then ask suspects to tell their story in reverse order. Typically investigators just have to act a little confused about their own recollection of the order of events to justify asking the same questions again. An example might be when an investigator says: "You said you went right to bed as soon as you got home [investigator scratches head in confusion]; can you tell me again where you were before you got home and what you were doing?"

Most people who tell lies about an incident have not memorized their alibis in reverse order. Consequently, liars get especially uncomfortable (obvious by their body language) and often omit information that they provided previously or get the chronological order of events mixed up. More important, if they completely omit (leave out) a critical event when telling the story in reverse order, that could be because the event never happened. This may be an indicator of deception and is certainly worth further exploring during the interview process and the investigation.

NOTE: As people age, their memories are often not as good as they used to be. Some others have problems concentrating. So don't convince yourself that people are guilty just because they can't tell a story backward. Want proof? Try saying the alphabet backward.

"Where" is also important when documenting the location evidence was obtained. Many investigators are trained to sketch, photograph, and/or videotape crime scenes. Any physical evidence obtained must have the retrieved time, date, and location documented so the information can be used later during a trial.

As a private investigator, I often obtain publicly available information off the Internet to aid in investigations and sometimes to provide to clients. Very often I ensure that I also log the URL number, date, and time that the information is downloaded, copied, or printed so that if I'm later asked "where" I got the information, I can answer honestly. It sure beats saying "I got this information off the Internet."

Why?

"Why" is an especially important question to ask a suspect so that the investigator understands what the suspect's motive or intent was at the time of the incident. Suspects might lie about the reasons. But it's still a question that must be asked.

TIP: Some interview and interrogation courses teach that interviewers should think about plausible reasons why a perpetrator may have committed the act under investigation and offer one or more suggestions to get a guilty suspect (who is reluctant to talk) to confess. (Remember, you never want innocent people to confess to something they did not do.) A technique often used is to "blame the victim."

For example, an investigator might say, "I think the reason you took your roommate's wallet was because you wanted to teach him a lesson about leaving his valuables unsecure. By losing his wallet, your roommate would know for the rest of his life not to leave money just sitting around. After all, if he hadn't left his wallet out, none of this would have happened."

The "why" question can also be important when the suspect(s) are unknown. Contemplating the "why" might identify the type of person who would have done the act(s) under investigation. For example: Why would somebody shoot a particular person at point-blank range and not shoot someone else at the same location?

Another example might be: Why would somebody steal only a valuable stamp collection in a house burglary when they could have also taken other items in the same house? (**NOTE:** Don't rule out that the stamps [or some of them] were never stolen and may not have existed in the first place. Always be skeptical!)

Another example might be: Why would a person kidnap a girl who was on the way home from grade school? Although the answer to this question might seem obvious—a child molester—don't rule out other possibilities: There could be parental custody battle going on or perhaps the other spouse has the child, the child could be lost or a runaway (if a runaway, don't rule out child abuse; the child might be hiding), the child might have been injured and is in a hospital, or the child may have elected to stray from normal routine and stop off at a friend's house. Maybe the child is still at the school and just stayed after.

War Story 3.9

On Halloween night, a young child reported that after opening the sealed packaging on a small chocolate candy bar, he found a pin stuck inside the candy bar. Because the child had not trick-or-treated very far from his home, it was reasoned that the suspect lived nearby and that other local children might have also received pins in their candy bars given out at the same house.

During a more detailed interview of the child, the original packaging material was obtained and held up to a light where it was determined that there was no pinhole in the torn-off packaging material. Evidence indicated that the pin was put into the chocolate candy bar after it was opened.

The child subsequently admitted that he stuck the pin in the candy bar himself and was influenced to make the false claim after watching a television special the night before on what dangerous items kids and parents should be on the lookout for before eating their Halloween candy.

Another good question is "Why not?" If suspects deny any involvement in an offense, you could ask them why they would not have done it. Sometimes the reason they give can be used against them in the interview.

War Story 3.10

During a sexual assault interrogation, the suspect continued to deny having any involvement in the matter under investigation. I asked the suspect why he would not have committed the sexual assault, and he said his mother raised him not to do things like that. Much later in the interview, I was able to mention how bad he must feel because his mother taught him the difference between right and wrong but he made a mistake. I then added that his mother probably also taught him to own up to his mistakes and to learn from them. The suspect agreed. More important, he did not reject my implication. It wasn't too long after that the suspect admitted his involvement in the sexual assault (and he actually felt relieved to get that off his chest). Thanks, Mom!

How?

When conducting investigations, learning how something happened is very important. If you were investigating a burglary, you'd want to know how the burglar gained entry. You'd also want to know how the burglar exited and how he or she got the stolen items out of the house.

If investigating a counterfeit credit card ring, you'd want to know how the criminals:

- Obtained the credit card numbers.
- Got the plastic to make the cards.
- Got the logos on the cards and printed them.
- Determined where and when to use the cards.
- Determined who would use the cards.

You'd also want to know where the purchased merchandise was brought and how the criminals profited, among other things. (Don't forget: You also want to know "where" the stuff is now!)

Another example of asking the "how" question might be: How could this have been prevented? Preventing a wrong or loss from occurring in the first place (or in the future) would save everyone grief.

War Story 3.11

When conducting a bribery investigation that was also a contract fraud case, I reviewed the pertinent government's contract award files in detail, including all of the government contracting officer's notes. I started by reviewing about 100 contract files awarded by the same government contracting officer to a certain vendor. All of the contracts awarded were for less than $25,000. Before awarding each contract, the government contracting officer was supposed to obtain telephone quotes from three different vendors. The vendor with lowest bid price should have been awarded the contract.

While reviewing the contract files, I noticed that the vendor who was called last (Vendor 3) always provided a price quotation that was less than those of the other two vendors. I came to that conclusion because Vendor 1's price was listed on the left, Vendor

2's price was listed in the middle, and Vendor 3's price was on the right. You'd think once in a while, the low bidder's price would have come from the first or the second vendor called. But that was never the case; the vendor who was contacted last (Vendor 3) always provided the lowest bid price.

In my opinion, this was an indication ("red flag") that the government contracting officer routinely provided Vendor 3 with the other bidders' price quotes.

Since I had already uncovered evidence that Vendor 3 had paid the government contracting officer several thousand dollars in bribes, it appeared that I now had circumstantial evidence to show what the government contracting officer did in return for the money. (He unlawfully eliminated fair competition and provided inside information to Vendor 3.) But I knew it would strengthen the case if I was able to obtain a voluntary (truthful) confession from the government contracting officer.

When I later interviewed the government contracting officer at his home, he strongly denied giving Vendor 3 the price quotes provided by the first two vendors. He said he knew it was illegal to provide competing vendors with inside information. I politely challenged him and showed him the pattern of evidence I uncovered, which indicated that he did provide Vendor 3 with the competitors' price quotes.

But then the government contracting officer provided his side of the story. He said that he often telephoned Vendor 3 and asked the vendor to offer price quotes to provide certain items. After Vendor 3 provided the price quotations, the contracting officer would say, "If you really want this contract, you'll have to quote a lower price." This continued until, eventually, Vendor 3 underbid the competition. Rationalizing his own illegal behavior, the government contracting officer told me, "I never once provided inside information to anybody. I never told anyone what the other vendors' bid prices were."

Regarding the several thousands of dollars he had received in bribery payments, the government contracting officer said, "I don't like to call them bribes. I like to think of them as loans which I know I'll never be able to repay."

In his own mind, the government contracting officer could rationalize all the wrongs he had done. We shook hands when I left, and he later pled guilty to several felony counts and was sentenced to prison.

How Much?

Determining "how much" helps determine the value and/or quantity of the alleged loss. For example: A stolen wristwatch could be valued at as low as a few dollars to as much as a few thousand dollars. A contract might be worth $10 million, but the loss might be only $20,000. Possessing 10 pounds of marijuana is a lot different from possessing a rolled marijuana cigarette.

Because many investigative agencies have dollar thresholds that must be met before full-scale investigations are initiated, learning the value and quantity of items missing, damaged, or lost is very important. The value also can make a difference for prosecutors, who also might have dollar thresholds to meet before accepting cases. In addition, the value is important to any insurance companies that might have an interest in the loss.

War Story 3.12

When I was an MP investigator, a younger uniformed MP handed me a plastic bag containing several pills along with a completed evidence receipt. He had made an arrest before meeting with me, and he asked that I conduct a chemical field test of the pills and secure them as evidence.

The pills were suspected to be amphetamines, and the MP had recovered them while searching a drunk driver. The evidence receipt that the MP completed indicated there were 9 pills in the plastic bag. But I counted the pills twice and found 10 each time. I handed the plastic bag back to the MP and asked him to recount the pills. He also counted 10. The MP's response was "I didn't count them very good." I saw no need to reprimand the young MP; he felt dumb enough as it was.

Investigators who conduct thorough investigations and obtain answers to the seven questions will have done a good job of investigating. But when it comes to this line of work, you should not be satisfied with just conducting "good" investigations.

Chapter 4 provides insight on how to take "good" investigations and turn them into "great" ones.

Chapter 4

Expanding Investigative Efforts

"A good investigator can connect the dots. A great investigator can find the dots to connect."

—Charles E. Piper, CFE

Every investigation can be taken to the next level. If catching one bad guy is good, catching two is even better. If finding evidence that suspects committed one crime is good, then finding evidence they committed more crimes is even better. It has been my experience that the most common mistake made by many investigators is thinking singular instead of plural when conducting investigations.

All too often investigators try to solve just the case they were assigned—and that's it! The reason many investigate in that manner is because that's how they were taught to investigate. Others who know how to conduct more thorough investigations sometimes rationalize not doing so because of other concerns (often because they have too heavy a caseload or have other personal commitments).

War Story 4.1

Over the years, I've worked for several supervisors who possessed a bean-counter mentality when it came to assigning cases and monitoring case progress. Those bosses seemed to think that all cases required the same amount of time and effort. In reality, some cases take longer to complete than others, and some have better results than others. When I worked general crime investigations, I had as many as 50 open cases at any given time. Each case was actively investigated for approximately one week to three months.

When I worked drug cases, my average caseload was between 25 and 50. Each case was actively worked for about the same amount of time as general crimes.

But when I worked complex fraud investigations, my caseload varied between 5 and 20 cases, and the cases were actively investigated for time periods between six months and five years (yes, years!)

One of the biggest complaints I had about some of the fraud investigative supervisors I worked for is they would sometimes say, "You've put enough time in that case, you need to work on some other cases." In contrast, my way of thinking is "If you are catching bad guys committing major fraud, what difference does it make which cases you are working?"

For many years I thought those leaders simply didn't know how to investigate properly (and sometimes that was true). But I later learned that some of them were being evaluated on how long cases were open. The supervisors were not necessarily held responsible (or as responsible) if the investigators in the office never solved/proved any wrongdoing.

However, investigators usually were evaluated on the number of people/entities they investigated that were charged with crimes or civil violations. Obviously, the supervisors' objectives conflicted greatly with the investigators' objectives.

The bosses wanted new cases brought in and all cases to be worked quickly. But investigators wanted to catch bad guys. One of my bosses told me to close an existing case that was slowly progressing and to reopen it under a new case number so it wouldn't look so old. (I knew what money laundering was, but he wanted me to launder cases!)

I informed the supervisor that his way of skirting around the case-age requirement eventually would bite us in the rear because evidence would be assigned to two different case numbers. I also told him that closed cases technically could be released to the general public (including suspects) under Freedom of Information Act requests. In contrast, open investigations would not be released. Plus, if the case ever went to trial, it would be a nightmare because things would be filed in two separate cases. My boss was risking the success of the investigative efforts just because he wanted to keep his job performance evaluation scores up high. But in fairness, he was just following guidance directed by his own "leaders."

NOTE: For the purpose of this book, it is assumed that readers have strong desires to conduct thorough and complete investigations and their supervisors will support those efforts. (If your bosses don't share that goal, keep reading anyway because sooner or later one of you might get transferred—I hope.)

Comparisons

The collection and comparison of fingerprints and/or DNA evidence demonstrates the success that can be had when investigators conduct thorough investigations.

Years ago, the FBI started collecting inked fingerprints of people arrested. The inked fingerprints were on cards and were filed. As time passed, the FBI and other law enforcement agencies were able to solve many cases by examining lifted prints from crime scenes and comparing them to already filed fingerprint cards. Criminal history checks could/can also be conducted by comparing inked print cards to existing fingerprints on file. Today, many fingerprint submissions and comparisons are done electronically or with computer/electronic aids.

DNA evidence also allows law enforcement and other investigators to cross-check and/or compare evidence to prove or disprove whether suspects had involvement in certain matters. The FBI's Combined DNA Index System, more commonly known as "CODIS," is a coordinated system of federal, state, and local databases of DNA profiles. Today, DNA evidence identifies suspects even years after they committed the crime. It also has proven that people sentenced and imprisoned for felony offenses never actually committed the crimes they were convicted of.

Sometimes the federal investigative agencies that conduct forensic examinations come under scrutiny. For example, on July 17, 2013, the *Washington Post* reported, "An unprecedented federal review of old criminal cases has uncovered as many as 27 death penalty convictions in which FBI forensic experts may have mistakenly linked defendants to crimes with exaggerated scientific testimony, U.S. officials said."

In a guest column printed in the *Commercial Appeal* (Memphis, TN) on August 18, 2013, Peter Neufeld, codirector of the Innocence Project, wrote an article titled "DNA Exonerations Hold Many Lessons." According to Neufeld: "Since 1989, 311 people have been exonerated by DNA evidence. Eighteen of these individuals served time on death row . . . Of the 311 DNA exonerations, 72 involved erroneous hair analysis."

Although the examination and comparison of DNA evidence has proven to be a useful tool to charge criminals, the preceding paragraphs demonstrate that all investigations should be thorough and complete.

When investigators make or request fingerprint and DNA searches and comparisons, they often make use of new and previous existing information for the purpose of obtaining evidence about an existing and/or previous investigation. Well-trained law enforcement officers and investigators will utilize these two tools regularly (or at least as needed). Perhaps one of the reasons the two are used so frequently (besides their incredible value) is because they are relatively easy to utilize. Requesting fingerprint and DNA checks and comparisons is kind of like purchasing a ticket at a church raffle—you have nothing to lose (as long as your goal is to establish the truth).

However, DNA testing can get expensive. On November 13, 2013, The Commercial Appeal (Memphis, TN) reported that the Memphis Police Department "pays $225 per rape kit for serology (a preliminary test to determine if there is enough DNA present to screen) plus shipping and DNA tests cost $500."

Compiling, searching, and querying legally obtained information can be of immense value. For example, a component of the FBI's Critical Incident Response Group, commonly referred to as "CIRG" is called the National Center for Analysis of Violent Crime (NCAVC). It assists federal, state, local, and international law enforcement officers and security agencies when investigating violent crimes (including street gangs and terrorism) that include unusual or repeated offenses based on behavior analysis. This proves extremely useful when trying to identify serial offenders.

Another database worth mentioning is the Terrorist Identities Datamart Environment (TIDE), which is the U.S. government's central database of known or suspected international terrorists. This database contains highly classified information provided by the Central Intelligence Agency, the FBI, the Defense Intelligence Agency, and the National Security Agency.

From TIDE, the FBI extracts information that is compiled in a Terrorist Screening Database, which is utilized by law enforcement to help keep the United States safe from terrorists.

NCIC

Law enforcement personnel can also input and run checks on the National Crime Information Center (NCIC), which is run by the FBI. Records stored on the NCIC include missing persons, fugitives, sex offenders, arrest records, outstanding warrants, protection orders, stolen property (with uniquely described or serial numbers), Department of Motor Vehicle information (including stolen license plates, stolen vehicles' identification numbers as well as stolen boats and guns information, and so on). The use of NCIC is strictly controlled and for the use of law enforcement.

INTERPOL

INTERPOL is an international agency, headquartered in France that provides administrative liaison between member country law enforcement agencies. It maintains DNA samples, fingerprints, mug shots, lists of wanted persons, and other information while assisting law enforcement agencies around the globe to communicate and share information. Interpol can also track crime trends and criminals around the world.

NOTE: All of these details are publicly available information and often referenced by news media.

With the aid of computers and software, more useful investigative information is legally stored, searched, and analyzed, resulting in increased identification of patterns, trends, and anomalies that were almost impossible to be performed decades ago. (J. Edgar Hoover, the first director of the FBI, undoubtedly would have been quite impressed.)

Resources

Very often the reason some cases are never solved is the large amount of work required to solve them. Also, trying to solve one case at a time requires lots of resources. The more open-case investigations on the books, the more investigators who are needed. And each investigator needs his or her own equipment and tools as well as training, salary, benefits, and so on. With budget cuts affecting almost every government agency, many are being forced to try to do more with less. And as much as I hate when other people say it, I have to agree: Sometimes you need to work smarter, not harder.

War Story 4.2

As a new investigator back in the days when we still used typewriters to prepare reports and carbon paper to make copies and none of us had computers, I often volunteered to cross-check paper copies of local pawnshop receipt tickets stored at the local police department. The primary purpose was to attempt to identify stolen property by comparing serial numbers of reported stolen property with the serial numbers listed on pawnshop receipt tickets.

It was a long, tedious process of thumbing through numerous boxes of paper pawnshop receipts. Sometimes the pawnshop employees failed to write the serial numbers down or scribbled them (making the numbers illegible), which made it impossible to know if those pawned items were previously reported stolen.

Complicating things, many victims of theft of property did not know the make, model, or serial numbers of the items stolen from them. In the past, most investigators I worked with would say those cases were almost impossible to solve. I disagreed because there were too many other ways to gain evidence (witnesses, fingerprints at the scene, informants, admissions, confessions, and circumstantial evidence).

To make the pawnshop ticket searches even more productive, I made lists of the names of all suspects from the various property crimes my office investigated. While thumbing through the pawn tickets and checking for serial numbers, I also searched for suspects' names.

When I found suspects' names, I made copies of those pawn tickets. After returning to my office, I cross-referenced everything they pawned with the stolen property files. When appropriate, I called the suspects in to be interviewed. Very often, suspects would voluntarily confess to thefts. Many of those confessions pertained to the theft of property whose serial numbers victims did not know.

Taking these pawnshop ticket searches a step further, whenever I found pawn tickets that identified stolen property by serial number or by suspect name, I also wrote down the names of the people who pawned items right before them and right after them. It was not difficult to do because the tickets had unique ticket numbers and were filed in chronological order by date.

Sometimes I found that the same people always pawned items right before or right after a known suspect. My investigative theory was: Many people commit crimes in pairs, and criminals often hang out with other criminals. As a result of these efforts, I sometimes identified co-conspirators and people who stole other items. I then called those people in for interviews and often got voluntary confessions to more thefts.

Even though I was reviewing the same source of evidence that many other investigators had access to, I was able to solve many more crimes and recover much more stolen property because my mind-set was completely different from theirs.

Retailers have learned over time that a large percentage of items are returned (with and without receipts). Some of the returns involve fraud. For example, a customer might switch the $800 UPC code tag on a widget with a $50 UPC code tag of a similarly described item. After paying just $50 for the item, the scammer returns later (without a receipt or the lowered price UPC code tag) seeking a refund (or store credit) for the actual cost of the item ($800). To fight against this type of fraud, some retailers outsource the information about returns (and the people who made them) to other companies that catalog and analyze the information to help protect the stores from future scammed returns by the same individuals.

On November 16, 2013, an Associated Press article was published titled "IRS Issued $4 Billion to Identity Thieves." Along with numerous instances of identity theft mentioned, it was also reported that "the IRS sent a total of 655 tax refunds to a single address in Lithuania and 343 refunds went to a lone address in Shanghai."

As evident by the incidents mentioned above, investigators should strive not only to solve the cases in front of them but also to attempt to link or compare new and existing legally obtained information to other legally obtained information for the purpose of identifying more wrongdoers and/or more wrongdoing by the same individuals.

Seven Questions: Five Ws and Two Hs Plus "Else"

Chapter 3 listed seven key questions to be asked in any investigation. To conduct more thorough investigations (which will not only help solve the case in your hand but also assist in solving other closed, open, and yet-to-be-opened cases), investigators need to ask all those seven questions and then these seven additional questions:

1. Who else?
2. What else?
3. When else?
4. Where else?
5. Why else?
6. How else?
7. How much else?

Currently, Previously, or in the Future

When asking the seven additional questions, the investigator should consider the likelihood that the same or similar wrongdoing (or whatever matter is being investigated) is currently occurring, happened in the past and could happen in the future. Attempting to identify current and previous occurrences may or may not be difficult. Projecting possible future occurrences could result in a higher solve rate in the future and—better yet—might allow the investigator to suggest or implement measures to prevent the same type incident(s) from happening in the first place.

NOTE: Investigators do not always need to ask the additional seven questions aloud; sometimes investigators can ask them in their own minds. While reading the next few examples, remember the importance (and possible availability) of the FBI's NCAVC and other information sources previously described.

1. Who else?
   • Who else did this suspect victimize?
   • Who else was (or could have been) victimized by this same suspect?
   • Who else was (or could have been) victimized by this same type offense?
   • Who else was involved (before, during, or after)?
   • Who else may have aided, assisted (before, during, or after)?
   • Who else might have knowledge (before, during, or after)?
   • Who else might be a victim of this type of wrong in the future?
   • Who else might be committing this same type offense?

NOTE: It is also important to attempt to identifying co-subjects, co-conspirators, and others who might have contributed to or aided the main subject(s) before, during, or after the wrongdoing. The importance of identifying these types of individuals is especially emphasized during the investigation of street gangs, illegal drug sales and distribution, and terrorism. For example, after the terroristic bombings of September 11, 2001, and the 2013 Boston Marathon, law enforcement and investigators immediately combined their resources and conducted thorough, well-planned, and complete investigations. The investigative results were extremely impressive. Since being extremely thorough and thinking about who else was involved works well in those type cases, it would be wise to at least think along those lines when conducting most other investigations.

2. What else?
   - What else has this suspect done wrong/illegal?
   - What else would prove or disprove this case?
   - What (other way) could this have occurred?
   - What else was said?
   - What else was involved or could have been involved?
   - What (other) evidence is there?
   - What (other) evidence could there be?
3. When else?
   - When else did this suspect do the same type thing?
   - When else did this suspect do something similar?
   - When else did someone else do something like this?
   - When else was this victim victimized?
   - When else has this complainant complained?
   - When else has something like this happened?
4. Where else?
   - Where else did this suspect do the same thing?
   - Where else did this suspect do something similar?
   - Where else did someone else do this same thing?
   - Where else did someone else do something similar?
   - Where else would evidence be located?
   - Where else would witnesses be located?
   - Where else has this happened?

5. Why else?
   - Why else would the person do what they are suspected of?
   - Why else would the person not do what they are suspected of?
   - Why else did this happen?
   - Why else could this have happened?
6. How else?
   - How else could this have happened?
   - How else could the suspect have accomplished this?
   - How else could someone else have accomplished this?
   - How else can the investigator get what they are seeking?
   - How else can this be proven or disproven?
   - How else could this have been prevented?
7. How much else?
   - How much else has the suspect done wrong/illegal that has not already been proven?
   - How much else is inefficient that contributed to the matter investigated?
   - How much else was stolen, removed, damaged (etc.) that has not yet been reported?
   - How much else can the investigator do to identify facts pertinent to this or related matters?

Thinking Like Others

Early in my career, there were times when I could not solve some cases after exhausting all efforts. Then it occurred to me that I had to change my mind-set to think like different people so I could come up with different answers. At the surface that sounds like Dr. Jekyll and Mr. Hyde kind of stuff—and perhaps it is. But in a nutshell, it works like this:

Think: How would the suspect have done this?

Think: How would someone similar to the suspect have done this?

Think: How would someone not at all like (the opposite) the suspect have done this?

Think: How would you (the investigator) have done this?

TIP: If the suspect is not known, just think how the typical suspect would have done this.

NOTE: You also can think about the periods before and after the incidents being investigated in this way. For example, ask: What would you have done before doing this? What would you have done after doing this? By objectively taking four different mental approaches— thinking like your suspect, like someone like your suspect, like someone nothing like your suspect, and like yourself—you might (or often will) get four different perspectives on the same matter. Between the four mind-sets, very often you will find the answer to your questions (or at least get possible leads to follow up on).

War Story 4.3

When I was a patrolman in a city's high-crime business district, there were low-income government subsidized housing projects on both the east and west sides of my patrol beat. The one on the east was called "East Side Housing" and the one on the west was called "West Side Housing." (These are fictitious names, as you might have guessed.)

Main Street was a north-and-south road, which was basically right in the middle of my beat. Over time, I learned that if armed robberies, shootings, or other violent crimes occurred on the east side of my beat, the suspects often ran home to East Side Housing. And when those types of offenses occurred on the west side of my beat, the suspects often ran home to West Side Housing. Obviously it didn't always work that way, but sometimes it did.

One morning at about 7:00 (just before the end of a midnight shift), there was a report of an armed robbery (man with a gun) about a mile southeast of my beat. At about 7:15, there was a report of another armed robbery about a half mile from my beat. At about 7:30, there was a report of another armed robbery about one block from my beat. All of the victims provided the same type description of their robber: a tall, slender, black male wearing blue jeans and a white T-shirt.

As soon as I heard the third armed robbery call on the police radio, I floored my patrol car's gas pedal and headed toward East Side Housing. Sure enough, I saw the suspect fleeing on foot and heading right toward the same place I was heading. The suspect was fast as lightning, and his long running stride allowed him to cross the four-lane street in about three steps! I called in on my radio as soon as I saw the suspect. In a matter of seconds, I lost sight of the fleeing man because he ran between a group of houses that all looked alike and were close to one another.

I and a backup police unit headed in opposite directions searching for the man. A shoot-out with the suspect ensued. No one was injured, and the suspect subsequently was captured. Understandably the victims were kind of shaken up, but at least they got their money back.

Thinking like the suspect and making use of known information (including pattern and trends) can be of great value when conducting investigations.

CAUTION: Before reading any further, remember this: Don't get into an illegal "profiling" mode while investigating. Although you can capitalize on following trends and patterns with great results, illegal profiling can get your cases thrown out of court, and you and your organization might end up getting sued. It's one thing to think a certain way but another to act solely on those thoughts.

Not long ago, police got in trouble for making traffic stops of people and cars on Interstate 95 with certain characteristics because over the years they learned those characteristics were common denominators to drug trafficking. In August 2013, a federal judge criticized the New York City Police Department's stop-question-frisk policy, claiming that the policy discriminated based on race. Others argued that the stops were not made based on race but on where crimes took place.

In my opinion, there is no arguing that common denominators exist, but taking action based solely on the color of a person's skin, country of origin, license plate state, or type of car can get a law enforcement officer and/or investigator in a heap of trouble—and it's not fair to the people confronted. If you're going to play a hunch, make sure you can legally justify your actions. It often comes down to remembering to treat others the way you'd like to be treated. Based on recent trends, at some point the reason for your stop(s) or actions will be scrutinized. Make darn sure you play by the rules, obey the law, and thoroughly document your observations and actions. If there are witnesses to what took place, write their names down or, even better, get them to provide written statements.

Three Investigative Exploration Approaches

Although not a math wizard, I have utilized the next investigative exploration approaches successfully to solve both reported and unreported crimes:

- If A is true, so possibly is B.
- If A and B are true, so probably is C.
- If A, B, and/or C are true, so probably is D.

NOTE: The investigative exploration approaches can be expanded.

Next are some examples of how investigators can utilize the exploration approaches. But as previously cautioned, these approaches are ways of thinking and do not call for taking any action unless it is legally justified. Saying "I had a hunch" or "They fit the profile" will most likely get you in trouble and/or your case thrown out.

1. If A is true, so possibly is B.

   Example 1: A person who stole a laptop computer and pawned it probably stole other things and pawned them.

   Example 2: A person who sold illegal drugs once probably sold illegal drugs to other people.

   Example 3: A person who submitted one false invoice to one company probably submitted more false invoices to that company.

   Example 4: A person who paid one person bribes probably paid other people bribes.

   Example 5: A person who accepted a bribe from one person probably has accepted bribes from other people.

2. If A and B are true, so probably is C.

Example 1: A person who stole a laptop computer and pawned it and stole other things and pawned them probably stole other things and sold them elsewhere.

Example 2: A person who sold illegal drugs once and to other people probably knows others who are selling illegal drugs (as suppliers and/or distributors).

Example 3: A person who submitted one false invoice to one company and more false invoices to that company probably has submitted false invoices to other companies.

Example 4: A person who paid one person bribes and paid other people bribes probably has committed other unethical or illegal offenses.

Example 5: A person who accepted a bribe from one person and accepted bribes from other people probably has committed other unethical or illegal offenses.

3. If A, B, and/or C are true, so probably is D.

Example 1: A person who stole a laptop computer and pawned it and stole other things and pawned them and/or stole other things and sold them elsewhere probably has committed other wrongs that are totally unrelated.

Example 2: A person who sold illegal drugs once and to other people and knows others who are selling illegal drugs probably knows of many others who are involved in many other illegal activities.

Example 3: A person who submitted one false invoice to one company and more false invoices to that same company and has submitted false invoices to other companies probably has committed other unrelated frauds and/or white-collar offenses.

Example 4: A person who paid one person bribes and paid other people bribes and committed other unethical or illegal offenses probably knows others who have committed similar crimes.

Example 5: A person who accepted a bribe from one person and accepted bribes from other people and has committed other unethical or illegal offenses probably knows others who have committed similar crimes.

Essentially, conducting thorough investigations involves doing these things:

- Utilizing your training
- Making use of all the tools, resources, and techniques at your disposal
- Obtaining as much information as legally possible
- Comparing everything
- Altering your mind-set
- Thinking with an open mind
- Playing the odds
- Following the rules

Information that can be legally obtained and compared or considered could be endless.

Follow the Same Blueprint

We've all heard the phrase "There's no need to reinvent the wheel." If something already exists, works, and is effective, just keep using that (or doing that) to accomplish your objectives. Very often investigators work extremely hard to solve cases. Often the efforts also involve research and trial-and-error methods. But by the time the case is completed (usually beforehand), the investigator will have developed a blueprint of the crime, wrongdoing, or other occurrence, how it was accomplished, and how the case was solved.

Repeating the same exact investigative process (perhaps with a few adjustments) very often results in identifying other wrongs or offenses committed by the same suspect or similar wrongs/offenses committed by other suspects. Those cases will be solved in much less time than it took to solve the first case! Expending just a bit more effort often results in doubling, tripling, and even quadrupling the investigator's solve or recovery rate! (Feel free to read this paragraph again.)

War Story 4.4
When I was assigned full time to investigate the possession, sale, and distribution of illegal drugs, it was understood that all drug cases had potential investigative value. A doper who purchases

a small quantity of illegal drugs received them from someone and knows who that person is. Getting the suspect to voluntarily identify the drug seller helps the investigator work up the chain to get to the highest possible source.

When I was in the army, my division went on a 30-day training mission at Fort Irwin, California, in the Mojave Desert. Unlike the other soldiers who went there to train for war, my mission was to serve as an investigator to investigate real crimes that occurred while my division was in training. In fact, I was the only soldier there with real bullets in his weapon.

One day, a company commander told me that a single marijuana cigarette was found next to a rolled-up sleeping bag belonging to one of his young soldiers. The soldier in question was a low-ranking private (E-2). Normally the case would have just been written up as "found contraband." But all the troops and their belongings were searched before coming to the training so there was some concern about how the joint made its way to the training site.

Since I had nothing better to do, I interviewed the young private, and of course he denied the hand-rolled cigarette was his. I next told him that I would like to run a test on his hands to determine if they had touched THC (the active ingredient in marijuana) in the past 24 hours. Although I never conducted the test (and I don't think such a test even exists), he quickly admitted the marijuana cigarette was his. Part two of the interview was getting him to voluntarily tell me where he got the marijuana cigarette.

The private informed me that he was standing guard duty outside in the desert when a civilian contractor's truck drove up. The truck driver was supposed to clean/empty the portable latrines (bathrooms). The truck driver asked the private if he wanted to buy any marijuana, and he purchased a nickel bag ($5 worth).

Part three of the investigation was ascertaining if the soldier was willing to work undercover for us. I explained that we (the government) would give the soldier five dollars to make another drug purchase from the same man while standing guard duty at the same location. I explained that some other undercover MPs and I would conduct covert surveillance of the purchase and photograph it. We photocopied the currency before giving it to the suspect, who was now our informant. The informant also wore a body recorder for us.

The next day, everything went as planned, and the toilet cleaning civilian sold the young private $5 worth of marijuana. Over the course of a week, several more controlled purchases were made from the same toilet cleaner; the quantity and price continued to climb until it progressed to one pound of marijuana.

On the day of the larger purchase, we put our team together and even called in the local police to be on standby. After the sale of the pound of marijuana, the toilet cleaning suspect was immediately arrested for wrongful possession and sale of illegal drugs.

The drug dealer was then turned over to the local authorities for questioning, and hopefully the local authorities pursued the investigation further. My work on that case ended after the last on-base drug deal . . .

The point is, those who investigate illegal drug cases understand the importance of not thinking singular (and always thinking plural). The same is true of investigators who conduct street gang and terrorism investigations. Treating each incident as just an individual occurrence is counterproductive. Don't think singular; think plural.

Chapter 5 outlines how to conduct up to 10 related investigations simultaneously including searches for systemic weaknesses as well as waste and abuse.

Chapter 5

Fraud, Waste, Abuse, and Systemic Weaknesses

"QUESTION: What do you call someone who is willing to pay $800 for a toilet seat?
ANSWER: General."

—1980s political joke

While serving as a federal agent, my case assignments included but were not limited to investigating fraud, waste, and abuse affecting the organization for which I was employed. My responsibilities also included simultaneously attempting to identify any systemic weaknesses that may have caused or contributed to the fraud, waste, or abuse.

Fraud

Many sources define the term "fraud."

Dictionary.com defines fraud as:

1. deceit, trickery, sharp practice, or breach of confidence, perpetrated for profit or to gain some unfair or dishonest advantage.
2. a particular instance of such deceit or trickery: mail fraud; election frauds.
3. any deception, trickery, or humbug: That diet book is a fraud and a waste of time.
4. a person who makes deceitful pretenses; sham; poseur.

Thefreedictionary.com defines fraud as:

1. A deception deliberately practiced in order to secure unfair or unlawful gain.
2. A piece of trickery; a trick.

merriam-webster.com defines fraud as:

a. deceit, trickery; specifically: intentional perversion of truth in order to induce another to part with something of value or to surrender a legal right
b. an act of deceiving or misrepresenting

Black's Law Dictionary defines fraud as:

A knowing misrepresentation of the truth or concealment of a material fact to induce another to act to his or her detriment.

The Association of Certified Fraud Examiners and many other anti-fraud organizations define fraud as:

The use of one's occupation for personal enrichment through the deliberate misuse or misapplication of the employing organization's resources or assets.

Waste

Waste might be described as an incident or practice that results in the expenditure of resources in excess of actual need and/or results in unnecessary costs.

Abuse

Abuse might be described as a practice that is inconsistent with sound fiscal business practices and results in unnecessary costs.

In short, both waste and abuse often result in wasted expenditures.

NOTE: The definitions of waste and abuse are paraphrased from descriptions provided by the U.S. General Accountability Office.

Systemic Weaknesses

A systemic weakness might be described as something that causes fundamental problems with the efficiency and effectiveness of a system or process.

When I conducted criminal, civil, and administrative investigations for the federal government, my final investigative reports had to mention whether I had identified any systemic weaknesses during the course of the investigations. If I did identify systemic weaknesses, I had to prepare a separate report identifying the weaknesses and make recommendations for corrective action and/or improvement.

As an agent, I didn't get paid any extra for identifying systemic weaknesses, writing the supplemental reports, or making suggestions for improvement. Supplemental reports identifying systemic weaknesses sometimes are called management control deficiency reports, fraud vulnerability reports, or some other similar name.

NOTE: Through the years, I came to realize that many successful investigators I knew never or seldom reported that they identified any systemic weaknesses during their investigations and therefore seldom (if ever) wrote supplemental reports or recommendations for improvement. After all, how could anyone prove whether an investigator identified any weaknesses or not? And if investigators never looked for systemic weaknesses in the first place, odds are they would not find any.

Simultaneously investigating fraud (criminal and civil violations), waste, and abuse as well as searching for systemic weaknesses is a lot to ask of an investigator. And to be even more thorough, the investigator also should include the investigative methods outlined in Chapter 4: attempting to link or identify additional offenses and/or wrongdoers.

As a private investigator and consultant, I still investigate in this thorough and complete manner unless my clients/employers want to limit the scope of the work. But my brain still thinks along those lines even when clients want less thorough investigations. Thorough investigations take more time to complete, but often the results are worth it.

Ten Simultanous Investigations

Utilizing this investigative methodology is the equivalent of conducting 10 or more separate but related investigations simultaneously:

1. Investigating for criminal violations
2. Investigating for civil violations
3. Investigating for administrative violations
4. Investigating to determine if the same suspect committed similar wrongful acts
5. Investigating to determine if the suspect committed other somewhat related wrongful acts
6. Considering whether others might have or might be committing the same type of wrongful acts
7. Considering how others might commit the same or similar acts in the future
8. Investigating for indications of waste/abuse
9. Investigating for indications of systemic weaknesses
10. Considering ways the system can be improved to prevent future occurrences

NOTE: Whenever investigating any one individual, the investigator should always be mindful of possible involvement of accomplices, co-conspirators, and others who may have assisted before, during, or after the offense(s).

As mentioned, the missions of many investigative agencies/organizations are only to investigate criminal violations and perhaps also civil violations. It may not be their responsibility to perform the other eight types of investigative efforts. In the closing paragraphs of this chapter I address some of the shortcomings of conducting those less thorough investigations.

Someone who has committed fraud often can be considered for both criminal and/or civil prosecution. However, suspects who have been involved only in wrongs resulting in waste and/or abuse normally are not considered for criminal prosecution and usually not for civil prosecution. They could, however, sometimes be held responsible administratively, demoted in rank/position, reassigned, or perhaps have their employment terminated for such actions.

Although not accurate to do so, I often use the words "waste and abuse" interchangeably because they both involving misuse of assets and/or use of assets for purposes for which they were not intended. Most legitimate organizations and entities want to get the most bang for their buck. (Well, at least the taxpayers, business owners, and/or stockholders do.)

The federal government has a (well-deserved) reputation for wasting tax dollars. So for federal investigators, identifying instances of waste and abuse is sometimes as easy as just looking up from their own desks (maybe even at their own desks).

War Story 5.1

The very first instance of waste and abuse within the federal government that I became aware of was when I was a private in the U.S. Army and serving in a combat engineer unit in Germany. (**NOTE:** I served in the engineers for my first year in the Army before joining the military police.) While my unit was preparing for an inspector general (IG) inspection, we had to paint almost everything that wasn't moving olive drab green. We also had to make sure that 100 percent of the items and equipment that we were previously issued were accountable for. Our company commander's job evaluation depended greatly on how he/we did in the IG's inspection. And in the Army, this saying holds true: "Crap rolls downhill." We all knew it was imperative that we pass the IG's inspection.

The IG's inspection team didn't know it, but whatever items our unit was short of, we borrowed from other units that were not going through an inspection. We just paint-stenciled our company's name on the items for the inspection. Afterward, we repainted the items and returned them to the original units. From what I could gather, all the companies on our base did the same thing.

There was also a lot of barrack thievery going on in my company right before the IG's inspection because each soldier had to be in possession of the items they were issued. We were all issued gas masks, which had to be stored on top of our wall lockers (along with our sleeping bags and field gear). But fellow soldiers kept stealing others' unsecured gas masks. The reason for the theft was that many of the soldiers used the tubes on their gas masks to smoke hashish. Since they didn't want to get caught with hash residue on their own masks, they'd steal other people's masks.

This created a domino effect, because even nondopers started stealing other people's gas masks after someone stole theirs. (As an aside, our unit's clothes drier never had a lint screen in it because dopers kept cutting screens for their hash pipes from it.) Dope (especially the use of hashish) was a big problem in my unit; I could write an entire chapter just about that.

Let me get back to the IG's inspection and the story about waste and abuse. In addition to needing to possess everything we were issued, our unit was not allowed to possess any government property that we did not have receipts for. So anything that was excess had to be gotten rid of. Many of the guys who lived off base brought trunkloads of government equipment home to hide until after the inspection.

But the strangest thing that I witnessed was when I was asked by my supervisor to help carry a large wooden crate to a nearby Dumpster. The crate was very heavy and nailed shut. On the way to the Dumpster, I asked one of the sergeants what was in the crate. He said, "It's a brand-new radiator for a deuce-and-a-half truck. But we can't find the receipt for it so we have to throw it out."

Even as a dumb private, I knew this was waste. But in the end, our unit passed the IG's inspection with flying colors, and our company commander awarded everyone in the unit with a three-day pass!

War Story 5.2

Four or five years later, I was serving as a Military Police investigator when two young privates wearing civilian clothes came into my office. They insisted that I take them to a specific isolated area in the woods so they could show me something.

I gave the two privates a ride in my unmarked police car as they gave me verbal directions to the wooded area. On the way there, the privates told me they were both getting kicked out of the Army and for the past several days had been assigned a bunch of "crap details," like painting and cleaning latrines. They said their intelligence unit was getting ready to undergo an IG inspection and earlier that same morning, their company commander ordered them to take some excess government equipment to the woods, destroy the equipment, and bury the evidence.

The two privates said that a third private was with them at the time, but he was back at their barracks. I asked what happened to the equipment, and one of the privates said, "We were ordered to smash and destroy all of it—including night-vision devices and other expensive stuff—and then told to dig a big hole in the ground to hide the pieces." Having experienced IG inspection preparations in my old unit, I had no reason to doubt what the privates told me.

When we arrived at the isolated area, I parked my car and the privates exited looking puzzled. When I walked up to meet them, I looked down and saw a six-by-six-foot hole in the ground. One of the privates shouted, "They dug the stuff back up and it's empty!"

I asked the privates what was going on and was informed that they had done what they were told and smashed up all the equipment and buried it; but someone had since dug the hole back up and removed everything. One private pointed to a nearby tree and said, "You can see the marks on this tree where we smashed the night-vision devices and stuff against it." I looked closely. It was obvious the tree had been struck numerous times, and there were even olive drab plastic fragments on the ground next to the tree.

Just about that time, an Army jeep approached us. Frankly, I wondered how anyone found us because we were in the middle of nowhere. The two privates yelled to me when they saw who the driver of the jeep was: "It's our company commander!" They also told me that the young man sitting next to their commander was the third private who had smashed up the equipment and buried it with them earlier.

The uniformed company commander (a captain with two silver bars on his fatigue shirt collar) stepped out of the jeep, followed by the young private passenger. The private was wearing civilian clothes but was barefoot.

The company commander stepped right to the freshly dug-up ditch, walked a full circle around it, and seemed to be inspecting the inside of the ditch. He never said a word to me or anyone else while doing this. I was wearing a suit and tie at the time, and all the soldiers knew that the only people on base who wore suits were either CID or MPI. Factually, my pay grade was only a corporal (two stripes), but nobody could tell that while I was wearing civilian clothes.

Next, the captain walked right up to me and said with a cocky tone, "Well, Mr. Investigator, it looks like the only thing you got here is a big hole."

The captain's arrogance and condescending tone irked me, but I was accustomed to dealing with bigger jerks than he. Without hesitation, I replied in a *Dirty Harry* tone, "Captain, why don't you park your ass back in your jeep and meet me at the MP station and we'll see what I got."

Quite honestly, that was the first time in my career I talked to a commissioned officer in that manner. But his lack of respect for me and my position as an investigator made me think of him as just another criminal.

The captain became furious because I talked to him the way I did, and he quickly turned to walk toward the jeep. Simultaneously, he told the barefoot private to come with him. I yelled out, "Not so fast, Captain. That private is coming with me!"

The captain immediately responded, "But he doesn't have any shoes on."

I replied, "You're the one that brought him out here like that. And he's coming with me."

The captain drove off in the jeep by himself with his tail between his legs.

The three privates all started laughing out loud at the same time. For a moment, the four of us enlisted guys had had our revenge. Plus I knew that I was about to make that captain's life even more miserable.

I intended to photograph the scene and retain the plastic fragments on the ground as evidence. I also would obtain written statements from the three privates and write a detailed report describing the captain's unexpected arrival at the scene and what transpired. But after I had taken the photographs, the MP dispatcher called me on the radio and ordered me to return to the MP station as soon as possible.

When I arrived at the MP station with the three privates, the MP desk sergeant looked at me and said, "You are in big trouble, and the MP operations officer [MPO] wants to see you in his office right now!"

I asked the three privates to have a seat in the front of the MP station while I walked to the office of the MPO. The MPO was an Army major. As soon as I stepped in, the MPO verbally reprimanded me for showing disrespect to a commissioned officer (that captain). I tried explaining to the MPO what had transpired, but he would not listen. The MPO ordered me to stop conducting the investigation and to not open a case on the matter. I was told that the three privates would be escorted back to their units by other MPs and I was to have no further contact with them.

I felt like I was in the middle of a *Twilight Zone* episode. I was just doing my job, the captain was a crook, and I suspected the privates were going to get in even more trouble for talking to me. Anyone who has served in the military knows that rank rules, especially in the Army. There's no talking back, and you have to follow orders. If you don't do what you are told, you'll pay the consequences.

This was just another example of waste and abuse inside the military (and the government). But I can tell you that this kind of stuff goes on a lot more often than people might think.

War Story 5.3

A couple of years later during the month of September, I was a sergeant (three stripes) assigned to that same MPI Office and a MP staff sergeant (three stripes and a rocker) came in and asked how many investigators worked under me. I told him 10. The staff sergeant then said, "I'm ordering you 11 new desks."

I told him we didn't need any news desks because ours were fine. He said, "The fiscal year ends on September 30 and we have money left over. If we don't spend it, we won't get the same dollar amount for our annual budget next year."

NOTE: The U.S. Government's fiscal years starts on October 1 and ends at the end of September. I have found this end-of-the-year spending practice to be the same in every single military unit, federal organization, and agency that I know of in the three decades I served in the federal government. During my tenure I saw taxpayer money intentionally squandered on a regular basis just so the organizations could receive the same amount of money (or more) the following year. The assumption was/is that if the units/organizations needed that dollar amount this year, they must need the same amount (or more) the next year. The budgets grew every single year!

War Story 5.4

One August, about 22 years after the desks incident, I was serving as a federal agent in Las Vegas, Nevada, and my supervisor told me to make a trip to Reno and spend a couple days doing liaison with federal prosecutors and other federal investigative agencies. I told my supervisor I didn't have time for that and I also did not have any cases in Reno. My supervisor said that it didn't matter because our region needed to spend money before the end of year. The supervisor told me some agents in Arizona were being sent to California to meet with agents from other agencies (even though the agents in Arizona did not work cases in California).

Worse yet, I was also told that other regions in our own agency needed funds to travel to work cases and were seeking travel funds from our region because we had a surplus.

Rather than sharing the funds with agents in different regions of our own agency, my supervisors were telling us to spend funds unnecessarily so our own region would get the same dollar amount for traveling the following year. If they surrendered money to another region, they'd get less the following year. What really surprised me was a few weeks later, the highest-ranking superior in our field office sent an e-mail to all of the subordinate agents that read something like "Congratulations, you spent all the money." Predictably, that supervisor got another promotion after that!

War Story 5.5

My agency, which was supposed to investigate fraud, waste, and abuse, seemed to enjoy spending money on training (along with the travel costs, meals and lodging expenses that went with it). I know of one agent who was told by his supervisors to stay in a hotel at government expense to attend training even though he lived five minutes from the hotel and there was nothing wrong with his house. He spent three or four nights at the hotel (at taxpayers' expense).

In my opinion, there is no way the expense could be justified. It seemed that my supervisors wanted to keep the training budget as high as they could to ensure they could get the same amount (or more) the following year.

Very often my agency would hold annual in-service trainings at locations where almost all the agents had to incur travel, meal, and hotel expenses instead of holding the training at a location where several agents worked and lived.

For example, one year, two regions (about 80 agents) traveled to and spent several days in Reno, for in-service training, even though we didn't have an office in Reno and, as far as I knew, we had no open cases there. This meant that many agents had to fly to get to the destination. We could have had held the training in an area that was more centrally located—and/or where some agents could have stayed at their own homes overnight. But we never did. It was all about spending taxpayer money, so the agency could get more money the next year. Once my supervisors made us have training at some lodge in the mountains in Colorado. Other times we stayed at beachfront hotels. What a waste!

War Story 5.6

In my opinion, one of the biggest wastes of taxpayers' funds in my own agency involved the funding of certain leadership training. Select investigators and supervisors were allowed to pursue master's degrees in a business management field at a prestigious university in or near Washington, DC. I may not have had as much heartburn about it if the courses were taught online and completed on the employees' own time. But that was not the case, and many of the investigators pursuing the degrees were not managers and had no intentions of becoming managers.

The taxpayers not only paid the cost of the tuition and books but also for the employees' airfare to fly to and from classes, their hotel stays, their meals, and incidental expenses. Worse, those investigators weren't doing any investigative work while they were traveling to and from school or in class. Some people are under the impression that furthering education is always a good thing. But this arrangement was, in my opinion, a complete waste of tax dollars and resulted in many investigators getting master's degrees that were totally unrelated to their jobs! Just like many other government programs, once they start, they usually never stop. The kicker was that this agency was supposed to be the one investigating fraud, waste, and abuse.

I could devote another entire chapter to war stories involving the waste and abuse within the federal government, but I think I touched on the topic sufficiently.

As stated in Chapter 2 and elaborated on later in this chapter, some law enforcement and/or investigative agencies investigate only "criminal" violations, never administrative matters or waste and abuse. It has been my experience that sometimes wrongdoing involving the misuse of assets actually is a criminal and/or civil violation. But when the prosecutors elect not to accept those cases for prosecution, those cases have to fall into some other category, which might be waste and abuse. For example, if an employee uses his company credit card to put gas into his personal car, but no one will prosecute it, is it still a "crime"? If a supervisor purchases 11 desks that are not needed, is that a crime?

If an agency's leader allocates funds for employees to travel nationwide to and attend college courses that will not enhance their job performance, is that a crime?

Also, sometimes cases are not accepted for prosecution because government personnel or the government's policies and practices caused or contributed to the wrongdoing.

War Story 5.7

I conducted an investigation involving allegations that a government contractor supplied defective electric cable that was to be used on U.S. Navy nuclear aircraft carriers and submarines. I had the cable tested by a laboratory, which reported that the cable did not meet the required flame-retardant specifications and had other defects. According to the laboratory, if the wire had been installed, it could have caused fires on the vessels and endangered the lives of everyone on board.

My investigation showed that the government contracting officer improperly listed (or allowed to be used) a 10-year-old military specification in the contract instead of the newer specification. I subsequently learned that the cable provided by the contractor did meet the 10-year-old specification but not the newer one.

During the investigation, I also inquired whether the government ever inspected the cable before accepting it (which is most often a requirement on such a critical item). I learned that in this case, the government failed to require inspection of the cable before accepting it.

In short, government employees dropped the ball. There were so many problems with the case that I knew no one would be prosecuted criminally, where we had the burden of proving criminal intent beyond the reasonable doubt. As a formality, I presented the case to a federal criminal prosecutor for consideration and also told him about all the problems we'd face trying to prove criminal intent on the contractor's part. The federal prosecutor rightfully declined to prosecute.

I took the case downstairs to a civil federal prosecutor, who accepted it because the burden of proof is much less in civil cases. In a civil case, we only needed to prove willful neglect by the preponderance of the evidence. The contractor certified (in writing) that the cable would meet the more current specification. In that case, we were able to pursue recovery amounting to three times the damages under the False Claims Act.

I wanted to further investigate what other government contracts the same contractor had been awarded in the past, and I intended to research what other similar electric cable contracts the government awarded to anyone else. I didn't know if this was an isolated incident or just the tip of the iceberg. But my supervisor said I had too many other cases and could not open an investigative project to look into these other matters.

As I stated earlier, part of my job responsibilities were to simultaneously investigate for systemic weaknesses that caused or contributed to the matter being investigated. So, at the conclusion of the investigation, I told my supervisor I was going to write a management control deficiency report describing the government employees' failures to do their jobs correctly and intended to make recommendations for improving the system.

My supervisor's response was "Don't bother writing a management control deficiency report; the government never does anything with them anyway."

I could not help but wonder how he got promoted to that position because he had absolutely no business making such a decision. The supervisor essentially told me not to do my job! Worse yet, he essentially told me not to look out for the safety of military service members. I ignored the request and prepared the report anyway.

NOTE: By the way, that supervisor received two more promotions after that case. (A scary thought, huh!?)

Had the civil prosecutor not accepted the case, it would have had to fall under another category. Under those circumstances, by definition, the matter would not have been either criminal or civil wrongdoing (because it would have been declined both criminally and civilly). If a wrongdoing is not criminal or civil, the wrongful acts must be administrative, waste, and/or abuse. (A military veteran might instead just use a more appropriate acronym to describe the situation: "SNAFU" [situation normal: All f— up.])

War Story 5.8

Another case example where the government screwed up so badly that it weakened the criminal case against the wrongdoers involved defective clothing material. (Yes, I know that sounds boring.) This case involved a multimillion-dollar U.S. government contract to provide shirts to the Saudi Arabian army under a foreign military sales contract.

The wool material the contractor was trying to use on the contract was old and defective. Besides failing for physical characteristics (like shrinkage), it was also kept failing for being the wrong color (off shade to be precise).

After a series of failures, the material samples submitted for testing for Lot 20 suddenly passed government testing. I flew to Philadelphia, Pennsylvania, and met with the government sample material examiner. She showed me evidence that most of the cut samples that passed testing for Lot 20 were cut from the same roll of material. (The cut lines from separate samples lined up perfectly with others like a jigsaw puzzle.) She said separate samples were supposed to have been individually cut from each individual roll of material that was going to be used on the contract (about 94 rolls). Instead, apparently most of the samples had been cut from one "good" roll of material in a scheme to get more passing test results.

A government quality assurance representative (QAR) was supposed to cut the test samples on all of the separate lots from each numbered roll of material at the contractor's plant. Then the QAR was supposed to personally tag each cloth sample with the unique roll number it was cut from and then personally mail the samples to the government for testing. When I interviewed the government QAR, she told me that she alone cut all the samples from each separate roll of material for every lot. The vice president of the company verbally corroborated this. When I pointed out to the QAR that someone cut most the samples from one roll of material, she yelled, "You need to wake up and smell the coffee; that contractor is honest!"

I was surprised that a government QAR would yell at a federal agent conducting a criminal investigation, and I was also surprised how insistent she was that the contractor was honest—almost as if she had a personal relationship with the company. The QAR's reaction made me think of her as a suspect.

The QAR later admitted that on one lot (long before Lot 20), she did allow the contractor to cut separate samples from each roll of material. But she insisted that she personally mailed the samples to the government for testing. The QAR said it was faster for the contractor to cut the samples while she was not there.

In effect, the QAR admitted she did not do her job properly on at least one occasion (which might explain why she was so defensive). I guess in her mind, if she could convince me that she and the contractor were honest, then I must be wrong. But I knew the government material tester in Philadelphia and I was not wrong.

When I confronted the company vice president again with the evidence, he said it would be impossible to determine which employee cut any particular samples because it was a "crap detail" assigned to employees who weren't doing their jobs very well.

I replied, "It's not impossible; it's just difficult. I want the names of every employee who ever cut samples from rolls of material on this contract, and I don't care how many people were involved. If you can't figure out who cut samples, then I want the names of every employee who works in this facility."

To make a long story short, I proved the case by getting handwriting samples of the main suspect employee and sending them to a government crime laboratory. I asked the lab to compare the suspect's handwriting samples to the handwritten numbers (representing individual roll numbers) that were on paper tags and stapled to each fraudulent sample of material in Lot 20. The lab later reported a positive match indicating the primary suspect (the company's own quality control representative) wrote the numbers on the tags affixed to the fraudulent samples.

The company's vice president and the suspect tried denying everything until they realized there was no escaping. The vice president subsequently admitted that for Lot 20, he ordered his employee (the company's quality control representative) to cut samples from one good roll of wool material and to falsely label each sample with different roll numbers.

But I also learned that the government QAR failed to do her job more than once. The company's vice president told me that the government QAR *never* cut any of the samples of material from any rolls and instead just gave the contractor preaddressed, post-paid boxes to mail the samples to the government. That way, the government QAR got to go home early every day. The vice president later pleaded guilty to his involvement.

At the conclusion of the investigation, I wrote a management control deficiency report regarding the government QAR's failure to do her job properly. I'm not sure if she was ever penalized for her actions—her boss previously had been a suspect in another investigation for receiving bribes on other clothing and textile contracts.

War Story 5.9

In the early stages of a multimillion-dollar fraud investigation, the assigned federal criminal prosecutor asked a well-known FIA to assist in my investigation.

Based on my experience, the allegations indicated that in addition to there being possible criminal violations, there were also some major systemic internal weaknesses that allowed the wrongdoing to occur. If I was correct, there might be additional similar instances of wrongdoing to investigate.

I also knew that as part of my job responsibilities, besides determining if there was criminal wrongdoing, I had to simultaneously attempt to identify any other systemic weaknesses that allowed the wrongdoing to occur, and later I would have to make recommendations for improvement.

To conduct such detailed investigations, more questions need to be asked and more interviews needed to be conducted. During a meeting with the FIA and the prosecutor, I laid out an investigative plan to accomplish those objectives.

As soon as I finished, the FIA agent announced, "We are the lead investigative agency on this case." And his FIA supervisor immediately followed up on that statement by saying to me, "I'm sorry, but our agency does not investigate waste and abuse." Without hesitation I replied, "Well, thank God somebody does."

Suggestions for Improvement

Listed next are just four examples where I made recommendations for improvement after the investigations were completed. They are listed so the readers can get an idea how investigations often can best be concluded.

1. I investigated a pharmacist for stealing painkillers from his employer's pharmacy. The pharmacist secretly accessed the pharmacy's computer system and obtained the names and insurance policy numbers of people who previously had prescriptions filled there. The pharmacist

then submitted false claims to the insurance companies under those beneficiaries' names. To cover his tracks, he made cash copayments into the pharmacy's cash register. The insurance beneficiaries never knew the pharmacist had used their names and policies.

My recommendation was for healthcare insurance companies to periodically (preferably at least quarterly) send every insurance beneficiary an individualized listing of all prescription drugs filled under their names, along with the prescribing physicians' names, the types of medication (and quantities), and the locations and dates the prescriptions were filled. Essentially this would be the same as receiving an explanation of benefits form just like the ones insurance beneficiaries receive in the mail after being treated by a doctor or dentist.

Implementing this would at least allow beneficiaries the opportunities to review summaries of all prescriptions that were filled under their names within a somewhat reasonable time period. If beneficiaries noted discrepancies, they could inform their insurance companies, which could conduct further inquiries and/or investigations.

2. In the case where the government failed to include the correct military specifications in the electronic cable contract and failed to inspect the cable and accompanying certifications prior to acceptance, I made recommendations to improve the check-and-balance systems in both areas to ensure all requirements were met before awarding contracts and before accepting the products.

3. In the case where the contracting officer circumvented the telephone vendor bid process and awarded contracts to a vendor who was bribing him, I made recommendations to improve oversight and review of all contracting officers' contract files on a regular bases to be alert for certain red flags.

4. In the case where the government QAR went home early and let the contractors cut their own samples of material and mail them to the government for testing in a preaddressed and stamped box, I made a recommendation to require QARs to certify that they personally selected and obtained samples, maintained the chain of custody, and mailed the boxes of test samples to the government laboratory. Copies of the certifications would be included in the QAR's work files, and a copy would be provided to the contractor. If the

certifications were later determined to be false, the QAR could be considered for prosecution and/or other administrative action.

Focusing entirely on criminal violations does not serve the complete needs of an investigation or its victims. If an agency's policy is to investigate criminal matters only and not to attempt to rectify the problems that caused the crimes or wrongdoing to occur, a vicious circle of crime will continue.

For some investigative agencies, the more crime that occurs, the more resources the agencies will gain in order to fight the crime. Thus, the agencies will grow.

To assist in the effort of an investigative agency to become larger (and have its budget increased), ensuring publicity of the agency's investigative successes (arrests and convictions) will cause many politicians to have no qualms about increasing that investigative agency's annual budget. In many ways, this is like continuing to spend end-of-the-year money unnecessarily to ensure equal or higher dollar amounts are received the next year. Many consider it just part of the game.

Also, when an investigative approach involves conducting only criminal investigations, there is a tendency to initiate undercover operations (with catchy names) with specific targets to obtain evidence of wrongdoing. When completed, "Operation Catchy Name" will get national media coverage, resulting in more positive feedback, which results in more funding for more investigators, and so on, and so on.

War Story 5.10

I once attended a healthcare fraud training seminar attended by investigators and federal agents from the local area. Most of the investigators in attendance worked for agencies whose mission was to conduct criminal, civil, and administrative investigations involving fraud, waste, and abuse while simultaneously searching for systemic weaknesses that allowed the fraud, waste or abuse to occur so that the weaknesses could be corrected.

One of the guest speakers (trainers) was a federal agent from a well-known FIA who received national recognition for a large-scale healthcare fraud investigation that resulted in several criminal convictions. That FIA investigated criminal violations only. Its investigation coined a catchy operation name.

That speaker from the FIA went on to tell the group that there was no need to review boxes of patient and billing records when conducting healthcare fraud investigations; they said it is much easier to conduct an undercover operation (like a sting) and get the evidence on tape. The agent added that once confronted with the audio and video evidence, the suspects would have no choice but to plead guilty. At the conclusion of the presentation, the agent received a large round of applause and a plaque.

I'm not sure how many in attendance realized how shortsighted that agent's investigation really was. The agent was actually telling everyone that the FIA's way of conducting healthcare investigations (criminal cases only) was smarter and better than their own.

I don't want to discount the superb undercover work performed by that agent and the other assisting agents, but their investigation was incomplete! It was the equivalent of a football team returning to the locker room for a victory celebration after scoring a touchdown in the first quarter.

By not reviewing the patient records and previous claim forms submitted by the crooked physician(s), no one would ever know how much money was lost due to prior frauds. (In this case, it could have amounted to millions of dollars.)

But at the conclusion of the undercover operation and prosecution, the FIA and prosecutors held a press conference where they mentioned the catchy operation name and the criminal convictions they obtained. It appeared that the FIA did a marvelous job, and all the agents involved probably got big awards. Based on the press releases and press conferences, the general public and politicians can't help but (wrongly) conclude that the FIA is better at conducting healthcare fraud investigations than other investigative agencies that conduct more thorough investigations.

What if, instead, an undercover operation was completed and then a document review and analysis were completed? What if attempts also were made to determine what else that provider did wrong? What if attempts also were made to determine who else was doing the same thing? What if attempts were made to determine how the fraud occurred and how it could be prevented in the future?

Doing all of these things, and more, would require a bit more time and resources. But it could result in larger dollar recoveries (by also pursuing the case civilly) and identify others committing more fraud. Most important, it could have stopped the same type fraud(s) from recurring.

But instead, the FIA got good publicity, its annual budget increased, and it hired more agents to investigate healthcare fraud. Meanwhile, the resources of other healthcare fraud investigative agencies were not increased. (They don't know how to play the game.)

Without question, there are times when speedy and expedient investigations are paramount, and there is no time to conduct simultaneous investigations to identify systemic weaknesses or waste and abuse. There are times when the best method to obtain evidence of wrongdoing is to conduct undercover operations and not look through boxes of documents. I totally understand and agree with that. But that cannot and should not be the preferred method of conducting investigations. Doing so serves the needs of the agency only, not the general public and certainly not the victims.

The goals actually should be to conduct thorough investigations and reduce crime and/or wrongdoing. Efforts at some point (even if it's at the conclusion of the original limited or "focused" criminal-only investigation) should be made to investigate all relevant facts and attempt to stop the same crimes/wrongs from occurring again in the future.

It is not a compelling argument to state that media coverage of the arrests and convictions serves as the deterrent. If media coverage of convictions alone stopped crime, there would be no crime at the time of this writing. Media coverage of arrests and convictions mostly provides fuel for the FIA to get increased funding to continue the same investigative practices in the future.

Investigative efforts need to include attempts to ascertain the causes and contributing factors that allowed the wrongdoing to occur. Follow-up recommendations for improvement need to be made to correct the shortcomings. In the end, this more thorough investigative approach will reduce funding needed for later investigations.

With less need for investigations, those resources can be trimmed. Having fewer investigators also will reduce the number of employee pensions to be paid and other postretirement funding. The end result will be savings for the taxpayers, business owners, and/or stockholders. Incorporating the methods outlined in this and the previous chapter will result in more bad guys/gals getting busted, more victims being assisted, and more crime being prevented.

I've often compared the two types of investigations with this analogy:

- One doctor tells a cancer patient that he/she is real good at cutting out cancer.
- The second doctor says he/she is real good at cutting out cancer and doing everything possible to ensure it does not come back.
- If you were the patient, which doctor would you want looking out for your well-being?

Some FIAs know how to play the game. It has worked well for them for many decades and still works as of the time of this writing. Well, guess what? A management control deficiency report or vulnerability report needs to be written to fix the system. (Maybe I just wrote it—if this book gets in the right hands.)

There's an old saying, "If it ain't broke, don't fix it." Let me add to that, "If it is broke, it needs to be fixed . . . and it needs to be fixed as soon as possible."

Chapter 6

Summary Reports

"Which 'he' are you referring to?"
                    —Investigative supervisor to subordinate

One objective of this chapter is to provide useful information in
a unique format that will assist investigators and fraud fighters
write quality summary reports. This chapter should not serve
as your sole source on how to write investigative reports. In fact, numerous books describe how to write reports, paragraphs, and basic sentences.
Every investigative training academy emphasizes the importance of including answers to the Five Ws: (who, what, when, where, and why) in
summary reports (I added how and how much). This chapter provides
the author's insight and select tips to consider when writing these reports.

No matter how effective an investigator is at solving wrongdoing and crimes and perhaps getting voluntary truthful confessions
from criminals, the case may fall apart if the investigator is unable to
communicate investigative activity and findings effectively. Therefore,

it is imperative that investigators continually strive to improve their written and oral communication skills.

NOTE: Chapters 11 and 12 provide more guidance for making case presentations and providing testimony.

War Story 6.1

While I was serving as a supervisory detective, an investigator on my team turned in a report for review that was covered with correction fluid and pen-and-ink changes. The investigator had a reputation as a go-getter and always volunteered for extra missions. He always displayed great enthusiasm when conducting investigations. He also was an effective interviewer who often obtained voluntarily and truthful confessions from wrongdoers.

Usually I just made minor corrections to his reports because he seemed to take it as a personal insult if anyone insinuated his work was anything less than perfect. I also saw no reason to add to his workload by sending reports back to him for minor corrections because he was already working 80 hours per week. But the sloppiness of this particular submission concerned me.

I sent the report back to him with a note clipped to the top that read something like "Joe, you did a great job on this case! Unless you are painting a fence, please refrain from using the gallons of white paint on your reports. Keep up the great work, but please retype this report and resubmit." I also added a line reflecting that an investigator's written reports are a reflection of his or her overall professionalism.

About five minutes after I dropped the report in Joe's in-box, he stormed into my office and handed me the note I just wrote and told me to read it. I did and then handed the note back to him. Joe then replied, "You misspelled professionalism." We both laughed.

Types of Investigative Reports

Investigative reports typically are written when cases are initiated and after completing any investigative activity. Preliminary investigative efforts normally are documented and often followed with the writing of an official case initiation. As previously described, wherever possible, both the preliminary investigation and the case initiation should include answers to the Five Ws and Two Hs: who, what, when, where, why, how, and how much.

During an investigation, reports should be written describing investigative activity (regardless of the outcome). If surveillance was performed, it should be documented. If photographs were taken, the photos should be documented. If interviews were conducted, the results should be documented, and so on.

NOTE: Typically I document my investigative activity so that anyone who reads my investigative reports can tell exactly what I did. Even if people read those reports 10 years later, they will still fully comprehend what I did. Writing detailed reports also helps refresh my own memory when needed.

Some investigators and/or investigative agencies might prefer to maintain only a detailed investigative case journal or "working file" as the investigation progresses and to later include all of the investigative information in one final summary report. As long as the investigation is not overly complex, large, or lengthy, a single summary report might suffice.

NOTE: As a PI, I find that many clients have limited budgets or are extremely cost conscious about the number of investigative hours expended on their cases. (PIs often charge by the hour.) To meet the financial needs of those clients, the best option sometimes is to write only one summary report at the conclusion of the investigation (instead of separate reports describing each activity) that provides a detailed summary of investigative activity. I draft the summary report as the investigation progresses rather than waiting until the investigation is completed.

Official Files and Working Files

Many investigators have two files for each case: the official file and the working file. The official file contains the original final reports, copies of evidence receipts, select photographs, and the like. Each official file might have an index sheet that chronologically lists all the documents and report dates. Normally the official case files are kept in a secured location (like a locking file cabinet) and maintained with other similar case files. Many investigative agencies are going paperless ("going green") and may maintain their investigative files electronically.

TIP: As a PI, I typically file copies of any invoices and payments received on the top left side of the official case file.

Working files might include copies of the same items as in the official file but usually also include the investigator's notes, copies of written correspondence or telephone conversations, an investigative plan, and just about any other papers, documents, business cards, and information that the investigator might find useful. Working files also might include a suspect's background information, a company's organizational chart, license plate and telephone number check results, and the like. If the information might be important, investigators often file it in the working file.

Many organizations also require investigators to submit and/or or store their final reports (or copies of their final reports) electronically at other locations. The electronic submission and storage of documents certainly allows for more efficiency, including wider access and timely distribution. Investigators should ensure that a secure environment exists for such submissions and storage and that backups always will be available. In fact, the security of all case-sensitive information is critical, whether storing paper copies or electronic ones.

Other Reports

Numerous other reports might be completed during an investigation, including: laboratory reports, polygraph examination reports, auditor reports, financial analysis reports, information reports, referral reports, management control deficiency reports, fraud vulnerability reports, and case closing reports. There probably are as many different types of reports as there are ways to cook shrimp.

If the investigator conducted investigative activity and/or obtained information, it should be documented. If a decision is made to not document it in the official file, it should at least be documented in the working file.

TIP: While on surveillance, I've found utilizing a small digital audio recorder can be very beneficial. When the recorder is on and you are driving through a parking lot, you can say out loud the license plate numbers you see or other observations a lot faster (and with less suspicion) then you can write them. Later you can listen to the recording and write down the information on paper and file it with your case notes.

Preparing to Write

Generally, the more experience investigators have, the better reports they write. One of the most frequent sayings of my college English teacher was "The key to effective writing is rewriting." I hated every time she told me that because it meant I had to rewrite something. Although I despised her for making me invest more time on the same projects, she was right. But I also learned that it is even better (and more time efficient) to try hard to write correctly the first time!

Depending on the complexity of the topic, it is often useful to create an outline before writing a report. It also is useful to write the information in chronological order unless there is a reason not to. Even a rough outline will ensure that you include all of the important facts in the writing. There's nothing worse than realizing you accidentally omitted important information from a report and that you then have to write a supplemental report to add the information. In fact, writing a supplemental report that adds previously omitted information might raise the eyebrows of the opposing legal counsel. A criminal defense attorney whom I do work for as a PI said this about police officers' reports: "If it's not written in the police report, it didn't happen." That statement should be enough to remind you to write detailed investigative reports. When it comes to writing reports, quality matters.

War Story 6.2
When I first started working as a supervisory detective, several of the investigators on my team boasted about the frequent successes of Rick, one of the other investigators who was known to

constantly solve cases. Rick frequently came into the office on the weekends to catch up on his report writing. One Saturday afternoon, I came into our office building to do some work and heard the radio blasting rock-and-roll music in Rick's office. His fingers were banging away on his keyboard. I stepped inside and asked Rick to turn down the radio, and he said, "I work much faster when listening to music while I type."

Sounding like a grumpy parent of a teenager, I replied, "Well, I can't think clearly with all that noise so you need to plug in some headphones." After entering my own office, I found that Rick had already turned in about a dozen reports for me to review. After reading three of them, I concluded they were the worst reports I had ever read.

NOTE: I believe that enthusiasm is one of the most important ingredients to being successful at anything—especially in investigations. And in this case, I was very conscious of the fact that Rick was voluntarily working on the weekend and he was a great investigator. I certainly did not want to spoil his enthusiasm for his job. However, I had to tactfully instill in him the fact that speed-writing was not the name of the game. (He might have despised me, as I did my college English teacher, but he learned.)

TIP: Law enforcement and investigative supervisors should remember it's not their job to just rubber-stamp and approve reports. They must review reports to ensure that all of the necessary facts are included, that critical information was not omitted, and that all necessary work was completed. Summary reports of interviews should also be reviewed to ensure that quality interviews were conducted.

War Story 6.3
When I was a rookie city cop during probationary training, I initially worked the swing shift (4 P.M. until midnight). Red, the

officer assigned as my field training officer, made me write all the reports for every incident we responded to. After responding to calls and taking action, he'd park our patrol car in an isolated area where nobody could see us and then he'd call out of service, meaning the dispatcher could not send us on any other calls. Red sat in the driver's seat and read the newspaper while I wrote the reports. I had no qualms about writing the reports because I had written thousands of them as a MP and as an MP investigator.

But after finishing each report, Red pulled out a red-ink pen and wrote all over my reports like a third-grade English teacher grading a dunce's book report. As soon as he finished bleeding all over a report, Red would say, "Do it over."

I had several problems with the way Red worked. First of all, we should not have been sitting in an isolated area where nobody could see us. Parking a squad car where the public could see us would deter crime and traffic violations and make us accessible to anyone in need. We also should not have called out of service to write reports because that made our patrol unit about as useless as a rusted tin can sitting in a vacant parking lot. We were just wasting time as I kept rewriting the same reports over and over again.

About a month later, I was transferred to midnight shift, and the field training officer assigned to train me, Danny, was the complete opposite of Red. Since our patrol beat was in a high-crime area, Danny made sure we maximized our time in an effort to respond to as many calls as possible, catch as many criminals as we could, and prevent as much crime as possible during our shift. To this day I still think of Danny (a fictitious name) as the best cop I've ever known.

Danny always took notes at every call we responded to and after every arrest we made. Immediately after returning to our squad car, he'd call the dispatcher and obtain a case number for each incident. After scribbling down the case numbers, Danny placed his handwritten notes under the driver's-side sun visor, and we quickly resumed patrol trying to catch more bad guys— or at least trying to prevent crime.

Danny told me that crime decreased in our area once the sun started coming up, and he concluded that writing the reports at that time would make the best use of our time. So as soon as the sun came up, Danny parked our patrol car in front of an open commercial establishment to prevent robberies. He varied the location each morning to ensure we didn't establish a pattern for the crooks to follow. Then he'd start writing all of the reports one after the other.

During the first few days, Danny wrote all the reports and let me read them when he was done. After a couple days, he started assigning me some reports to write. Because he never called out of service while we were writing, occasionally we'd get dispatched to other calls, and we'd have to work late to finish all of our reports. Danny said we shouldn't charge the city any overtime when that happened because it was our own decision to delay writing the reports. Not only did I learn a great deal from working with Danny, I enjoyed every minute of it and tried to emulate and teach his work habits to others whenever possible.

War Story 6.4

While working as a PI consultant, I reviewed a police report on a civil rights violation case and found that the arresting officer did an outstanding job of describing minute details of what occurred before, during, and after an arrest. However, the officer's report omitted critical information about a second officer who responded and physically assisted in making the arrest. The report also omitted facts about another suspect who complained of injuries received at the scene. Without providing all the details, the omissions were, in my opinion, evidence of a false report. The officer demonstrated his ability to record minute details but elected to omit critical information that coincidently was the subject of the complaint. In short, sometimes it's the information that is intentionally *not* included that makes the information false and/or misleading.

Length of Reports

Some investigative agencies and organizations dictate that investigative reports must be short. An agent from a FIA that I often worked major fraud cases jointly with said that reports should never be longer than one or two pages. In one instance, we conducted a four-hour interview of a suspect, which covered about five different fraud schemes. My typed summary report was about five pages long. The FIA agent insisted that the report should only be one or two pages. Factually, since that the interview was not electronically recorded, intentionally omitting information would not have adequately described what was said in the interview. That FIA is very well respected, but its policy of limiting the amount of information in reports sometimes fails to describe investigative activity accurately. A report should be as long as it needs to be.

Attachments and Exhibits to Reports

Including attachments or exhibits to reports when appropriate often helps readers fully comprehend the information provided. For example, if a burglar pawned a stolen stereo and a pawn ticket listing the serial numbers was later recovered, it would be a good idea to write a report that references how and when the pawn ticket was found and recovered and for the report to include a copy of the pawn ticket.

A partial summary of such a report might read something like this:

> . . . A review of the store's pawn tickets identified ticket No. 1234, dated December 23, 2012. The make, model, and serial numbers on the pawn ticket matched those of reported stolen by Jones. The pawn ticket reflects that item was pawned by John Smith, Attachment (1).

Attachments also can be copies of photographs taken or of other documentation (like a false invoice) that could help the report be as informative as possible. Attachments can include self-generated link analysis, bar graphs, and other visual aids that help provide useful information. (See the sample visual aids in the appendix.)

War Story 6.5

While working jointly with a highly respected FIA, I reviewed several boxes of printed e-mails that the FIA obtained as evidence. During my review I found several e-mails that provided incriminating information against the suspects of a multimillion-dollar fraud scheme. It took me about a week to review the printed e-mails, after which I wrote a report describing where the documents were obtained from, when they were obtained, when they were reviewed, and a generic description of the contents of the e-mails. The description also included the names of the individuals who received or sent the e-mails and the time frame the e-mails were sent.

I wrote the report as a relatively short summary of the contents of the boxes in the event we ever needed to reference those materials in the future. I should note that during that investigation, we acquired dozens of boxes of documents so staying organized was very important.

However, after reviewing my report, the prosecutor said he did not want any reports to be written describing the contents of the boxes. I was baffled by this instruction because the e-mails contained incriminating information against the suspects, not exculpatory information.

Then one of the FIA agents said, "Why don't you do it the way our agency does it: just write some notes about what you found and place the notes in your working file?"

I later learned that the prosecutor and FIA's rationale for not writing detailed reports was to prevent the defense counsel from possibly obtaining copies of the reports during discovery. They wanted to make the defense team have to look through all the e-mails rather than give them a hint of what we knew. This was just one of the many tactics they used to help them "win" in court. Not to sound like a Holy Joe, but my objective as a federal agent was to document facts, not hide them. In the end, I still wrote my report and placed it in my official file.

Reports Should Stand Alone

Each report should stand on its own. Do not assume that readers will have reviewed any previous reports. For example, if John Smith is the victim, the report should reflect that information. Don't assume that the reader reviewed previous reports, and don't make the readers do so just so they can understand another report.

Include all relevant information, not just the information that makes the suspect look guilty. The investigator's job is to identify the facts.

If conducting an internal investigation, include all relevant information, not just the information that makes the alleged wrongdoer look innocent.

NOTE: Investigators who are assisting a defendant prove his or her innocence may have different investigative priorities from investigators working for/with the prosecution. Those investigators assisting the defense might focus their investigative efforts on obtaining information that will discredit the prosecutors' cases. Anyone who is accused of wrongdoing in a court of law is entitled to a strong defense. The report-writing requirements for investigators working for the defense may differ from those for investigators working for/with the prosecution.

Report Formats

In every government organization I've worked for, sample template reports (also known as go-bys) were available that investigators were required to follow when writing reports. Most of the templates, however, were prepared using fictitious "simple" cases involving one or two suspects who committed one crime together.

Because I tended to expand investigations and link other criminal activity to the same suspects or additional ones, standard report formats usually were inadequate to communicate case facts. But since most government investigative agencies are paramilitary, uniformity usually dictates report-writing formats, even though different format styles might work much better.

War Story 6.6

At the conclusion of one of my federal investigations, approximately 60 interviews had been conducted, 40,000 e-mails reviewed, and numerous criminal violations identified that spanned several years. Ten individuals were titled as suspects for criminal violations, and many lived in different states. I wrote so many reports during the investigation that those reports along with their attachments filled a couple storage boxes. This investigation involved millions of dollars, several different complex white-collar fraud schemes, and possible conspiracies in which the overt acts occurred in different states.

When preparing the final investigative summary report, it would have been ideal to include some visual aids—in particular, link analysis and timeline graphs. Presenting them at the beginning of the report would have allowed readers to more easily comprehend the magnitude and complexity of the criminal activity. Those visual aids also would have served as useful references while reading the report.

However, my agency insisted that I follow the standard report template format, which made it very difficult for readers to comprehend the criminal violations and who committed them. I was not permitted to include the visual aids in the final report. Also, my agency's report template required the listing of every interview in the order it was completed rather than in an order that proved the wrongdoing.

The end result was a 250-page report that included all of the case facts but in a format that did not allow the information to be comprehended easily. The management mind-set was "That's the way we always do it" and "All reports must be uniform and in compliance with the agent's manual."

In short, the agency's report template was fine for simple cases. But in highly complex fraud cases with multiple suspects involving multiple different crimes at several different locations, the required format was self-defeating.

In my opinion, investigators should be permitted to occasionally deviate from the standard report format when necessary as long as the final work product produces the intended results and contains all required information.

NOTE: As the owner of my own private investigation company, my report formats are customized so I can best communicate investigative activity and results. Very often I copy photographs, graphs, and tables and paste them in the body of written reports with descriptive captions under them. My clients like detailed investigations that are well documented, well organized, easily comprehendible, and presented as a professional final work product.

Common Report-Writing Mistakes

Listed next (in no particular order) are some mistakes investigators often make when writing reports or verbally communicating.

Too Generic

During my career, I've read reports that have included things like this: "John Jones was interviewed and provided no useful information." Frankly, I have no idea what an investigator means by the word "useful." The investigator should add a paragraph or two and describe something more informative about the interview. Further, by detailing the information that was provided, if the opposing counsel later interviews the same person and gets different results, the investigator might be able to refute their testimony by comparing the two different accounts provided. In fact, reporting that a person had "no useful" information implies the interviewer had an agenda and the information provided did not correspond with that agenda; therefore, the information was not "useful." Don't play games; report the facts.

High Vocabulary

A few investigators have the vocabularies of English professors, and they sometimes chose to utilize their arsenal to impress readers. However, all too often readers become confused when reading those reports because they do not understand the meaning of the chosen words. So as booksmart as those investigators are, they often fail to communicate effectively when writing investigative summaries. The general rule when it comes to report writing is to keep the sentences short and simple.

Overutilization of Acronyms and Abbreviations

The overuse of acronyms and abbreviations can render sentences almost meaningless. As most know, the U.S. government loves to use acronyms. When I first started as a federal agent, the senior agent in my office constantly included acronyms when speaking to me. On my first day when discussing a case he said to me, "The PCO told the ACO to review the FAR and then contact the QAR." When I asked the senior agent what the heck he was talking about, he laughed hysterically and walked away.

NOTE: He meant that the procurement contracting officer told the administrative contracting officer to review the federal acquisition regulation and then contact the quality assurance representative.

My own federal agency required its agents to use abbreviations in reports wherever possible. For example, if I was investigating a company named Alpha Bravo Charlie Widgets, Incorporated, I was required to spell out the company's name the first time in the report, but after that I'd have to refer to the company as AWI or ABCWI. (I would have preferred to use "ABC Widgets.")

Using only the abbreviated capital letters wasn't always so bad, but very often several company names were listed in the same report and I also had to abbreviate their names. By the time I started the second or third page of the report, there would be abbreviations and acronyms all over the place. Reports sometimes got so confusing that I needed a cheat sheet to understand what I had written. An example might read: "AWI provided defective products to AHW, which shipped them to THA to be stored at the DPSC warehouse."

Confusing Pronouns

The proper use of pronouns is essential when writing investigative reports. Examples of pronouns are: I, you, he, she, and it. There's nothing more confusing than reading a report like this one:

> Michael Jones and John Smith were involved in a verbal altercation that turned into a physical altercation when Smith hit Jones with a metal pipe over the head. Jones then cut Smith with a knife. He was transported to the hospital where he was

treated by Dr. Spock. He fell on the floor and hurt his back while there. Jones was subsequently arrested while sitting in a parked car with Mark Most. A search of the vehicle found three handguns. He said the guns did not belong to him. They wrote written statements.

Some questions that beg to be asked are "Which 'he' are you referring to?" and "Who wrote written statements?" In short, it's best to be specific when referring to individuals and use their last names. Always be conscious that the use of pronouns might be confusing to the person(s) to whom you are conveying the information. Even though it might sound redundant, use the person's last name most of the time. If the personnel involved have the same last name, add their first initial or first name before their last name. (By the way: This also applies when verbally providing information.)

Tense Switching

Investigators (including myself) have a tendency to write reports or statements that switch back and forth from past tense to present tense (and vice versa). An example of this might be:

On January 3, 2013, at 1400 hours, I received a call from the police dispatcher to respond to a shots-fired call at 123 Elm Street. Upon arrival, I observed a white male, later identified as John Smith, with a pistol in his hand. I ordered Smith to drop the weapon and to fall to his knees. Smith began jumping up and down and insisting he did nothing wrong. I then began grabbing Smith's arms to place him under arrest. Smith kept on resisting so I began pushing his head into the cement. I think Smith must have banged his own head on the cement a couple of times while he resisted. After handcuffing Smith, he started spitting on me. Smith must have tripped after that because he fell again before I got him to the police car. Paramedics examined Smith at the scene but Smith refused treatment. I transported Smith to the city jail where he was booked on charges of Wrongful Possession of a Firearm by a Convicted Felon, Disorderly Conduct, and Resisting Arrest."

You will note that starting with the third sentence of the paragraph, the action went from past tense (received, observed, ordered) to present tense (jumping, insisting, grabbing, resisting, pushing). Everything in the paragraph is comprehensible, but the tense unnecessarily switched from past tense to present tense. If it already happened, try to use past-tense words. (Yes, I realize that I violated this rule several times in this book.)

Use of the Word "That"

One of my previous supervisors constantly removed the word "that" from every sentence in every report. I agree that I often use the word "that" too often. But sometimes the word is needed and if it is removed, the meaning of the sentence will change.

For example, if I wrote that a witness said "He said that I hit him," my supervisor would remove the word "that," causing the sentence to read "He said I hit him." Removing the word "that" makes the sentence almost appear that the suspect confessed to hitting someone when the witness actually was alleging that someone else struck the witness.

To ensure our final reports weren't changed by that supervisor after we submitted them, most agents used the search command on their computers to locate every sentence with the word "that" in it so they could reword the sentences before submitting the reports. We also had to make sure the supervisor did not remove the word "that" from direct quotes. Instead of searching for "bad guys," we were searching for "thats."

NOTE: That same boss (yes, I used the word "that" again—on purpose) was also anal about counting the number of spaces between sentences and measuring the margins on reports. It would have been tolerable except whenever he found errors, he'd call us on the phone and yell like we just shot his dog! Needless to say, the morale in the office was always in the gutter.

War Story 6.7

That supervisor was anal about a lot of things. We all had to wear ties and white long-sleeve shirts (no other colors) when he visited our office, and our work cars always had to be immaculate.

Before he arrived from his out-of-state office, we also had to make inquiries with nearby hotels to ensure he could get a hotel room where the shower head was a certain height so he wouldn't bump his head. He also made it a requirement that all federal agents under his control had to back in their government cars when parking. His rationale was that too many accidents were caused when drivers backed out of parking spaces.

NOTE: We were not first responders and our government cars didn't have blue lights or sirens. There was no reason for us to "combat park" like police officers who respond rapidly to emergencies.

So no matter where we were driving to, we had to look for parking spaces that we could back into. As you know, some parking lots have arrows on the pavement and cars can legally travel in only one direction. The diagonal parking spaces are designed for cars to pull in forward to park, not back in. But our leader said we could not park in those spaces and should keep driving around until we found parking spaces where we could back in.

The agents in the field office all got a chuckle when one of our agents backed into a parking space and accidentally smashed into that supervisor's personally owned vehicle! The accident never would have happened if the agent just pulled in forward and parked like a normal person.

War Story 6.8

This story really doesn't pertain to investigative report writing, but it's a spin-off of the story above. Another one of my supervisors was anal about requiring employees to forward their government credit card billing statements to the him as soon as the credit card statements were received in the mail. The supervisor felt agents had to reconcile every cent of every credit card purchase as soon as the information became available.

The supervisor wouldn't approve employee travel or vacation time toward the end of any month because that's when the credit card billing statement would be received in the mail. Another problem was that the supervisor's office was located in a different state. Rather than being permitted to just fax or e-mail a copy of the credit card billing statements to the supervisor, we had to send the original credit card statements to him via a costly overnight delivery service.

One month I didn't use my government credit card at all, and the supervisor still made me overnight the credit card statement to him. (The taxpayers paid for that shipment.) A few days later, I received a supplemental notice in the mail that my credit card account was awarded an 18-cent credit as a bonus for previously using the card.

Nothing throws a bean counter off more than having a surprise financial credit when trying to reconcile financial statements. My supervisor instructed me to call the credit card company to find out exactly why my account received the credit. So after 30 minutes, I got an answer. Next my boss made me fax copies of the notice to three different offices. I also had to make about a half dozen other long-distance phone calls about the matter in between. And finally I had to ship the original notice about the 18-cent credit to my supervisor via the overnight delivery service.

In short, I spent about four hours, made about six long-distance calls, and sent three faxes and one overnight shipment— all because of an 18-cent credit. Yes, that supervisor received two more promotions after that—and received several job performance bonuses (paid for by the U.S. taxpayers).

Report writing is an essential part of completing any investigation. Unless the case is unfounded and closed, odds are the summary investigative reports will be reviewed by several individuals. Those individuals often know absolutely nothing about the investigation except what they read in the reports. Detailed and thoroughly conducted investigations that are well documented impress readers as to the quality of the work performed. Those reports also serve as historical references that describe the investigative activity performed. A quality report is also a reflection of an investigator's overall professionalism. One other thing to keep in mind is that once in a great while, cases are appealed or tried again. More often these days (especially because of the use of DNA), cold cases are reinvestigated sometimes several years after the original investigations. For these and other reasons, it's important that every investigation be well documented.

Chapter 7 describes some of the resources, tools, and techniques utilized by investigators to assist in learning the truth.

Chapter 7

The Investigator's Toolbox: Resources, Tools, and Techniques

"Measure twice, then cut."

—Carpenter to an apprentice

Although it's gratifying to accomplish something completely on your own, gaining assistance from others and/or maximizing the use of internal and external resources often provides the best results.

There are times when it is in an investigator's (or their client's) best interest to focus only on one case at a time. But as this book has illustrated, broadening your investigative scope and efforts usually will yield more bang for your buck. Expanding on and utilizing available investigative resources, tools, and techniques often will allow you to

131

accomplish much more, in less time, and often at a lesser cost (in the long run).

Did you ever notice how frequently good managers delegate responsibilities? Investigators should also consider the benefits of delegating and/or working as a team where appropriate so that responsibilities can be shared.

NOTE: Technology keeps on improving, and it will continue to allow investigators to access, collect, and share legally obtained information in many useful ways. This chapter is not an all-encompassing guide to all tools, techniques, and resources available to investigators but should serve as a source and reminder to consider all available resources when planning and conducting investigations. If you are ever in doubt, consult legal counsel to determine the legality of investigative activity before it is conducted.

Investigative Resources

Resources come in many forms, including people and places as well as tangible and intangible things. This chapter provides some examples where investigators might find resources to accomplish their objectives.

Organizations

The following list provides examples of how investigative personnel might seek assistance from others:

- A corporate investigator might seek investigative assistance from the local police department, which has authority to conduct more encompassing investigations.
- The local police might seek assistance from the county police to work jointly on certain cases.
- The county police might seek the assistance of one or more state investigative agencies.
- The state investigative agencies might seek assistance from other state agencies and FIAs.
- FIAs might seek assistance from one or more other FIAs and possibly other state, county, or city investigative agencies.
- PIs might seek assistance from other PIs or consultants (and/or obtain publicly available historic police reports).

- A federal agent might contact INTERPOL when a suspect travels overseas.
- Any of the listed agencies or individuals might seek investigative assistance from each other or from financial institutions, insurance companies, or other entities that might have an interest in the outcome of the investigation or in the subject matter being investigated or simply might be able to lend their expertise.

A perfect example of working together and making use of resources might be when investigating an insurance fraud scam in which several people conspired to use two or more vehicles to cause an innocent driver to be in a traffic accident for the purposes of filing a lawsuit.

Let's say two cars were driving on a highway in the same lane at a high rate of speed.

- Car 1 is occupied by four fraudsters, one of whom is driving the car.
- Car 2 is occupied by an unsuspecting motorist who follows behind Car 1.
- While traveling at a high rate of speed, the driver of Car 1 slams on the brakes and causes Car 2 to crash into the rear of Car 1.
- The police later respond and issue a traffic citation to the driver of Car 2 for following too close.
- The occupants of Car 1 report fake injuries and are examined and treated by a co-conspiring physician.
- The co-conspirators eventually involve a co-conspiring attorney who files lawsuits against the driver of Car 2 and that driver's insurance company.

A preliminary investigation into this traffic accident could be handled a lot of different ways. It could be considered an isolated incident, or efforts could be made to determine if this was part of a statewide or even national insurance fraud ring. It's up to the investigators (and/or the investigator's supervisors) to know about other resources that might be able to assist in the investigation. Sharing the information could help in uncovering a much larger fraud scheme or fraud ring.

TIP: The best way to gain knowledge of other investigative resources (and schemes) is to make additional professional contacts. Some call that networking. Keep in mind that every one of your professional contacts has contacts of his or her own that the contact may be willing to share. In a scenario such as the one just described, you might want to contact the National Insurance Crime Bureau, which has many resources to prevent, detect, and deter such crimes.

War Story 7.1

When conducting healthcare fraud investigations as a federal agent, I knew of several other federal agencies that also investigated healthcare fraud. Having attended various related working group meetings, I also knew that several private insurance companies also had their own investigators who worked in this field. Of course, each state also has its own healthcare programs and investigators. By sharing information, we often learned that the same individuals who defrauded one insurance company or program were defrauding others as well. Working the cases jointly allowed us to accomplish more and allowed us to share the workload among different agencies/organizations. We also strove to avoid duplication of efforts. The prosecutors liked this approach because by identifying more victims, we identified higher dollar losses. This added to the appeal of the cases and usually resulted in larger dollar recoveries (and more attractive press releases).

War Story 7.2

All too often when conducting investigations as part of a task force or joint investigative team, some investigators will not contribute much or at all, yet they always take credit for 100 percent of the accomplishments. The term used to describe that is "coattailing" because those investigators just ride other investigators' coat tails throughout the investigation.

During my 20 years as a federal agent, I found there was one highly respected FIA that was notorious for coattailing. Its agents sent me e-mails every 30 to 60 days asking for updates on cases we were supposedly working together. They'd even ask for copies of my

90-day case summary reports so they could update their superiors even though they did not contribute any of the work accomplished.

I can understand that sometimes well-meaning or overworked investigators get tied up with other cases and can't contribute as much as they initially hoped. But I worked one case where an FIA kept transferring the case we shared to different agents every few months, even though none of its agents ever lifted a finger to help. The continued reassignment of the case indicated that the supervisors probably were aware of the coattailing but continued to let it happen.

I wondered why the FIA didn't just close the case since no one wanted to do any of the work. But its agents sure were there at press release time after the suspects pled guilty! The coattailing investigators claimed full credit for the investigative accomplishments. As long as those agents got numbers in the stat columns, they received good evaluations. Plus, their agency got credit for the case and got to claim credit for the stats. Good stats for the year often result in higher budgets. Higher budgets usually equate to increased billets (employees) for the agency. "And the wheels on the bus go round and round . . ."

Other Professionals

In addition to other agencies and organizations, many other professionals regularly assist investigators. An entire book could be written about the types of professions that routinely provide invaluable assistance to investigators. Those individuals include but are not limited to:

- Administrative assistants
- Auditors
- Analysts
- Computer forensic examiners
- Forensic laboratory personnel
- Crime scene analysts
- Compliance personnel

- Human resource personnel
- Quality assurance personnel
- Court reporters
- Transcribers
- Information brokers
- Information technology (IT) personnel
- Paralegals
- Certified Fraud Examiners
- Nurses and other medical professionals

Patrol officers conduct detailed preliminary investigations that often make a huge difference in solving cases.

War Story 7.3

One rainy night at about 4 A.M., while serving as a city cop, I was dispatched to check on three suspicious men sitting in a parked car in a residential neighborhood. It was pouring down rain and many of the streets were partially flooded. I drove to the area, waited for my backup unit to arrive, and then approached the driver's side of the suspect's vehicle. The driver rolled down his window, and I asked what he and the other two occupants were doing sitting in the car for so long. There was a passenger in the front seat and another passenger in the rear seat.

The driver told me that he couldn't see while driving because of the heavy rain so he pulled over and was waiting for the rain to lighten up. The story made sense. But I still asked him for his driver's license, vehicle registration, and proof of auto insurance.

I then stepped back into my patrol car, which was parked right behind the vehicle, called the dispatcher, and ran a warrants check on the driver and a check on the license plate number to see if the vehicle had been reported stolen.

While waiting for dispatch to provide the results, I noticed the backup officer (Officer Talker) standing outside the suspect's vehicle. He was conversing and laughing with the passenger who was sitting in the backseat.

The dispatcher reported there were no outstanding warrants on the driver and the vehicle license plate came up clean. Just for the heck of it, I wrote down all of the information about the driver and the vehicle on a pad of paper inside my notebook. Then I walked back up to the driver and handed him back his driver's license and other paperwork and told him to move on as soon as the rain let up because they were making the neighbors nervous. Officer Talker and I then called back in service and departed.

About two hours later, I got dispatched to another call several blocks away in another residential neighborhood to respond to a report of "shots fired—man down." Those type calls were pretty common in the city. Upon my arrival, I saw a dead man lying on a residential driveway with a lot of blood all over the ground by his head. There was a metal tire iron lying on the ground next to his body.

Officer Talker showed up to assist again. Talker walked up to the dead man on the driveway and said to me, "Hey, that's the dude I was talking to. He was in the backseat of that car we checked out earlier."

The bloody driveway led to a front door of a house, and the front door was wide open. I approached the house with caution. After stepping inside the house, I saw a man sitting in a rocking chair holding the top of his head with blood dripping down his face. He was holding a revolver in his other hand. I quickly removed the revolver from his grasp and asked the man what happened.

The bloodied man said he had just come home from a night of gambling and parked his car in his driveway when he was attacked from behind by a few men. The man said something like "One of the men grabbed me from behind and tried to hold me still while another man repeatedly struck me on the head with a tire iron. Another man started going through my pockets trying to steal my money. I always carry a gun in my pocket when I go gambling so I took the revolver out of my pocket and just started shooting over my head. That guy lying on my driveway was one of the ones that got hit with a bullet. I think there were two other guys and they ran off."

I asked if he saw or heard a car drive away after the shooting and he said he could not recall. I immediately called on the police radio for an ambulance and also asked for my supervisor and the detectives to respond. Then I walked back to my patrol car, grabbed my notebook, and posted a BOLO on the police radio for the driver and the vehicle that Officer Talker and I had checked a few hours earlier. I had the suspect's name, physical description, address, license plate number, and vehicle information.

To make a long story short, a couple of hours later, the other two robbers were arrested. One had bruises all over his knuckles. When asked how he got the bruises, the suspect said that while they were committing the robbery, the guy swinging the tire iron kept accidentally hitting his hands while he was holding down the robbery victim.

Although there are a lot of lessons to be learned in this story, the fact is the second officer's observations combined with my own observations and actions are what helped us solve the case. Had we not worked together, the case might not have been solved—or at least not solved as quickly.

War Story 7.4
As a fraud investigator, I was examining numerous electronic files containing insurance beneficiary information in an Excel spreadsheet format. My intent was to run a few queries searching for fraud anomalies and other red flags. At the rate I was going, it would have taken at least a full day to accomplish my objectives. When I asked an investigative analyst how best to accomplish my objectives, she took control of my keyboard, viewed the monitor, and had all the information I wanted in less than 10 minutes. Although I knew what I was looking for to identify fraud, the analyst knew how to do it better and quicker. She knew how to run the queries, sort, and filter, but didn't know what schemes to look for as well as I did. We made a good team.

War Story 7.5

When conducting an investigation into internal corruption of a large organization, I learned that the suspects openly communicated about their wrongdoing via e-mail. During the investigation, I obtained several printed copies of their e-mails but later enlisted the assistance of a trusted computer forensics (IT) expert. We legally obtained mirror copies of the e-mails from their organization's computer server. But there were tens of thousands of e-mails to review.

I provided the computer forensics expert with some keywords to search for. He narrowed the number of e-mails for me to review to a manageable level and put them on a small portable hard drive. Without his assistance, I would have never been able to accomplish my goals in a timely manner.

War Story 7.6

I was assigned to investigate a complex cost-mischarging investigation where a contractor mischarged labor hours and material costs on a firm-fixed-price government contract to a government cost-plus contract. The contractor was going to receive a fixed dollar amount, no matter what, on the fixed-priced contract, but would be reimbursed more on the cost-plus contract depending on how much labor and materials billed. (It makes my head hurt just thinking about cost-mischarging cases.)

I immediately requested the assistance of an experienced and trusted government auditor who actually enjoyed entering the financial information onto computer spreadsheets and then analyzing the information.

It wasn't like I just coattailed the auditor's work. Based on the names on the time cards, I was able to conduct interviews with the employees whose labor was mischarged, and they told me which contracts they had actually worked on. Working as a team, the auditor and I were able to prove and quantify the fraud. Without the assistance of the auditor, I think I'd still be sitting at my desk trying to figure everything out.

War Story 7.7

Sometimes luck plays a role when conducting investigations. While working on a midnight shift as a city cop, I was dispatched to handle a traffic accident. The dispatcher gave me the names of the two intersecting streets. I could only find one of the streets on my map so I drove in that direction. After searching the area for several minutes, I decided to drive down a nearby isolated road near some warehouses.

It was about 3:00 A.M. and there were no streetlights in the area. After driving about 100 yards, I was about to turn around because it was obvious I was nowhere near an intersection and the road I was on wasn't even paved.

But at a distance ahead, I saw what appeared to be someone trying to wave me down with a white flag. As I approached, I saw a vehicle parked on the side of the road. How could anyone have a traffic accident out in the middle of nowhere at that late hour? I wondered.

As I pulled up to the vehicle, I saw that the lady waving the white flag was actually naked and the white flag she was waving was actually her bra! Standing next to her was a man wearing blue jeans and a torn T-shirt with scratch marks down his neck. The lady yelled out, "He raped me and is trying to drag me into the bushes!"

I quickly pointed my pistol at the man, ordered him to his knees, and handcuffed him. The scratch marks on his neck and torn T-shirt made it obvious there had been a struggle. After searching the suspect and placing him in the backseat of my patrol vehicle, the woman informed me that she had met the man at a nightclub and he offered to give her a ride home. But instead of taking her home, he took her to the isolated area, raped her, and was dragging her to the bushes on the side of the road until he saw my patrol car's headlights. The woman was confident that the man planned to kill her.

I called on the radio to have my supervisor and detectives respond to the scene. Ironically, it was only because I couldn't find the traffic accident that I was able to save the woman from further injury and make the arrest.

How does this story demonstrate teamwork? My police training officer had embedded into my brain always to know where I was while on patrol in case I needed a backup, but I had no idea where I was when I made that arrest. To tell the detectives and my supervisor where I was, I had to go to a secondary channel on the police radio (this was before the use of GPS devices and cell phones) and describe to the dispatcher my surroundings and the last known street I crossed. A more senior officer who previously patrolled the area recognized the description I provided and showed up a few minutes later so that the crime scene could be preserved and processed. Then I took the lady to the hospital for treatment and so medical personnel could collect evidence utilizing a rape kit.

War Story 7.8

NOTE: This story is an example of large-scale national systemic weaknesses that cause or contribute to huge dollar losses in which, unless things have been improved, everyone pays.

While conducting a counterfeit credit card investigation, I contacted the security investigator at a bank that issued credit cards to employees of my government agency. I asked the bank investigator what investigative progress was being made on a few known counterfeit credit card transactions.

The bank investigator told me that the bank was not investigating those particular transactions because the bank did not suffer any financial loss; instead, the merchants (store owners) who accepted the counterfeit cards over the telephone suffered the financial losses.

I explained that those small store owners did not have the investigative resources to investigate the use of the counterfeit cards. I also emphasized that the same counterfeit cards were used to make unlawful in-store purchases for which the bank did suffer losses. The bank investigator said, "If I investigate incidents in which our bank did not suffer a loss, I'll get fired. We do not investigate anything involving M.O.T.O."

I learned that M.O.T.O. stood for mail orders and tele-phone orders (including Internet charges). The bank investigator explained that the merchants who accepted telephone, mail, and Internet purchases suffered the losses when counterfeit or stolen credit cards were used to make those purchases.

The bank investigator said that in-store merchants had a respon-sibility to compare the credit cards used with the customer's iden-tification cards to ensure the names and signatures matched. If the stores complied with those requirements, those merchants would not suffer the loss; the bank that issued the credit card would suffer the loss. If the in-store merchant did not check for a matching identifica-tion card and signature, the in-store merchant would suffer the loss.

I asked, "Don't you think you would have a better chance catching the thieves if you found out where items were shipped to [from Internet and phone orders] as compared to searching cash register videos from stores after the purchasers have departed?"

The bank investigator said that she agreed but repeated that she was not permitted to investigate anything where the bank did not suffer a financial loss.

I said, "Well, I can investigate it. Can you give me your entire database for the past five years on every known or suspected counterfeit or stolen credit card purchase that was ever made on credit cards that were previously issued to government employees associated with my agency?"

I later received the entire database. What I subsequently learned was that every large private entity had its own investi-gative staff that investigated its own losses only. Many smaller companies had no investigators so I assume they just wrote off the transactions as business losses. The credit card issuing bank(s) had a few investigators who investigated their own losses—and nobody was working together!

This pattern of not working together was true not only with the credit card issuing bank I was dealing with but with all of the other credit card issuers that I discovered also had been victimized by the same counterfeiters.

NOTE: The use of counterfeit and stolen credit cards and the failure to collectively and thoroughly investigate each and every unlawful transaction results in higher everyday costs to consumers, merchants, and credit card holders. I suspect that the credit card issuing banks probably can recover their losses by charging consumers and business entities higher interest rates and other fees.

Many of the crooks know how to avoid detection and do not make too many large-dollar purchases at the same stores or with the same merchants. They also know that most merchants will probably just write off the low-dollar losses rather than investigate them. In addition, many of crooks know not to carry more than four counterfeit credit cards at one time; if they are caught with more than four counterfeit cards, the feds will be notified. Meanwhile, many of the fraudsters are laughing all the way to the bank, and consumers, credit card holders, and everyone else are paying higher costs for goods, services, and bank fees to make up for the losses.

This scenario is a perfect example of investigators (or their employers) doing an inadequate job of investigating because they are thinking singular instead of plural and not working together.

Because I had access to all of the counterfeit card transactions and did not care who suffered the loss, I finally was able to trace all related transactions and link the criminal activity to known and previously unknown suspects.

NOTE: Many credit card companies are doing a superb job of electronically monitoring credit card purchases for anomalies and other red flags. When I was living in Tennessee, one of my credit cards was used in Las Vegas, Nevada, at a department store. The credit card company's security department immediately telephoned me to inquire if the charge was authorized. It just so happened that one of my daughters was on vacation in Las Vegas and made the purchase herself with one of my card accounts. Had I not answered my phone, the credit card company probably would have put a temporary freeze on that credit card to prevent any possible future fraudulent charges. So to that credit card company I say, "Good job!"

Public Records

Public records (sometimes called open records or open sources) are available to anyone, not just investigators. The information can prove extremely valuable when conducting any investigation, especially background checks and asset locations. Public records to check may include any of these and more:

- Marriage and divorce records
- Federal, state, county, and municipal criminal (felony and misdemeanor) and civil court cases
- Judgments and Uniform Commercial Code filings
- Federal bankruptcies
- Local police department incident reports
- Local police department response reports (sometimes official police reports are not written for all responses)
- Voter registration
- Vehicle registration
- Sexual predator and methamphetamine conviction listings
- Secretary of state business filing records
- County tax assessor records
- Inmate locaters
- Department of Vital Statistics (birth and death records)
- Professional licenses (filed with each state)
- Medicare exclusions list
- Government suspension and debarment lists
- Utility and telephone companies

Information brokers can provide investigators with background information (for a fee). That information might include:

- Addresses, previous addresses (and even neighbors' names and addresses)
- Telephone numbers
- Social Security numbers (or partials)
- Date of birth
- Vehicles owned and license plate numbers
- Associates
- Arrests
- Bankruptcy filings
- Current or previous employment

Many information brokers require investigators (including PIs) to provide copies of their current investigator license(s) before they will perform any searches/queries.

TIP: The amount of publicly available information is staggering. In fact, many experts in the field make a living at conducting public record checks. Be cautious about relying solely on records found on the Internet. To ensure those records are accurate, consider getting certified copies of them from the actual source.

Investigators who conduct background checks on personnel seeking government security clearances reportedly are required to conduct criminal history checks by going in person to courthouses to check the records rather than relying on the various "criminal history" checks available over the Internet. Keep in mind that, very often, felony offenses are reduced to misdemeanors to speed up the case or lessen the burden on the criminal justice system. Sometimes people who committed felonies assist in the investigation(s), and their charges are reduced. Also note that divorce records often contain some very "interesting" information or insight that might not be available otherwise. If using any information obtained to make employment hiring decisions, remember to follow all applicable laws, including the Fair Credit Reporting Act, in order to treat job applicants fairly and to avoid being sued.

War Story 7.9

While conducting white-collar investigations involving businesses and/or business owners, it's fairly common to check secretary of state records in the state where the suspect business is located and/or where the business owner resides. On several occasions I've found that the suspect business owners actually owned two or more additional companies and were committing the same type fraud with their other entities. In one case, I drove by the business address of the suspect company that was providing defective circuit boards to customers. The business address was actually a house in a residential neighborhood. After checking the secretary of state records by the address and by the business owner's name, I identified two additional existing companies and three more that had since closed down.

Investigative Tools and Techniques

I tend to think of investigative tools as the physical items used to assist in the progress of an investigation. I think of techniques as the methods used to deploy or utilize the tools.

When discussing tools, I can't help but think of the ones sold at hardware stores or located in my garage. I've got some tools that I've only used once, like a special wrench used to install a faucet. But I have some other tools that I use regularly, such as a hammer, screwdrivers, and portable drill. Duct tape and WD-40 have also become tools of necessity for quick fixes. Someone once told me, "If it's not supposed to move and it does, use duct tape. If it's supposed to move and it doesn't, use WD-40."

I once purchased a metal drain snake to unplug a clogged-up bathroom sink. For years I was afraid to use the 18-foot-long metal snake because I thought I'd accidentally break my pipes with it. But I got tired of pouring expensive chemicals down my drain (that usually didn't work) and paying plumbers $100 an hour. So, I finally utilized the metal snake, and I'll be darned if it didn't work great. Since then I've used that snake to clean out every drain in my house.

Along those lines, I can say that I was just as intimidated about using many investigative tools and techniques for the very first time. But once I did, there was no going back. And there are some tools that can be used for more than one purpose. Sometimes you have to improvise and make do with what you have.

TIP: When investigators are "legally" installing or attempting to hide audio and video cables/wires in false ceiling tiles and other locations, they can carefully affix the cable/wires a metal or a fiberglass snake or even a fishing pole to lead the cables/wires where they need to go.

War Story 7.10

As a private investigator, I once had to find out if a particular man frequently visited or stayed at a particular house. The reason was because my client's ex-wife started dating a convicted child molester (CM), and my client didn't want his kids (whom the ex-wife had custody of) to be anywhere near the CM. My client got a court order to ensure the CM could not be around his kids.

Because the house was located on a cul-de-sac, it was difficult for me to perform long-term vehicular surveillance of the house without getting burned. From a distance, I was able to photograph each time the CM's car drove to my client's ex-wife's house, but it was almost impossible for me to drive by and photograph the CM entering the house without being detected. Plus, I had to be able to prove that my client's kids were also in the house at the same time as the CM!

Since the kids got out of school at the same time every day, I filmed them going into the house after school and then maintained surveillance to show that the kids never left. I previously put a small pinhole-type camera inside a thick hollow clipboard which allowed me to approach the house with little suspicion. (It helped that the house next door had a "for sale" sign on the front lawn.)

The pinhole camera was not made to be used with the clipboard; it was just something I designed on my own. And I did have to use my drill to make a hole in the clipboard and the "handy-dandy" duct tape to hold the camera in place. As my time in the U.S. Army taught me, sometimes you have to improvise to accomplish your objectives.

Besides people, there are many "things" that greatly aid investigators. Without question, the number one "thing" is the computer (or smartphones/tablets) along with the Internet and various software and phone apps (I'll add books and manuals to that number one thing on the list—especially since you might reference this book!)

Internet search engines allow for instantaneous access to publicly available information almost anywhere. Social media sights also contain a wealth of information that individuals often voluntarily post for everyone to see. Reminder to check with legal counsel to ensure you are not violating any laws/rules before checking/accessing individual's social media sites. The rules are ever changing.

Data mining and other analytic software can proactively identify patterns and fraud without an investigator even lifting a finger.

GPS and camera video recording features—allow investigators to accomplish more and more every year but again, make sure you follow the letter of the law before utilizing.

War Story 7.11

While serving as a federal agent and investigating a public corruption case involving the awarding of several government contracts, I noticed while reviewing files that contract award prices of some of the same medical items (e.g., splints, crutches, bone screws, and other durable medical equipment and supplies) fluctuated greatly in a very short time. The pattern I saw suggested that prices seemed to be increasing rapidly on almost everything.

I asked one of the honest and trusted government employees at the facility to provide me with data so that I could review the price history of items of interest. When reviewing the data, I quickly concluded that pricing was out of control. The prices of some items gradually increased from as low as $50 per item earlier in the year to several hundred dollars later in the year. In fact, it seemed as if the rapid price increases for medical items was not the exception but the rule.

I asked a trusted contracting supervisor if he could explain why the prices could increase so rapidly. He scratched his head and said he was surprised to see how the prices became inflated so fast. He first reasoned that perhaps some items could be purchased at less cost in larger quantity or the price of some items might increase because of supply and demand. But even he agreed that something seemed wrong because the prices of too many items increased too rapidly.

I later determined that the contracting officials who were obtaining telephonic bid quotes were not checking price histories before awarding the contracts. Had they done so, they would have realized that the bid prices they received were way too high (not reasonable) to begin with. Bidders eventually figured out that they could bid whatever they wanted to and still get awarded contracts.

Many of the contracts were awarded after receiving just one bid price because (as policy dictated) the contracts were considered low dollar (less than $2,500). But all those "smaller contracts" can add up to a lot of money.

Later I figured out the scheme. Many bidders were paying bribes to the contracting officials who awarded those contracts. Some of the contracting officials were intentionally splitting contract awards to ensure the prices were kept under $2,500 so they did not have to get competitive quotes.

As soon as the contracting officers awarded one contract without competition for $2,450, they'd award another contract to the same vendor for about $2,475. Since each separate contract was under $2,500, they could award the contracts after receiving just one (inflated) price quote.

I'll have to admit that I didn't use any fancy software or computer program to identify the problem. I just printed out price histories and circled prices in red ink that didn't seem to make sense. But with today's technology (especially use of analytics and data mining), price anomalies like these should be easy to detect.

War Story 7.12

In Chapter 5 (War Story 5.8), I referenced a case where the contractor sent false material samples to the government for testing on a shirt contract. I did use a spreadsheet computer program to help with that case. While trying to figure out who sent the false samples of material to the government, I entered onto spreadsheets the dates that the samples were submitted for testing for each of 24 separate lots of material. Each lot had a different number of rolls of material in it. For example, Lot 1 might have had 98 rolls of material, Lot 2 might have 106 rolls of material, and so on.

Therefore, if 98 or 106 rolls were shipped from Contractor A to Contractor B, the corresponding amount of roll samples should have been sent to the government for testing after the rolls were received at Contractor B's plant.

Next, I entered the shipping and receiving dates into the computer. I just wanted to know when each shipment occurred. What seemed like a complete waste to me was that every time rolls failed government testing, Contractor B was supposed to ship the failing rolls back to Contractor A because those rolls could not be used in the contract. Because more than 50 percent of the samples failed in each and every lot prior to Lot 20, it seemed to me that shipping the rolls of material back and forth would get very expensive and therefore cut into Contractor B's profit.

My guess was that Contractor B probably never shipped the failing rolls back to Contractor A. I later found I was wrong about that. I asked for and received the corresponding shipping and receiving documents and bills of lading and found that Contractor B did ship the failing rolls back to Contractor A.

But at Lot 20, all of a sudden, about 95 percent of the rolls passed testing (and you will recall that it appeared that they were all cut from one roll of material). What I found by looking at all the dates side by side on the computer screen was very interesting: The samples that Contractor B sent to the government for testing for almost every lot (including Lot 20) were sent to the government *before* the rolls were actually delivered to Contractor B.

In short, it would have been impossible for Contractor B to cut samples from rolls of material at its plant if the rolls of material had not yet arrived. Because each lot had different numbers of rolls of material, it was easy to prove that there were some shenanigans going on.

My spreadsheet looked something like the one on page 151:

If the samples had not yet arrived at Contractor B's plant, that meant everyone had lied to me not only about who cut the samples off the rolls of materials but the location where the samples were cut. Suddenly my primary suspect company became Contractor A, not Contractor B.

I brought my documentary evidence to Contractor A's plant and questioned some high-ranking executives about the cutting of the samples. They said that in order to speed the process, Contractor B asked them to cut and ship the samples of each roll of material and then ship the samples to Contractor B ahead of the actual shipment of rolls. (They even provided me with the

INVESTIGATIVE TOOLS AND TECHNIQUES

LOT #	Number of Rolls	Rolls of Material Shipped by A	Rolls of Material Rec'd by B	Samples Sent to Lab	Tested by Lab	PASS	FAIL	Failing Rolls Shipped Back to A	# Rolls "B" Shipped Back to A
1	98	01/12/09	01/19/09	01/15/09	01/21/09	28	70	01/28/09	70
2	106	02/01/09	02/07/09	02/05/09	02/10/09	40	66	02/14/09	66
3	87	02/16/09	02/20/09	02/17/09	02/21/09	27	60	02/24/09	60
...	...	...	...	...	...	...	...	...	...
20	94	12/03/09	12/09/09	12/05/09	12/09/09	89	5	No Record	Unknown

NOTE: Lots 4 through 19 not listed for brevity.

The spreadsheet shows that samples of each roll of material were sent to the lab *before* the rolls were even received by Contractor B.

Therefore, the samples from each roll of material could *not* have been cut at Contractor B's facility.

Notice the sudden increase in passing samples (and low failure rate) at Lot 20.

receipts that showed they overnighted the freshly cut samples to Contractor B's plant.)

Their rationale made sense. But I asked who cut the samples from Lot 20, and was told the samples were cut at Contractor A's facility and shipped to Contractor B. They said Contractor B was responsible for shipping the samples to the government for testing.

Now it was even worse because that meant both Contractors A and B were primary suspects for sending the false samples for Lot 20 to the government lab for testing. Instead of narrowing this down, my list of suspects got bigger!

Because I mentioned this story earlier, you know that I subsequently obtained handwriting samples from Contractor B's internal quality control supervisor and that a government testing laboratory concluded that his writing matched the writing of the numbers written on the roll sample tag numbers for Lot 20. Contractor B's vice president finally admitted that for Lot 20, he directed his internal quality control supervisor to submit samples that were all cut from a roll of material that previously passed testing.

On a side note, Company B's defense attorney was not very happy when I showed him the evidence that the samples had routinely been shipped for testing before the rolls of material were received. I distinctly remember the defense attorney's words to me: "There he goes playing with his computer again."

But the bottom line is, computers, along with careful analysis of data, can help detect fraud, waste, and abuse.

Cloud computing and data storage services allow investigators to store, access, and/or share information including photographs and videos with others very quickly.

Telephones, two-way radios, and other electronic group communication methods allow investigators to communicate instantaneously. With the use of smart phones, photographs and videos can be quickly shared. When on surveillance, the ability to talk hands-free certainly can avoid detection. We've all seen the Secret Service agents wearing earpieces monitoring radio transmissions. Similarly, investigators can use Bluetooth technology when performing covert surveillance. Having Bluetooth built into your car radio is very convenient and practical when performing surveillance.

TIP: When possible and practical, it's a good idea to use both two-way radios and cell phones to perform team surveillance because sometimes one is more practical than another. Plus it is good to have backup communication methods. Make sure the walkie-talkie batteries are replaced with new ones or charged (bring backup batteries if possible), and test the radios before you start your surveillance. Remember that unencrypted radio transmissions might be picked up by others—perhaps even on baby monitors. If using cell phones, don't forget the battery chargers.

Obviously, text messaging is great for investigators to communicate. In addition, legally obtained telephone text messages of others can be very valuable to investigators. Knowing what resources are available (and are legal to use) is important for an investigator. It should be remembered that sometimes your own professional contacts have access to additional resources. Many computer forensic investigators can professionally download, copy and save data, photos, videos and other information from digital telephones, GPS devices and computers. Just make sure you obey the law before trying to gather evidence.

War Story 7.13

As a federal agent, I often worked jointly with one of the largest and most respected FIAs in the country. Not only did they have a lot of agents, they also had a lot of resources. When they wanted surveillance done, they assigned it to their own surveillance team. When they wanted an analysis of bank records completed, they assigned it to one of their own analysts. When they needed covert recording equipment, they went to their own tech equipment experts, who installed the equipment. They even had administrative assistants to copy documents for them.

When I was an agent, I had to do almost all of that work myself because my agency did not have the same resources. The moral of the story is to become good friends with others because combining your resources can help accomplish your objectives more efficiently.

The computer hardware and software available to assist investigators is almost mind-boggling (especially to us baby boomers and our predecessors who were brought up using manual typewriters, carbon paper to make extra copies of documents, rotary telephones, reel-to-reel tape players, and film cameras that required separate flash bulbs to take each picture. Gee, it makes me feel old just typing that). That's why I say it's important to keep striving to learn more—and to make sure you know others in the field who can help you accomplish your objectives.

Since the time I was rookie investigator, I learned the importance of having templates and go-by samples to reference when preparing various reports. With the use of computers, there's no reason to re-create everything time after time when one "sample" report (template) can be edited and modified to accomplish your objectives. Just make sure you triple check your final report; you don't want the wrong case number or wrong suspect name in your final report. (Okay, I could have made a few war stories from that one, but I'll save myself the embarrassment.)

Speaking of computer stuff, I use Microsoft Excel quite a bit, especially when investigating white-collar cases or when conducting large-scale investigations. I also use it as a business owner to track my case inventory and to log my business expenses. Microsoft Access is an even stronger tool, but I generally rely on the analysts to use that. Microsoft PowerPoint has been my bread-and-butter when it comes to preparing visual illustrations and graphs to present information in an easy-to-comprehend fashion. I use Microsoft Word to prepare my documents and reports. I know some other professionals that swear by Apple's Mac products, and sometimes they amaze me with what they can do with those products. At the time of this writing, Adobe's Acrobat XI's (Standard and Pro) PDF creation software is an incredible asset for any investigator and investigative office. At the time of this writing, PDF Converter Professional 8 is a less expensive alternative to consider which I personally use.

As a PI, I've probably taken more photographs and video in any single year then I did in any five years as a federal agent. I've also electronically recorded more interviews as a PI than when I served in law enforcement. As a result, I often process/copy digital recordings, video, and photographs on my computer and make copies for my clients and for courtroom presentations.

As a PI, defense attorneys sometimes provide me with videotapes that were filmed by law enforcement officers. These tapes purportedly support the cops' cases for prosecution (**NOTE:** Sometimes those videotapes show that the cops did not follow proper procedures.) The format(s) for electronic media can vary.

War Story 7.14

Over the years I've gotten pretty good at shooting videos and clipping, editing, and enhancing them. For training purposes, I even started incorporating royalty-free music (that I pay for) into some of my advertising videos. One time a criminal defense attorney asked me to review a police video from a driving while intoxicated (DWI) traffic stop. The attorney wanted me to split the video into several separate segments so he could show particular segments of the traffic stop during his courtroom presentation. Using my Microsoft Windows Movie Maker software, I completed his request. The videos were created and saved in WMV format. Then I labeled and copied all of the separate video segments onto one DVD for him and made a few extra copies while preserving all originals.

A few hours later (still several days before trial was scheduled), the attorney informed me that the DVD I provided him with (in WMV format) would not play on his Mac computer. To correct the problem, I converted the videos into MP-4 format. The videos then played fine in both of our computers.

A few days later, the attorney called me and informed me that the small-town courtroom where the trial was to take place did not accommodate showing videos played on computers. He said the small-town courtroom only had a DVD player. Well, the MP-4 format would not play on the DVD player so then I had to convert the videos to DVD format.

The moral of the story is that when providing, requesting, or receiving electronic media (including video and/or or audio), make sure they are in the needed format(s).

Search Warrants

Law enforcement investigators have access to more investigative tools than non–law enforcement investigators. The best example is law enforcement's ability to obtain search warrants. Planning for and executing a search warrant can take a lot more time than many might imagine.

War Story 7.15

Prior to working white-collar cases, I investigated a lot of illegal drug cases while serving as a detective. With a team of other law enforcement officers, we planned for the safe execution of search warrants, knowing we also had to expect the unexpected. While working drug cases, there was an adrenaline rush each and every time we entered places with our guns drawn, not knowing what we would face with each step forward. Besides making arrests, most of the recovered evidence seized usually fit inside a single vehicle and sometimes in a single envelope.

However, when investigating white-collar cases, the search warrants I participated on often resulted in the collection of so much evidence that we had to rent trucks to haul everything away. We'd take countless boxes of paper records and electronic media. If it was a defective product case, we'd sometimes collect machinery and the actual manufactured items. One company illegally imported circuit boards, so we collected boxes full of circuit boards. One company made defective tape, so we collected all kinds of tape as evidence. One company made defective sealants used on airplane windows; for that one, we collected old glue as evidence.

In fact, on the defective sealant search warrant, I found in a desk drawer the "smoking-gun" journal in which an employee actually listed each order, the dates of shipment, the items ordered, and the inferior products substituted.

I never experienced any physical resistance while on search warrants of businesses. The chief executive officers or other high-ranking managers of the suspect companies usually just called their attorneys, and everyone cooperated. I don't think I ever even had to draw my weapon from my holster on a white-collar search warrant. The local news media usually showed up after an hour or two and later filmed us carrying out the evidence.

On one search warrant of a company, as soon as we showed up, a group of employees started running out the back door! They weren't even suspects on our case but were illegal immigrants who hightailed it out of there when they saw federal agent raid jackets. The prosecutors told us in advance just to let them run.

A federal immigrations investigator once asked me if I knew how they could tell which employees were illegal immigrants when the investigators arrived at construction sites. I responded, "I suppose you can tell they are illegal because they run away." The immigrations investigator replied, "No, the illegals are the ones working. They don't take their jobs for granted, and they break their rears all day long."

Subpoenas

Another tool often used by law enforcement is a grand jury subpoena. Once a federal criminal prosecutor accepts a case for criminal prosecution consideration, it's relatively easy for a federal agent to obtain a grand jury subpoena for records and even testimony. Reluctant witnesses who don't want to talk are sometimes issued subpoenas to appear before a grand jury and asked to testify to what they know.

War Story 7.16
As a federal agent working jointly with another FIA, I noticed that agents from the FIA usually preferred it when the federal prosecutor called witnesses to testify before the grand jury instead of our interviewing the witnesses at their homes or elsewhere.

Because I often conducted criminal and civil investigations involving the same matters simultaneously, I preferred that the grand jury not be the first choice as a way to get witnesses to tell what they know. The reason is that grand jury testimony usually is confined just to the criminal case (and considered "secret"), and that information cannot be shared with the civil case.

In contrast, if I questioned someone at their home (or anywhere except in the grand jury room), I could use the information obtained in both the criminal case and the civil case. But if the witness was subpoenaed and testified at a grand jury, the information could only be used in the criminal case. Later I could request a court order to release the grand jury testimony, but there is no guarantee the requests will be approved.

It took me almost 15 years to figure out why those other FIA agents preferred using grand jury subpoenas to obtain testimony. First of all, it was because those other agents only worked criminal cases and could care less about civil cases.

Second, because those FIA agents didn't have to personally conduct the interviews, they did not have to spend time preparing for those interviews. Instead, the federal prosecutor and the grand jurors asked the witnesses the questions.

Finally, if the witness testified before the grand jury, the FIA agent did not have to write a detailed summary report describing what the witness said. Instead, the prosecutor obtained an actual transcript of witness testimony and handed the transcript to the FIA agent.

In short, by using a grand jury to obtain witness testimony, those FIA agents only had to put in enough time to serve the witness with the subpoena. When I interviewed a witness outside of the grand jury, I had to plan the logistics of the interview, prepare the questions and strategy for it, conduct the interview, and write a report describing it. Obviously I invested much more time than the FIA agent did. But my interviews were more detailed and could be used in criminal and/or civil court.

Over the years, I learned that it usually was best for me to complete as much of each investigation as possible before briefing the federal criminal prosecutors because they often wanted to use grand jury subpoenas on the cases.

TIP: Sometimes a grand jury subpoena is the best investigative tool on the planet because recipients understand the importance of the request and seldom delay responding. Plus, because of their secrecy requirements the recipients can't tell the world (including suspects) that they received the subpoena. But if you are simultaneously conducting a civil or administrative investigation, you have to remember that there are many restrictions on how grand jury information can be utilized. Other types of subpoenas do not have the same type of restrictions. The bottom line is that grand jury subpoenas have their pros and cons.

Interceptions and Tracking Devices

Other techniques/tools utilized by law enforcement are interceptions of wire, electronic, and oral communication (like telephone calls, e-mails, and text messages) and the use of tracking devices. Prior approval often is needed from a court or through consent of one or more of the affected parties before implementing some of these methods. Investigators considering such techniques had better follow the letter of the law; otherwise, the evidence obtained might be inadmissible and the investigators may find themselves in a legal bind.

NCIC

As previously described, law enforcement personnel can also input and run checks on the National Crime Information Center (NCIC), which is run by the Federal Bureau of Investigation. Records stored on the NCIC include missing persons, fugitives, sex offenders, arrest records, outstanding warrants, protection orders, and stolen property (with unique descriptions or serial numbers). The stolen property entries also includes stolen license plate numbers, stolen vehicle identification numbers, as well as stolen boat and gun information and more. The use of NCIC is strictly controlled and for the use of law enforcement.

Mail Covers

As a federal agent, I often used mail covers to obtain useful information in white-collar cases. A U.S. Postal Service–approved mail cover results in a U.S. Postal Service employee's logging all the information listed on the return address labels of mail delivered to a specified address and/or a specified person or entity at an address. There needs to be justification before a mail cover is approved. Mail covers are typically in place in 30-day increments. Mail covers do not include the opening of any mail, just a listing of the information on the outside of the envelopes delivered. This information also includes the postmark, which has the date and location where the mail was processed.

War Story 7.17
The first time I used a mail cover as a federal agent, I learned that one of my suspects received mail from a few banks under her maiden name. With that information, I later found that bribery payments were laundered under her maiden name at one of those banks. I never would have known that information except for the use of the mail cover.

Trash Covers

Factually, some people throw in the trash useful and sometimes incriminating information. Then they put the trash cans on the curb. Many investigators have found useful information by taking the trash that was put on curbsides and then later (carefully and safely) sorting through it.

"Dumpster diving" was considered one of agents' "other official duties" when I was a federal agent. Dumpster diving involves going through large Dumpsters behind businesses, during search warrant executions. Phone bills, e-mails, and other correspondence often can be found mixed in with garbage. Investigators going through or taking people's trash should keep safety in mind not only in regard to the contents of the trash but about being confronted while attempting to secure such evidence. An investigator should check on the governing laws of the locale before even considering the implementation of a trash cover.

Undercover Assignments

Investigators sometimes utilize covert undercover techniques in their quests to obtain evidence. Cops work undercover to catch drug dealers, terrorists, and other wrongdoers. Many PIs also work undercover. Some FIAs conduct long- and short-term stings or operations. Large undercover operations often require an agency to expend valuable resources (man-hours, store fronts, car rentals, etc.) in order to safely and effectively complete the mission. But sometimes undercover assignments can be short term.

War Story 7.18
As a brand-new federal agent, I was tasked to work undercover as a civilian employee with a fictitious back injury. The senior federal agent in charge of the investigation told me to visit a certain physician, who was a suspect in the case, and to tell that doctor there was nothing wrong with me. I was also directed to ask the doctor to complete paperwork indicating I had a back injury that would prevent me from going back to work. I was to tell the doctor that I worked as a laborer at a warehouse.

The senior agent told me I should say something like "Doc, I need to pay child support, which I'm behind on, and want to collect temporary worker's compensation so I can go get a second job for a while and collect two paychecks. I wonder if you can write down that I have an injured back so I can get out of work at my first job."

When meeting with the doctor, I brought along a book that was hollowed out on the inside and contained an audio transmitter. I also wore a body-wire recorder under my shirt. I was told by the senior agent to tell the doctor that I did not need to be examined. The senior agent was sitting in a parked car outside the building recording our conversation.

NOTE: I forgot I was wearing a body wire and stopped in the men's room before going into the doctor's office. I'm sure the senior agent didn't appreciate my recording the sounds before and after the toilet flushing.

While seeing the doctor, I told him the lines from my script and was surprised when he told me to get undressed so he could examine my back. Frankly, I didn't feel like getting undressed plus I had the body wire under my shirt. I said, "There's no need for me to get undressed, Doc, because there's nothing wrong with me."

The doctor then told me that he was not willing to write down anything that indicated I had a back problem and he told me that I would not be billed for the visit. He then politely asked me to leave.

Perhaps if I hadn't been wearing the body wire and had been willing to get naked for the doctor, the plan would have worked. I thought it was odd that the doctor was willing to examine me after I had already told him nothing was wrong with me.

War Story 7.19

While serving as a federal agent, I worked closely with a federal investigative analyst who identified many instances where the government continued electronically depositing government paychecks into the bank accounts of government retirees who were dead. In some cases, the investigations determined the funds deposited since the time of death were just sitting in the deceased individuals' bank accounts. However, in several instances, the funds were being withdrawn from the accounts—often by caretakers who were not even related to the deceased retirees.

With approval of my agency, I conducted an undercover operation to determine if there was criminal intent to steal the funds. I used a fictitious name and acted as if I were a government employee from the payment office and legally recorded telephone conversations with suspects believed to have illegally withdrawn the funds from the accounts. Very often I obtained incriminating and/or useful information during those recorded conversations.

It was kind of fun when I later knocked on the doors of those same individuals and identified myself as a federal agent while asking them some case-related questions. They had no idea I was the person they had previously talked to on the telephone and often provided information that conflicted with what they said earlier.

One caretaker who unlawfully withdrew funds from a deceased person's account claimed she didn't know that the person was deceased. But I had previously obtained a photograph of her from the Internet taken while she was at the man's funeral; she had received a folded American flag during his gravesite service.

Another caretaker (half the age of the deceased) said she was the deceased retiree's common-law wife and she thought she was entitled to the deposited money after he died. A few days after the woman learned that she was going to be criminally charged with the theft of funds, she "slipped and fell" at a department store and obtained a quick out-of-court settlement, which she used to repay the government for the money she had unlawfully withdrawn from the bank account. Her efforts paid off; the judge dismissed the case against her because there was no dollar loss after she repaid the money.

Another caretaker (also half the elderly retiree's age) actually married the retiree (even though she was still married to someone else) and got him to sign over his car, condo, and just about everything else to her. Not long after, the retiree committed suicide in a hotel room (at least that's what the police and coroner ruled), and then the caretaker cleaned out his bank accounts—including the retirement checks electronically deposited after the retiree died. She actually forged his name on checks after his death. The case and evidence against her was solid, but for some reason the assigned prosecutor elected not to prosecute. The prosecutor said that there was a chance that the woman thought she was entitled to the money!

NOTE: On November 5, 2013, the *Washington Post* published an article titled "Government Fails to Keep Up on Deaths." The article included some alarming numbers: "In the past few years, Social Security paid $133 million to beneficiaries who were deceased. The federal employee retirement system paid more than $400 million to retirees who passed away . . . In 2011 auditors found Medicare paid $23 million for services provided to dead people . . ."

Photography and Video, and Audio Recordings

Almost all investigators use cameras, video recorders, and/or audio recorders. Surveillance is a common technique utilized to obtain information and evidence. Investigators need to be careful not to violate other people's legal right to privacy. Legally recorded evidenced can be extremely valuable and often irrefutable. As they say, "A picture is worth a thousand words." Getting film of a worker's comp employee who claims he can't walk, who is outside cutting his lawn, is pretty good evidence that there's a false claim in there somewhere. That type photo/video is often referred to as, "the money shot".

TIP: It's best to get back-to-back days of video showing allegedly injured fraudsters performing physical acts that they previously reported they couldn't do. If only one day of physical activity is filmed, the fraudsters likely will claim that they did take one day to see if they could do those things but they were in so much pain the next day that they realized it was a mistake. By capturing on film several consecutive days of people doing physical things that they said they couldn't, you can establish a pattern of fraud.

Another form of video that often assists investigators is the video from closed-circuit television systems used by business owners, corporations, private citizens, and government agencies. Security cameras are installed in many places these days. Very often, investigators can review and/or obtain valuable video evidence from those sources. This type of evidence was extremely useful during the investigation of the 2013 bombings at the Boston Marathon. Not only was law enforcement able to obtain photographs of the suspects; they were able to publicize the photos nationwide while seeking the general public's assistance. The investigation was solved quickly because of outstanding work by all involved.

War Story 7.20

As a federal agent, I assisted the local police in an investigation involving the death of an elderly military retiree whose decomposed body was found in a wooded area. The deceased man was also a widower. After a few months, I did some research and determined that the federal government was still making monthly electronic retirement check deposits into the man's individual checking account.

Later in the investigation, I learned that someone was making regular automatic teller machine (ATM) withdrawals from the dead man's bank account without authorization. In the months that followed, I obtained photographs from bank ATM machines across the United States when the withdrawals were made. As a result, I was able to identify the thief, who was later determined to be the former roommate of the deceased military retiree.

When questioned, the suspect admitted to obtaining the personal identification number of the military retiree's bank account and unlawfully making the ATM withdrawals from the retiree's bank account before and after he died. More important, he admitted to killing the retiree and dumping his body in the woods.

War Story 7.21

While serving as a PI, I was asked by a criminal defense attorney to reinterview a woman about the last time she saw a coworker alive. The woman was previously interviewed by police and testified in court. The attorney was defending a man who had already been found guilty of murder, but new information allegedly was found indicating that on the day of the murder, his client was nowhere near the coworker who was later found dead. The new evidence was a building's security videotape, which showed the victim walking down the stairs of her office building, but the client was not walking down the stairs with her. This conflicted with earlier testimony.

The person I was to reinterview previously testified that she saw the suspect walking down the office building's stairs with her coworker just before the coworker was later found dead. The suspect denied ever walking down the stairs with the victim that day.

During my interview of the witness, she stated she was certain she saw the suspect walking down the office building's stairs with her coworker just prior to her coworker's being found dead.

Further investigation determined that the building's security videotapes were not well organized and not date stamped. There were probably numerous videos of the coworker walking down the office building's stairs alone on many different days. Because there was no way of knowing the date of the "new evidence" video, it didn't have much value—at least in my opinion.

War Story 7.22
While serving as a PI, I was asked by a criminal defense attorney to watch and make duplicate copies of a police traffic stop video that was being used as evidence to support a DWI charge against his client. The video was obtained by a dash-mounted camera on the patrol car of the officer who made the traffic stop. The officer reported that his probable cause for pulling the driver over was that she was weaving in and out of lanes.

I objectively reviewed the film and observed that the driver never once crossed over into another lane of traffic. In fact, the driver stayed between the lines of her lane. I also watched the video of the driver's performance of the Field Sobriety Test and was of the opinion that she passed the test. Since the driver refused to take a Breathalyzer test, the only physical evidence was the police videotape. To make a long story short, the defense attorney was able to get the charges against his client dismissed—because of the police's own evidence.

TIP: Many companies, organizations, and financial institutions do not store their videos or photographs very long. The same is true of police dispatch tapes. Some even record over old tapes and digital media to avoid the expense of purchasing new tapes/digital media and to save storage space. If you intend to inquire about or try to obtain existing video, audio, or photographs from other entities or organizations, do it quickly and put it at the top of your investigative plan. The information/data may not be available for very long.

Laboratory Analysis

In early June 2013, the U.S. Supreme Court made a decision that would allow law enforcement officers/investigators to greatly increase their solve rate involving many violent crimes. The decision paved the way to allow police officers to take a DNA swab of anyone arrested for a "serious" crime. Up until that ruling, only the federal government and approximately 28 states followed this practice. One of the justices opined that the use of DNA for identification was no different from matching the face of an arrested person with a wanted poster or matching tattoos to reveal gang affiliations.

The ability to compare DNA that was legally obtained as evidence from previous (and future) crimes with the DNA from arrested individuals increases law enforcement's ability to think plural. Even if those arrested are not found guilty or convicted, their DNA can be compared to previously obtained DNA evidence.

Government crime and other laboratories often examine DNA, hairs, fibers, blood, fingerprints, handwriting, tool marks, tire marks, and the like. This chapter cannot cover all of the work that crime laboratories can do to assist investigators. Some war stories in previous chapters described the benefits of laboratory comparisons of fingerprints and handwriting. It should be remembered, however, that the chain of custody of all items to be examined by a laboratory must remain intact if the evidence is to be used in a court of law.

Perhaps the biggest advances made in law enforcement are not so much the techniques and hard work deployed by investigators but the ability to make quick use of evidence involving DNA, fingerprints, and mug shots. This is also true of the abundance of video and photographs that can be obtained from surveillance cameras and from individuals who have ready access to video recording devices on their smartphones.

The war stories that could be told about the use of laboratories to solve cases are endless and played up pretty well on many television shows. Labs assist in terrorism investigations, bombings, murders, rapes, and other investigations. The evidence is also used to prove individuals (including those previously convicted) were not involved in wrongdoing. When I was a burglary investigator, I used fingerprint dust powder at crime scenes about as often as a barber uses talcum powder. The next war story is more humorous than anything else.

War Story 7.23

While I was serving as a detective, a female employee of our large organization showed me a handwritten love note that she received from a newly assigned detective in my office. She wasn't offended by the note but questioned its appropriateness. The love note didn't have a signature at the bottom. Instead it had a hand-drawn smiley-face picture. Having been around that particular detective for a short while, I knew that he considered himself to be a ladies' man and was always trying to impress people. He even tried to convince outsiders that he was in charge of our detective's bureau.

One day I got a call from a woman who was the customer at a nearby post office. She reported that someone stole a $200 money order she had just purchased, which she had placed on a nearby counter while sorting her mail. The money order was not yet made payable to anyone. The woman recalled that just before the money order came up missing, a man dressed in a suit conversed with her and her teenage daughter in an overly friendly tone and seemed to be trying to get dates with both of them. After leaving the post office, she found a note on her windshield. The note included lots of flattering comments about both the woman and her daughter. There was no signature on the bottom, just a hand-drawn smiley face.

I called the rookie detective in and interviewed him about the theft, and he denied stealing the money order. But I later determined that he did steal it and cashed it at a nearby liquor store just before the interview. His smiley-face signature gave him away.

Informants

Information individuals provide to investigators sometimes sends the fact finders in the right direction. The informants' motives may vary from wanting to do the right thing, revenge, or even for money received for providing the information. Investigators need to ensure that information received from an informant is credible and reliable. Some informants request confidentiality before providing information.

Investigators should ensure they never mislead informants about the possibility of their having to later testify in court. Many law enforcement agencies have strict guidelines regarding registering informants and/or logging any information provided by informants.

Some law enforcement reports may refer to registered informants by assigned numbers rather than the informants' names. Both the informant and the investigator must be able to trust each other. It's not a one-way street. Although I do not discuss telephone hot lines in this book, some companies and organizations (including law enforcement agencies) use them. The hot lines allow callers to provide anonymous tips that can later be investigated. Keep in mind that the tips are not always accurate.

A few of the PIs I know have told me that they often provide cash for quick information. One said he paid a security guard to let him in a gated community. Another said he paid a hotel clerk to provide the room number a suspect was located in.

War Story 7.24
While working on an Army drug suppression team, the Army CID agent and I were using an informant who seemed to have ants in his pants. He could never sit still, and he was always

talking. At some point during a debriefing after a drug purchase, the informant insisted that we give him an undercover car and came up with some other crazy ideas he must have seen on television. The CID agent got frustrated and yelled at the informant, "Sit down, shut up, and tell me what happened!" (Of course, it's impossible to do the last two at the same time.) We used that line a few dozen times to rib that CID agent.

Polygraphs and Deception Detectors

The laws surrounding the use of polygraphs have changed over the years. Vocal analysis is another method used as an aid to detect deception. In some instances, investigators are not even allowed to ask if an individual would be willing to take a polygraph or voice detection examination. Law enforcement has been known to utilize polygraphs to determine if someone has lied and also to verify that someone has told the truth. That might sound like the same thing, but polygraphs have been used as a method to eliminate people from suspicion.

For example: If four people had equal access to a safe where $10,000 was reported missing and all four claim to have no knowledge about the missing funds, it could be that none of them had anything to do with the missing money. Eliminating them from further suspicion might work to everyone's advantage. Investigators must become familiar with and stay current on the ever-changing laws regarding the use of polygraphs and other deception detection tests before even asking someone to participate in one.

Analysis and Audits

As previously described, analysis and audits often prove very valuable when conducting investigations, especially fraud investigations.

Other Case Files and Police Reports

As a law enforcement investigator and as a PI, I've been able to obtain valuable information from old and other police reports and case files.

Closed police cases are usually available to almost anyone, and they can provide a great deal of useful information. Of course, law enforcement officials will be able to get access to much more than the non–law enforcement folks. Those old reports sometimes identify information about others, including: biographical information, associates, previous employment, where they were and whom they were with on certain dates, and even information about what others did or were suspected to have done. Closed investigative reports released by law enforcement to members of the general public and media often contain redaction marks (lines drawn through) so that Social Security numbers, juvenile names, and informant names are not released.

War Story 7.25

While I was serving as a supervisory detective on an Army installation, a civilian man was caught stealing an unattended purse from an office building while posing as a janitor. Because of my supervisory position, I received daily briefings of all the crime occurrences on the base and knew there were several recent reports of unattended purses having been stolen from office buildings. As part of his previous arrest processing, the thief had his mug-shot photograph taken.

For the next few days, I searched for and obtained all of the old police reports of purses reported stolen from office buildings on the Army installation in the past year. Many of the case files contained information indicating that witnesses saw a suspect in the area who matched the description of the recently arrested purse thief.

Next I put together a photograph lineup of suspects who looked like the suspect who was recently arrested and included his photograph too.

I arranged to meet each witness separately and prior to the viewing the photo lineup, I told each witness that the photos may or may not include the person seen in the area when the purses were stolen. Six different witnesses positively identified the recently arrested suspect as the man they saw in the area when their purses were stolen.

This case demonstrates that with a little more investigative work and by making use of old information, you can solve several old cases. In this case, the suspect served an extended period of time in jail because he was connected to previous crimes committed.

War Story 7.26

On that same Army installation, a soldier came to the police station in the middle of the afternoon on a weekday and said that he had just seen a man walking down the street wearing a tan trench coat that was stolen from his house. The soldier said his home was previously burglarized and several items were stolen, which he had already reported to the police. My first thought was how in the world could the soldier prove it was his coat.

Since not too many people walk around on military installations wearing tan trench coats, I drove up to the man and stopped him for questioning. He was in his late twenties and also wearing a nice three-piece suit, dress shoes, and even had a gold chain dangling from his suit connected to a pocket watch. The only thing that didn't make sense was that he was all dressed up and seemed to have lots of money but he was walking instead of driving.

For my own safety, I first conducted a pat-down search of the man and felt something that could be a weapon in his right front pants pocket. I removed the item from his pocket and found it was a roll of Kennedy half dollars. I looked closer at the paper roll and saw it had a name and telephone number written on it, neither of which matched the suspect's.

I told the man why I stopped him. He denied stealing the coat and said he purchased it himself from a store. Just for the heck of it, I called on the police radio to see if there were any reports of theft from a person with the name listed on the roll of Kennedy half dollars.

Sure enough, the person's name was listed as a reported victim of a house burglary that included the theft of a coin collection, and the victim lived right down the street from the house where the coat was stolen from.

I arrested the well-dressed guy on the spot and transported him to the police station. My more detailed search of him (after arrest) found a number of rings and other jewelry, which I was able to trace back to several other burglaries in the same area. Even the gold pocket watch was stolen!

During the subsequent interview of the suspect, he admitted to committing a string of burglaries in the area—including stealing the tan trench coat.

There are a lot of lessons to be learned from this story, including making use of old police reports and historic stolen property records to solve cases. Sometimes pursuing investigative leads that you don't think will be worthwhile can be very productive.

Ask

Investigators should also remember there is often one perfectly legal way to obtain evidence and other information: Simply ask for it. Law enforcement officers often ask drivers for consent to search their vehicles even though the officers have absolutely no probable cause to search their cars. Investigators can consider asking people to provide things that might otherwise be more difficult to obtain. During my law enforcement and investigative career, I have experienced great results obtaining evidence and other information simply by asking for it. But as many salespeople can attest to, you must use a lot of psychology when dealing with people, including the timing of some questions, tone of voice, and word choices.

Investigators should also keep in mind that if the purpose of their request is to obtain evidence or other information to possibly use in court, they will have to prove that they acted lawfully and that the items or information were lawfully obtained.

Sometimes consent is later contested. Some who provide consent may say they felt threatened, intimidated, or coerced and therefore the consent was not given voluntarily. They might even deny that they ever gave consent in the first place. Having a witness or two to the consent helps a lot, but it's even better to get the consent in writing. If the written consent says that they had the right to refuse, that's even better.

Also ensure that the person you are asking can legally provide what you are asking for.

For example, a person can't give consent to have their next-door neighbor's house searched. An employee may not be able to legally provide an investigator with an employer's proprietary information. Even though investigators may be acting in good faith, they must follow applicable laws and be able to prove and articulate their investigative activity and actions. I've got dozens of war stories about asking for things during investigations, and I provide a few of them next.

War Story 7.27

When serving as a patrol officer, I made a traffic stop of a vehicle for a minor traffic infraction. Upon approaching the vehicle, I observed a pack of cigarette rolling papers on the front passenger's side floorboard. Rolling papers are not probable cause to search cars where I come from. So instead I simply asked the driver for consent to search his vehicle. The driver asked, "What happens if I refuse?" My response was 100 percent truthful. I replied, "Then I will take appropriate action." The driver then immediately gave me verbal permission to search his vehicle, resulting in the recovery of illegal drugs, and I arrested the driver.

But the "appropriate action" I would have taken could have been a lot of things. I could have requested that a drug-sniffing police dog walk around the vehicle during the traffic stop. But actually, the "appropriate action" I probably would have taken would have been to let the driver drive away and I'd get back in my patrol car and leave.

War Story 7.28

When serving as a federal agent investigating a healthcare fraud case, I conducted a detailed interview of a former administrative employee. Toward the end of the interview, I asked if she had any documents that she wanted to provide. The former employee hesitated and then said something like "I've been saving some documents that show fraud for a couple of years. I didn't want someone to say that I was part of the crime. I have a box full of documents I'd like to give you."

War Story 7.29

While serving as a federal agent investigating a conflict-of-interest and contract fraud case, I asked a government contracting officer if he had copies of any e-mails that would support some of things he told me during the interview. The contracting officer printed out several e-mails and handed them to me.

War Story 7.30

While I was conducting a theft investigation, a witness often reviewed her own copies of documents before answering my questions. When the interview was almost completed, I asked, "Would you mind giving me copies of those documents you were looking at during the interview?" She provided the copies without hesitation.

TIP: While conducting an interview, it's usually best not to stop the interview to have the person immediately copy or obtain the item(s) or information you want. Instead, make a list of the items you will ask for on the right margin of your notepad. Toward the conclusion of the interview, ask for those things that will require the person to physically get up to retrieve them. (Exceptions, of course, would be things that require immediate action, such as the collection of evidence that could be destroyed or tampered with or items that could prevent safety or could cause harm if not immediately retrieved. Investigator discretion is advised.) The reason I suggest not ordinarily stopping the interview is that if the interview is going well, let it keep going that way. Interruptions are bad enough, but intentionally causing stop-and-go moments can be counterproductive.

TIP: Be mindful of your own safety if you allow people (particularly potential suspects) to leave the room alone to return with evidence or other items. They might come back with something more powerful than you are expecting or they might not come back at all!

As previously mentioned, this chapter does not list all possible resources, tools, and techniques available to investigators. In fact, I have hardly mentioned one of the most important and effective tools to be used in almost every investigation, that is the mother of all investigative tools: interviewing, which is discussed in greater detail in Chapter 8.

Chapter 8

Interviewing

"Liar, liar, pants on fire!"

—Child to a fibber

Interviewing is the Swiss Army knife in the investigator's toolbox because well-planned and thoroughly conducted interviews will contribute greatly to the success of any investigation. Interviews often prove helpful even when all other tools fail to provide good results. However, the techniques applied when using the interviewing tool vary based on the user's training and experience.

I could tell enough interview and interrogation war stories to fill another book. In fact, trying to summarize into one chapter all of the useful information an interviewer needs to know would be challenging to say the least. This chapter provides information and war stories about interviewing that should be valuable to any investigative interviewer.

I learned many of the interviewing techniques I've utilized during my career by accident, by trial and error, from conversing with or watching other interviewers, by completing training courses, and by reading books. (I learned absolutely none from watching television or movies.)

NOTE: In this chapter, I often use the word "interviewer" rather than "investigator" because the job positions of many professionals who conduct interviews may not be officially designated as "investigators."

In War Story 3.2, I described being a young investigator who obtained my first admission/confession from a thief when he admitted stealing a television (which I didn't even know had been stolen) when I actually was investigating the theft of a radio. The lesson I learned was that when conducting interviews or interrogations, interviewers should usually act as if they know more than they actually do. When interviewers project an air of confidence (not cockiness), the person being interviewed (the interviewee) will more likely think that the interviewers know all or most of the case facts. That's a nice way to start an interview. But you still must go into every interview prepared.

Interviews and Interrogation

There is a difference between conducting interviews and conducting interrogations. Interviews usually are conducted by soliciting information and (one hopes) receiving truthful responses from individuals. Interviews are nonaccusatory.

Interrogations are different because they usually involve the interviewer directly or indirectly challenging the truthfulness of the person being questioned in attempt to learn the truth without the use of threats or coercion.

An interrogation often occurs when the interviewer informs the person being interviewed that the interviewer believes he or she lied. Obviously, accusing someone of wrongdoing or not telling the truth could result in a confrontation. It's been my experience that it's sometimes best to avoid a confrontation if possible. In contrast to directly accusing a person being interviewed of lying, you could consider just insinuating that the person has not told the truth (or the complete truth). By insinuating (rather than accusing), you can avoid the predictable challenge or strong denial that the person accused would offer. However, note that sometimes a direct accusation is a valuable technique to use when beginning interrogations.

War Story 8.1

During interviews of deceptive suspects, after I've listened to the interviewee's (fictitious) story, I often preface accusatory or likely confrontational questions about their criminal involvement, by saying something like "You know, I expect a person who is accused of doing wrong to deny it when they first sit down with me. Denial is almost a natural reaction. Because almost everybody does it, I don't hold it against them for at first trying to wiggle out of the situation. I know it's sometimes hard to tell the truth. But the facts uncovered during the investigation are not going away. So when someone continually denies they did anything wrong, even when the evidence shows otherwise, that makes them look even worse. Because then they look like a wrongdoer and a liar. Does that make sense?"

The response I'm given by that last question often tells me what I'm up against. If the interviewee agrees that it makes sense, I'll know that the person will at least be open-minded about continuing the questioning. By saying that I understood why someone would lie, I demonstrated that I am a reasonable person. But if the person being interviewed stands up and says, "Are you calling me a liar!?" or "Are you calling me a thief!?" I know I might have a challenge on my hands.

Of course, my response to such an outburst often would be an honest answer, like "How about you just listen to what I am saying; I haven't called you anything."

Rapport

Over the years I have learned that building rapport with the interviewee before even starting the interview is extremely important. Just shooting the bull for a bit with the individual will help him or her to be more comfortable around you. If you can get that person to like you (as compared to disliking or resenting you), that will be very helpful as you proceed.

War Story 8.2
As a new MP investigator in the U.S. Army, I received on-the-job training before going to the Army's MP investigative academy. By sitting in on other investigators' interviews or by watching them through two-way mirrors, I learned how they conducted interviews and interrogations.

Most of the investigators' interactions with suspects were very professional, and the investigators used a lot of tact, empathy, and compassion. But sometimes all hell broke loose during interrogations. Sometimes investigators threw ashtrays, case files, or anything else that was handy across the room but away from the person being interviewed.

The interviewers' intent was to use a form of psychology on the suspect to get them to confess. Of course, after watching this technique used several times, it wasn't long before I too started throwing stuff around the interview rooms and yelling at suspects! I was never angry at any of those suspects; it was all an act.

As a more experienced interviewer, I think back to those very early interviews almost in disbelief because they were so unprofessional. But the fact is, much psychology is used when trying to elicit voluntary truthful confessions, and very often that psychology can be planned before even starting an interview. Even building rapport with the person to be interviewed is a form of psychology. But sometimes what happens during an interview can surprise you.

War Story 8.3
During one investigation, my boss and I had two suspects in custody who were believed to have acted together in a series of burglaries. They were questioned separately, and both denied having any involvement with the crimes. My supervisor had the bright idea of putting the two suspects in the same interview room together and for us to watch them through a two-way mirror.

Since we had told both previously that they were subject to being monitored and recorded, neither said anything to each other while we were covertly watching them.

But one of the suspects took out a very small piece of paper (about three inches by three inches) and wrote a note on it. He then handed it to the other suspect, who quickly read it and then crumpled it up and put it in his mouth.

My boss ran into the adjacent interview room and told the suspect to spit out the note. Then the guy started chewing real fast! Next thing I knew, my boss had his hands around the suspect's throat and was yelling at the suspect to spit out the note! I don't know what my boss thought he'd get out of that tiny piece of paper after the guy had been chewing on it. I don't remember the outcome of those interviews; I just remember laughing.

Listen and Then Talk

It's very important for interviewers to be good listeners. I'm not talking about having superb hearing; I'm talking about listening skills. All too often, interviewers think it's their job to keep talking—and even interrupting. Let the people you are interviewing talk! And actually listen to their answers!

In fact, the best thing to do is to ask open-ended questions, which almost forces the other person to provide elaborate answers. During an interview, the person being interviewed should do most of the talking. During an interrogation, however, the interviewer should do most of the talking (leading to the possible confession).

During the interview phase, if the people interviewed tell lies or untruths, it's usually best to not correct them. Just let them keep on lying for a while because they are giving you ammunition to fire back at them later. If you stop them at the first lie, they'll probably say that they made a mistake and correct it. If they tell 10 separate lies, it's pretty hard for them to later say that they made 10 mistakes.

War Story 8.4
One time I called a suspect to be interviewed in my office on a burglary case. He knew he was free to leave the interview at any time because he was not in custody. I had him sit in a chair a couple of feet away from mine. After I asked his name, date of birth, and address, he lifted his thigh off the chair slightly and then squinted. Next he released a loud stinky scent of gas from his rear end. I looked at him in disgust and told him to knock it off. And then he did it again!

Now, that was a day where the suspect won the psychological battle. I yelled at him to get his nasty rear end out of my office! I have no recollection of ever calling him back in to be reinterviewed. Those were my younger days, and I would have handled the whole thing differently years later. What would I have done differently? I guess I would have let him go sit on the pot for half an hour and then started the interview over.

Note Taking

Notes can and should be taken when conducting interviews. Some say its best for the interviewer to write something down after each answer, not just when the person says something of interest that was not previously known. The interviewer must remember that people being interviewed are always studying the interviewer. If you're not careful, they'll figure you out before you figure them out. In contrast, during the interrogation, usually you don't take notes while attempting to elicit a (truthful and voluntary) confession.

War Story 8.5
Prior to conducting one interview, I made a list of all the people I interviewed and planned to interview and placed the list in the left pocket of my folder. During a subsequent interview of a suspect,

I bent my folder in half because it made it easier for me to write. While I continued asking questions of the suspect, I noticed he seemed to be staring at the back of my folder. I didn't realize it but I was accidentally showing the suspect my interview list, which I didn't want him to know about.

But as I said, I learn from my mistakes. Of course, never again did I unintentionally leave case planning sheets out for the suspects to see, but sometimes I made up fictitious information sheets and let suspects "accidentally" see those pages during the interview. Then the suspects would think they were slick and outsmarted me, but in reality, they did what I expected them to do. The sheets of paper containing fictitious information were just props.

War Story 8.6

Another time I completed a detailed investigative plan to target a ring of possible corrupt government employees. I called a federal agent from another FIA and asked him to meet me inside a warehouse at a government storage depot. I gave the FIA agent a paper copy of the investigative plan, which also identified all of the government employees suspected to be accepting bribes. Some of the employees were pretty high ranking. We discussed the plan in detail, and the federal agent said he would assist in the investigation.

A few days later, my boss got a call from a high-ranking government employee from the government storage depot. He told my boss that one of his employees found a folder inside a warehouse at the government storage depot containing information about a corruption investigation. My boss later retrieved the folder, and we learned that the FIA agent had left his folder inside the warehouse.

Although my boss was furious, I didn't give the agent a hard time about it when I returned his folder to him. I know accidents can happen. But we scratched the thought of conducting the investigation because we had every reason to believe our efforts had been compromised.

Corroboration

Interviewers should keep in mind that even when a suspect admits to wrongdoing or confesses, that's not the end of the investigation. Next, you will want to try to get that confession witnessed and/or in writing. Then you should try to corroborate the information provided by the suspect.

If the suspect tells you where evidence is located, you'll have to do your best to legally retrieve it. You might want to even take the suspect with you to show you where it is. If the suspect describes something about the crime scene that would be known only if he or she had been there, you'll need to corroborate it. Don't ever make the mistake of thinking that a confession alone will be sufficient to get a conviction in court—especially if it was not electronically recorded, witnessed or if a written statement was not obtained.

By corroborating the information obtained in the confession, you'll also feel confident that you did not obtain a false confession. The last thing you want is for an innocent person to confess to something he or she did not do.

TIP: Keep in mind that complainants, victims, and witness sometimes lie or are mistaken about the information they provide. Don't always assume that 100 percent of the information provided to you is accurate. Try to corroborate the information.

Examples of people who provide inaccurate information are:

- Someone making false or inflated insurance claims
- Attention seekers
- A driver involved in a hit-and-run accident who later claims the car was stolen
- Someone being in a place where he or she shouldn't have been when something wrong happened (examples: a cheating spouse or an employee injured off duty but reporting the injury as if it occurred while on-duty)
- A person who mistakenly wrote down the wrong license plate number of a car seen in an area
- People looking for revenge

The list of possible untruth tellers and their motives is endless.

Word Choice

TIP: Some say it's best for the interviewer to ask a suspect who has voluntarily confessed to write an "apology" or a "statement." The reasoning here is that if you use the word "confession," the suspect will associate that word with jail, prison, or other consequences and might not want to write or sign anything.

Car salespeople often use a similar technique when trying to get customers to sign a contract. Instead of saying "Let's sign a contract" they might say, "Let's put together an agreement." They know the word "agreement" is a lot more pleasant to the ears than the word "contract."

An interviewer's choice of words can make a big difference in obtaining cooperation when questioning people. In the early stages of the interview, say "take" instead of "steal." Instead of "molest," say "touch." Instead of "assault," say "hit." You can obtain additional details of the crime as the interview progresses. But if suspects hear legal terms, such as "assault," they probably will associate it with criminal charges, jail, or other consequences, and they might clam up.

Similarly, an investigator could knock on a residential door and (after showing identification credentials) lead off with a statement like "My name is Investigator Joe Blow and I'm trying to ensure this neighborhood stays safe from crime. Can you tell me if you've seen any suspicious people in the neighborhood recently?"

By prefacing any questions with a purpose, residents probably will be able to better relate to the investigator because they believe the investigator is acting in the residents' best interest. So when time permits, think about your word choices. You might be able to make improvements and get better results.

War Story 8.7

When I was a detective, a supervisor periodically inspected and inventoried each detective's credentials. The credentials consisted of a unique photo identification card and a badge contained in a wallet-size black leather case. The credential cases were government issued so they all looked the same. One day during an office meeting, the supervisor called out, "Creds check!" The investigators knew the boss wanted to see everyone's credentials, and all the detectives tossed their credential cases on the table for the boss to inspect. It only took a few seconds and then everyone picked up their creds off the table and went back to work.

A couple of hours later, two of the detectives came back into the office laughing. They were asked what was so funny and said they just went to a reported burglary together and right after they showed their credentials to the female victim, she said, "That's not you!

The detective (who was a white male) immediately inspected his own credentials and realized that after the credential inventory, he accidentally picked up the credentials of a black male detective. The investigators had to undergo a second credentials inventory to get everything straightened out.

Planning

One of the most important stages of any investigation is the planning of the interviews.

There are actually two parts to interview planning. The first part is planning the order in which the interviews most probably will be conducted. Typically you'll interview the victim(s) and complainant(s) first and then the witnesses. Suspects usually are interviewed last, and the main suspect usually is the very last one interviewed.

Sometimes I'll interview main suspects earlier just to hear what they have to say (even though I don't expect them to tell me the truth). The only problem with that strategy is once suspects officially tell you some lies, they often have a more difficult time later admitting to the truth because they will have to admit they lied earlier.

Consequently, later you will have to try to get them to admit to two wrongs: the one you were investigating in the first place and also the lies they told when they were first interviewed. Suspects often can rationalize why they committed the original wrong, but it gets harder for them to rationalize why they also lied about it when questioned earlier. So they might not confess because they'd also have to admit that they lied earlier. In other words, a suspect might not mind being labeled a crook who acted on impulse on the spur of the moment, but he or she doesn't want to also be labeled a liar.

The second part is planning for each interview separately. Obviously there will be some key questions you'll want to ask during your interviews, and many of the questions will be unique to the individuals interviewed. Creating a unique interview question list (or outline) for each person to be interviewed will ensure that you actually ask all of the questions that you intend to.

By having most of the questions prepared in advance, you'll also be able to review them long before the interview starts to determine the best order and the best format to ask the questions.

For example, if you start by asking an open-ended question, like "Tell me what you did yesterday," the interviewee can start wherever they want and talk as long (or short) as they want. Just remember to listen and don't interrupt (unless they go too far into left field). You can guide the interview as it progresses. Regardless of their answers, they are locking themselves in to their own statements (for better or worse).

During the interview, avoid asking too many closed-end questions, which require only yes-or-no answers. Your goal is usually to get suspects to talk and elaborate.

Don't suggest answers to the person being interviewed. For example, it would be ill-advised to ask, "You didn't have anything to do with this, right?" Odds are the person will just agree with you since you suggested the answer.

Don't ask compound questions either. I've heard interviewers ask three or more questions in one sentence. Usually the person interviewed answers only the last question, and the interviewer accepts it. Here is an example of a compound question:

Question: Where were you last night; I mean, were you with Bob and Terry? About what time did you get home?

Answer: I got home at about 10:30 at night and went in the house by myself.

In this example, the suspect was given three questions to answer at the same time, and he chose to answer the last question, which he answered truthfully. The answer implied he was not with Bob and Terry, but he never said that. So technically, the suspect never lied. He gave a truthful answer to very poorly worded questions.

Don't neglect to ask good follow-up questions. Too often, interviewers ask questions and accept responses that don't even answer the questions. Sometimes the person interviewed will almost invite the interviewer to ask follow-up questions but the interviewer fails to ask them.

Body Language

It has been said that people communicate more nonverbally than they do verbally. You know that's true if you've seen people roll their eyes after they hear someone say something they didn't agree with. You do not have to be an expert to observe body language, but as an interviewer you would do well to study kinesics, which is the interpretation of body language. Hand gestures, facial expressions, and even body movements often provide nonverbal communication and clues.

One of the best methods of interpreting body language is to first study people's norm. By asking nonthreatening simple questions early in the interview, you'll be able to observe their norm. In the beginning, they'll probably be facing you in an open position with their feet flat on the floor. They'll probably look you in the eye when they answer questions. Even if they don't, you'll still be establishing their norm.

When you later ask critical questions of suspects, they may suddenly turn their body away from you or react completely differently from when you asked them the simple questions. Their reaction does not necessarily mean they lied; it just means that something happened inside their brain to cause them to physically react. Of course, it could be that they just were uncomfortable and needed to shift around. It's only through a series of questions and responses that the interviewer might be able to observe constant deviations from the person's norm. That's why the question formation during the planning stage is so important. With proper strategic planning, the interview can be extremely productive.

Just because someone had an abnormal or significant reaction to a question does not mean the response was a lie. Nonverbal behavior should be evaluated by clusters (several different responses to several different questions), not just one single response. The interviewer should explore more deeply those areas that triggered the physical reactions. Just remember that body language alone does not prove deceit.

It's worth repeating that during an interview, you should let people answer your questions and don't interrupt. Very often the interviewer's silence will cause interviewees to volunteer additional information because they are uncomfortable with the silence. In other words, periodic and well-timed silence can be deployed as an interview technique. To experiment with this, the next time you are engaged in a conversation and you ask a question, just keep looking (don't stare) at the other party after they've answered. Almost instinctively they will continue talking.

Sometimes all an interviewer needs to do is repeat a portion of the other person's response and that person will elaborate even more on the topic. An example of this might be:

Question: Where were you last night?
Answer: I went out with my friends.

Question: You went out with your friends?
Answer: Yes, we went to Club Soda and had a few drinks.

Question: We went?
Answer: Yeah. Me, Tom, Carl, and Mike had a few drinks.

Question: A few drinks?
Answer: Well, maybe more than a few.

Props

In the early stages of my investigative career, I accidentally stumbled on the benefits of using props during interviews and interrogations. Props are physical items that the interviewee sees before or during the interview that cause them to draw their own assumptions or conclusions.

War Story 8.8

During the later stage of an investigation, I called a primary suspect into my office to be interviewed concerning the theft of thousands of dollars of government equipment. Since I had already completed many other interviews of other suspects and witnesses during the preceding weeks, my case file was quite thick. I possessed strong evidence indicating that the suspect I was preparing to interview was the mastermind behind the theft of the property.

During the interview, the suspect repeatedly denied having any knowledge about the theft. Not wanting to share with him the actual evidence I possessed, I held my case file in front of him and said something like, "I didn't call you in here to waste your time. I've conducted an extremely thorough investigation and interviewed everyone involved. They've probably even told you that they've been interviewed. I've got written statements in this case file from every person I've interviewed, but I'm not permitted to show you them. Now, you can sit there and tell me you don't know anything about this, or you can tell the truth."

The suspect paused and then confessed to masterminding the theft and told me where the stolen property was. With his consent and assistance, all of the stolen items were recovered.

Everything I told the suspect in the interview was true. I *did* conduct a thorough investigation, and I *did* have written statements in the file from everyone interviewed. The evidence that he committed the crime was overwhelming. But I realized that it was his seeing the thick case file that made him accept that the evidence was overwhelming.

After that, every once in a while on cases that had been open for a few weeks, I used thick case files as props to demonstrate to suspects that lots of investigative work had been accomplished prior to the interview. Sometimes the case file contained mostly blank sheets of paper, but the suspects didn't know that.

Over the years, I've learned to use other items as props, including boxes marked with evidence tags, blank videotapes, and even fake fingerprints. What might be surprising is that I never lie to any of the suspects interviewed. I never actually say I possess evidence that I don't actually have. I don't like lying to people—even bad guys. But I have no problem outsmarting them.

When working burglaries, I'd leave a prop out in the open and never even mention it. Suspects would see it and assume that the prop was evidence against them. If I showed a suspect a set of lifted fingerprints, I'd ask if he could tell me why his fingerprints would be found at the crime scene. But I never said that the fingerprints I just showed him were from the crime scene or that they were his fingerprints.

Sometimes I'd leave a videotape marked "evidence" on a nearby table. Then I'd ask suspects if there was any reason why they would be seen on video in the area where the crime was committed. I never said that I had a video of them in the area where the crime was committed.

War Story 8.9
While conducting an investigation jointly with an agent from another FIA, we were preparing to conduct an interview of a white-collar crime suspect in the FIA's office. Prior to inviting the suspect to the interview room, the agent gathered all the boxes of evidence we had (which were actually just case-related documents), and wheeled them into the interview room on a dolly. The agent said to me confidently, "We do this a lot in our interviews."

A few minutes later he called the suspect into the room to be interviewed. The suspect didn't even seem to notice all of the boxes stacked up on top of each other. After exchanging pleasantries, the federal agent handed the suspect a stack of papers and asked him what they were. The suspect looked them over and said, "That's the government contract I was awarded." The federal agent replied, "Oh."

In effect, the federal agent blew the interview because he quickly demonstrated that he did not have a grasp of what was being investigated. Wheeling in a dozen boxes of props wasn't going to convince the suspect that agent understood the case facts.

In short, all the props and airs of confidence in the world won't do you any good if you don't prepare for the interview.

War Story 8.10
While I was teamed with another investigator on surveillance, our target pulled into a parking space, exited his vehicle, and entered a restaurant. My partner decided to peek in the passenger-side window of the target's unoccupied car. I was initially against him doing this out of concern he might get caught peeking in the target's car window. When the investigator returned to our car, he said something like, "I know where he's going next."

I laughed and asked how he knew where our target would be going. My partner said, "He had a list of all the places he's going today sitting on the front passenger seat." Well, my partner hit a home run because after the target finished his lunch, he drove right to where my partner said he would. For the rest of the day, we knew in advance where the target was going.

TIP: From that day forward, I made sure I never left anything in my parked vehicle that might give a clue as to who I am, what I do, or where I'm going. However, I have placed props in the interior of my parked cars just in case someone decided to peek inside. I've intentionally left files on the passenger seat that give the appearance I work for an insurance company, construction company, and others. I have no idea if doing so has ever paid off, but I make sure to make it difficult for people to find out anything about me and what I'm doing unless I want them to.

War Story 8.11

While serving as an investigator, I had to conduct numerous consecutive interviews inside an office that belonged to the business entity that had been victimized by its employees. I worked in that office for several days straight, and it became obvious to me that most of the employees resented me conducting the interviews and questioning their integrity. I always made it a point never to throw anything of investigative value into the office trash container.

But it occurred to me that since some people might dig through the trash can searching for clues as to what I knew, I could feed them some misinformation. Then word might trickle out that I had more evidence against the suspects then I actually had.

So at the end of every day, I wrote some fictitious information on a sheet of paper, wadded it up, and threw it in the office trash can. The wadded-up notes said something like:

- Interviews conducted: 16
- Confessions: 3
- Witnesses: 6
- Videotape Evidence: 2
- Other Evidence Obtained: 18

I have no idea if anyone ever went through that trash searching for information. But if they did, I'll bet it scared the heck out of them!

Finish the Job

During an interview or interrogation, I also attempt to have the suspect voluntarily tell me where the evidence is (and/or provide me with it) and ascertain the reason why the person committed the crime or wrongdoing.

I want to emphasize again that the purpose of an interview is to learn the truth. Even when a voluntary and truthful confession is obtained, the information should be corroborated. I repeat: You don't want innocent people to confess to something they did not do, and you don't want to rely on the confession as your only evidence.

Empathy

Since my early days as an investigator, I've tried to empathize with suspects I interview. I try to consider what I'd be thinking if in their shoes. (Actually, I think that's why props work so well.) I ask myself, "What would make me voluntarily confess if I had committed the wrong that they seemed to have committed?"

You'll recall that my way of investigating is extremely thorough, so very often by the time I interview suspects, I already have sufficient evidence to prove their guilt. Obtaining a voluntary and truthful confession very often just seals the lid on the case.

Obtaining a truthful and voluntary confession also makes it less likely that suspects will want to take the case to trial. They know the evidence is overwhelming and that they voluntarily confessed to the wrongdoing. If you don't have to spend time preparing for trials, you can keep investigating other cases.

But I also try to empathize with suspects at the conclusion of the interviews/interrogations, especially after they've confessed. I know they must feel relief but also concern about their own future. Suspects might also be thinking about the public humiliation they might experience. (White-collar criminals tend to get very concerned about possible publicity of their wrongdoing. In fact, their concern about publicity often delays their confessing.)

Although there are some criminals who aren't worthy of anyone's pity, I try to allow suspects to keep their dignity and treat them with respect. I'm not the judge and jury. I also don't want them hating me or hating others in my profession after the interview. Statistics have shown that many of those same suspects, even the ones who don't confess, will be interviewed again about some other wrongdoing at some point in the future.

Statement Analysis

There are many benefits of having complainants, victims, witnesses, and even suspects provide written statements during an investigation. Obviously having the person's own words (and own choice of words) documented and in the case file can help refresh the interviewer's mind at any point in the investigation. Written statements can be shared with others (with a need to know) by making copies and/or providing electronic facsimiles. A written statement makes it very difficult for the writer to later tell a drastically different story. But one of the biggest benefits of obtaining written statements is that is allows the interviewer to analyze the words and sentences used (and not used), which often can provide clues.

War Story 8.12

When I served in the U.S. Army's Military Police Corps, the MPs were required to obtain sworn written statements from everyone interviewed. The MPs even had a special form for this: DA Form 2823. For example, when responding to reports of theft, we'd interview the victims, take notes, and then ask them to write a sworn written statement.

Part of our job was to ensure they included all the necessary information in their statements. Sometimes we'd have to ask them to include whether stolen items were secured, how they were secured, the names of others who had access to the property before the theft, the value of the items, and so on. Some MPs were better at taking more detailed written statements than others. As a uniformed MP, my own personal objective was not to just complete an initial response report but to help solve the case.

As a result of my job performance as a patrolman, I was later selected to be a plainclothes investigator for the Army. Investigators also obtained written statements from everyone interviewed. But as an investigator, I also had to type those statements on an electric typewriter. (This was before computers.)

I didn't know how to type when I first started but later became one of the quickest two-finger typists around. Even while typing this book on my laptop computer, I still use just two fingers to type, but I'll be darned if I know how people can just use two thumbs to type on a smartphone.

Just as our bodies are responsible for much of our communication, so are the words we use (or omit) and sentences we make (or don't make). If an interview was videotaped, viewers could later closely watch the video to better analyze body movements and facial expressions. But by then it's usually too late unless you plan on conducting a second interview of the same person.

An audio recording of a person's verbal statements (or interview conducted) could also allow for a later analysis of the speaker's choice of words, change in tones, delays in responses, coughs, and other features.

NOTE: The next points about statement analysis apply both to listening to others' word choices and when reviewing their written statements.

Pronouns

Analyzing written statements is an often-overlooked valuable investigative tool and technique. In fact, the analysis of written statements is a topic seldom taught in investigative training classes. As I pointed out in Chapter 6, writers' use of pronouns often is confusing because of the lack of clarity. Similarly, a person's use of pronouns may provide great insight.

An indicator of deception might be the lack of the use of the word "I." Sometimes people subconsciously try to remove themselves from the scene even though they were actually there. In their statements, they might completely omit the pronoun "I." For example, they might say, "Got the gun" instead of "I got the gun."

Rather than say "I," they might say "we." For example, they might say "We got the gun" instead of "I got the gun." In fact, overutilizing the word "we" throughout a statement (when they should say "I" or be more specific) is an indication of deception.

There's another thing interesting about the pronoun "we." The word "we" is often used to indicate togetherness. You've probably noticed that in sports, fanatics often say when their favorite team wins, "We won." But when their favorite team loses, they say, "They lost."

If someone makes a complaint that a complete stranger made them go somewhere against their will but the complainant often uses the word "we," that could be a red flag and worth further exploring. Such a complainant might say, "We went to (blank)" instead of "He made me go to (blank)" or "He took me to (blank)." You should consider the words "We went" to possibly imply togetherness and possibly voluntary action. The choice of words is *not* conclusive evidence of deception. But statements such as those just described should at least arouse the investigator's suspicion.

Some deceptive people will change the pronoun "my" to the adjectives "the" or "a" to avoid showing ownership or to try to create greater distance between them and the person or object. For an example, a deceptive person might say about his girlfriend named Jane, "I picked up a gun and accidentally shot the girl." But it might have been more accurate for the person to have related, "I picked up my gun and accidentally shot Jane."

Often people also try to generate some distance from a person by referring to them as "he" or "she" rather than by name when they actually know the name. For example, if a man refers to his recently murdered wife only as "she" and never says "my wife" or never uses her first name, that could be an indication that he's intentionally generated some distance. Similarly, if a man says something like "I did not have sexual relations with that woman," many might speculate that he was trying to create some distance by saying "that woman" instead of calling her by name (which he knows). Also, the choice of words "sexual relations" is pretty broad.

Partial Truths Equal Deception

When people are pulled over for driving while intoxicated or asked if they had been drinking during their lunch break, they might respond, "I had a beer." Factually, they are telling the truth. But a more accurate statement might be, "I had several beers." When given a choice, people prefer not to lie. This is an example of why it's important to conduct interviews thoroughly. The way the questions are phrased is important, and follow-up questions are also important. Follow-up questions should be asked to obtain clarification.

Specificity

In the early stages of an interview or interrogation, the interviewer needs to be careful about being too specific when asking certain questions. For example, the interviewer might ask, "Did you grab him by his left arm and drag him to the floor?" It could be that the person being interviewed could truthfully answer no to the question because she grabbed the person by his *right* arm. If later challenged with evidence that she did grab the person by the left arm, the suspect could say she denied it earlier because she thought she grabbed the person by the right arm.

If the interviewer asks someone if he ever had sex with a certain person, and the interviewee replies that he never had "sexual relations" with that person, the interviewee never answered the question. In that case, the interviewer should repeat the question and ask even more specific questions to ensure that the suspect answers. Don't allow suspects to avoid answering your questions by providing broad or nonspecific responses.

Minimizing

Previously I mentioned that it's better to not use the legal word such as "assault" or "molest" to a suspect because the person being interviewed will associate the word with jail, prison, or consequences. You may find that some interviewees will choose words that seem to lessen the impact or severity of the incident. For example, a person might say, "I hit Jim" instead of "I punched Jim"; or "I touched her upper body" instead of "I grabbed her breast." In other words, people may try to minimize the seriousness of their actions by using softer/gentler words.

Can't Recall

Very often people who don't want to communicate all they know will say, "I can't recall" or "I can't remember" or "I'm not sure" or "to the best of my memory." Factually, it could be true that they can't remember, but it could be they just don't want to provide any more information. Conducting a more detailed interview could result in obtaining additional information.

NOTE: Just as when interpreting others' body language, it's usually best to try to establish people's norm and then watch for deviations. Also remember to consider clusters of behavior rather than individual incidents or reactions. For example, if a man referred to a person as "Jane" at first and later refers to Jane as "that girl," "her," or "she" when describing a critical event, it could be that during that time, something changed dramatically at the scene.

Think Plural

As stated throughout this book, in order to conduct thorough investigations investigators should think plural, not singular. In the case of interviewing, the interviewer's initial primary questions should be specifically directed toward the incident under investigation. If you don't focus your efforts, the people interviewed may lose confidence in you. Stay on track at least until you obtain all the information you need for that particular investigation. It's okay to ask a few (seemingly) off-the-wall questions, but basically stay focused on your objective.

Let me throw in a couple sports analogies: In a football game, a receiver's primary thought has to be to catch the ball and then run. But we've all seen receivers who take their eye off the ball just before the catch (because they are thinking about running after the catch), and then they drop the pass. When conducting interviews, you need to remember to concentrate on what you are doing and don't get ahead of yourself regardless of what's going on around you.

Many football receivers glance across the field so they have an idea where the hole might be after they make the catch. But some smart receivers might intentionally glance at an area where they are not going just to throw off the defenders. Very often you can make interviewees think you are heading one way when you're actually heading in another.

In other words, during interviews and interrogations, you need to be thinking about more than one thing at a time. But there are times when you need to focus completely on one thing. All professional sports athletes practice and prepare before the games. Interviewers should practice and prepare before conducting interviews. Just as professional athletes participate in training camps before the regular season starts, professional interviewers should regularly train to improve their interviewing skills and related knowledge.

Interview Notes

Interviewers should save any notes taken during interviews/interrogations and ensure that the notes are secured/safeguarded in case they are needed or asked for later. It is advisable to sign or initial each page of notes along with writing the date of the interview and perhaps the time. Many interviewers place their interview notes in separately marked envelopes in the official case file once the investigation is completed.

Interview Room Sketches and Photographs

The job of defense attorneys includes finding holes and deficiencies in the prosecution's cases. A common tactic is to claim that clients believed they were in custody or thought they were not free to leave the interview room. They may even claim that their client's path to the door/exit was intentionally blocked by the interviewer(s).

For that reason, it is a good idea for the interviewer to either draw a sketch or take photographs of the interior of the room/location where the interview was conducted. Obviously if the interview is legally videotaped and depicts the entire room, you'll have proof of how the interview was conducted. If you draw a sketch and/or take some photographs of the interview room setup, place them in the official or working file. You might also want to initial and date the photos or sketches.

War Story 8.13
While I was serving as a patrol supervisor in the Army on a midnight shift, we kept getting calls to respond to alarms going off at the Base Exchange store (which is like a small department store). Each time, the responding units checked the doors and windows and determined the building was secure. After about the tenth time, a manager of the store was called to respond because it was determined that it was the motion detectors inside the store that were triggering the alarm.

Upon the store manager's arrival, the MPs entered the building along with a K-9 police dog and dog handler. A couple of burglars were caught inside. (The police dog deserves the credit for sniffing the hiding burglars out.) It seemed odd that there were no signs of forced entry into the building, but the burglars obviously got in somehow.

The MPs handcuffed and transported the two burglars to the Army CID's office. Upon arrival, the CID agent told the MPs to take the handcuffs off the prisoners and to lock them in two separate interview rooms. MPs were posted as guards outside of the interview rooms to prevent the prisoners from escaping.

About 15 minutes later, the CID agent entered one of the interview rooms, and one of the suspects was gone! He just completely disappeared. Then the CID agent opened the second interview room door, and the second suspect was gone too! They just both vanished into thin air.

As the CID agent started verbally reprimanding the two MPs standing guard, another MP said he heard footsteps from above in the false ceiling tiles. Next, an athletic MP climbed up into the false ceiling and started carefully looking around for the suspects. About a minute later, the MP's foot came crashing through one of the ceiling tiles, which caused all of us who were standing around to burst out laughing.

A few seconds later, from a distance down the hall, we heard the sound of a large crash followed by running footsteps. We all ran toward the sound and saw the ceiling was completely caved in near the exit door and ceiling tile debris was all over the floor. We also saw the two suspects running toward the exit door, which they pushed open and sprinted away from the building.

One thing that's not fun is having to run as fast as you can chasing people after you've been awake for almost 24 hours. One of the MPs quickly caught one of the subjects, and the other suspect was caught not long after.

The way the two suspects escaped from the interview rooms was the same way they had been committing burglaries. The suspects later admitted that they entered the Base Exchange store while it was open. Just before closing time, they hid up in the store's ceiling tiles. Several hours later, when the store had closed, they climbed down and selected expensive merchandise to steal. They later admitted to burglarizing not only that store but several others on base.

War Story 8.14

When I was a city police officer and serving in a high-crime inner-city area, there were constant burglaries of small mom-and-pop business establishments. Fortunately I had an excellent training officer who taught me how to prevent and detect burglaries while on patrol. Briefly, the way to accomplish that is by being aggressive while on patrol, stopping and questioning suspicious persons, shining a spotlight on windows to ensure there is a reflection (we had a lot of smash-and-grabs in the area), and looking for unusual things like window air conditioners being moved out of place or fire escape ladders being pulled down.

"Roof jobs" were pretty common too: The burglars would get on the stores' roofs and ax their way in. Those crooks were almost like termites or rodents, and for every one you got rid of, others would take their place. The worst thing you could do was stop patrolling your beat for a couple of hours to write reports because the bad guys would break into everything. (I caught one guy putting an entire newspaper machine in the backseat of his car just to steal the coins.)

Liquor stores that were closed for the night were special targets of burglars. The thieves sometimes worked in large groups and used sledgehammers to pound holes through the stores' cinder block walls. Then they'd enter and steal cases of wine and booze. The funny part is that they'd often leave a trail of full liquor and wine bottles that they dropped as they ran away. Sometimes you could catch them by following the trail of full bottles like bread crumbs.

Detectives later investigated the burglaries, not the patrol officers. If the detectives did their jobs properly, they'd conduct detailed interviews trying to connect similar burglaries in the area. I hate to say it, but in those neighborhoods, it often seemed like it really wasn't a question of who was stealing stuff but who *wasn't* stealing stuff.

War Story 8.15

Similar to the last war story, just as my midnight shift was about to end, I got a call to respond to a report of a burglary of a small mom-and-pop breakfast grill that was just getting ready to open up for the day. Earlier in the night, burglars broke in and stole meat and cooking equipment. The owner was understandably furious as she tried desperately to prepare meals for arriving customers.

I felt pretty bad about the burglary because it happened on my patrol beat. I had never been assigned to patrol that particular area before and didn't even know the restaurant was there (it was located in an isolated area and there was absolutely no exterior lighting around it).

As soon as I walked inside the restaurant, the business owner verbally scolded me and said that I should have done a better job of protecting her property because she gave cops free breakfasts every morning. I replied, "I feel real bad that this happened. But just so you know, I've never accepted a free breakfast from anybody." (She should have bought some exterior lights and an alarm system instead of feeding the cops for free.)

TIP: Don't ever think that people give you things while on duty without expecting something in return. My training officer taught me not to accept even a cup of coffee at no charge. When waitresses refused to take our money, we'd leave money exceeding the purchase price on the counter as tips.

NOTE: It's true that patrol officers in particular are usually underpaid. Both my training officer and I were notorious for moonlighting before or after our shifts (sometimes both). My training officer said he often used his moonlighting money to pay informants for information.

NOTE: Investigators, law enforcement personnel, and other interviewers need to ensure they follow all laws when conducting interviews or interrogations. Interviewers should also respect individuals' legal and other rights before, during, and after all interviews. Have the common courtesy to let persons interviewed use the restroom when they need to. Offer them something to drink after a while. It's also a good idea to make notes as to when you offered or allowed those things (because defense attorneys might say the confessions were coerced). Consider seeking legal counsel and/or completing professional training before initiating any interviews/interrogations. Before conducting any interviews, consider rights to legal counsel, to remain silent, and to union representation as well as the rights of juveniles/parents and the rights of mentally challenged personnel and others. The bottom line is to make sure you follow the rules and laws so that any information you obtain will hold up in court. (Yes, that is a long C.Y.A. note.)

Chapter 9 helps investigators and fraud fighters create useful plans before initiating investigations.

Chapter 9

Case Planning

Planning is one of the first steps to take when initiating any detailed investigation. I intentionally postponed discussing the topic until I had outlined other important aspects of conducting thorough and complete investigations. Between the information already provided in this book and perhaps along with your own previous training and experience, you should have a pretty good idea of how you want to approach each investigation. Armed with all of this knowledge, your investigative goals are probably much larger.

Just like any other worthwhile project that requires an investment of time and/or resources, an investigation is more likely to be successfully accomplished and completed in a timely and efficient manner if you create and follow a well-drafted plan. But keep in mind that your plan probably will change as the investigation progresses.

The first things you must determine are what needs to be investigated, why it needs to be investigated, and what needs to be accomplished in order for the investigation to be considered complete.

If the goal is to solve a case and possibly hold the wrongdoer(s) criminally and/or civilly accountable, it is important to know which criminal and/or civil statutes may have been violated and what the statues' elements of proof are. That's important because in order to charge/convict someone of a specific violation(s), evidence needs to be obtained that proves all of the elements of those statutes/laws and that the specified suspect(s) did it.

In an administrative employee investigation, undoubtedly there will be some policies and procedures, job descriptions, or other documentation that describe the dos and don'ts that the suspects employees should have known. You can't prove that an employee violated company policy if the employee was never made aware that the policy existed in the first place. You'll want to obtain copies of the applicable rules that were said to have been violated, proof that those rules applied at the time of the violation(s), and proof that the alleged violator knew or should have known about the rules.

War Story 9.1

When conducting a healthcare fraud investigation, I reviewed a medical facility's insurance claim forms and noticed that the actual provider of services was not listed on the claim forms. Instead a supervising physician's name was listed. My review of patient medical records indicated that the treatments had been provided not by a physician but by someone with less education. The insurance company paid more money when reimbursing the claims because it believed a licensed physician provided the services.

My first thought was that the doctor would probably tell me that he didn't know that he was not allowed to sign the claim forms when he did not personally perform or directly supervise the treatments. But the insurance company told me that when the doctor signed up to be an approved provider, he agreed that he would follow and stay up to date on all the insurance company's claim rules and procedures before providing services and/or submitting claims for payment. In essence, this agreement was a catchall that removed the wiggle room for approved providers who submitted false claims that might try to be excused because they didn't know the rules.

To prove the case, in addition to obtaining evidence of the false claims, I also needed to obtain a copy of the doctor's signed provider agreement showing that he agreed to follow and stay up to date on all of the insurance company's claim rules and procedures before providing services and/or submitting claims for payment. I also needed the insurance company's written policy (along with the date implemented), describing that the name of the actual provider of services had to be on the claim form. In short, a lot of documentary and other evidence needed to be obtained before a violation(s) could be proven.

TIP: Whenever possible, the investigator should learn about (or become aware of) other similar occurrences involving the same area, same vicinity, same modus operandi, and/or similar activity as the possible suspect(s). The more historic information you know, the better prepared you will be to expand the investigation if and when you so desire. Although it is not always essential to have detailed knowledge of any historically related information before initiating an investigation, it is important at least to be thinking in that direction while conducting the investigation. Also, as previously discussed, during an investigation, you should be thinking (and probably asking) about what caused the incident(s) to occur and how those instances can be prevented or avoided in the future.

I begin my investigative plans with pen and paper in brainstorming sessions. Usually I just draft the first things that come to mind, expand on those thoughts, think about previous related investigations I worked and how actions I took before might apply to the new case, and then fine-tune the investigative plan into an organized format. (I also shred all but the final drafted plan.) You must consider the (possible) existence of evidence when developing an investigative plan as well as the tools, techniques, and resources that might be useful to obtain the evidence and/or to complete the investigation. Last, you must prioritize each investigative step with consideration given to the benefits and possible consequences of initiating some steps before others as well as how the timing of steps might aid or detract from your investigative efforts.

In many ways, planning and conducting an investigation is like playing a game of chess. There are possible benefits and possible repercussions to each move you make—especially the timing of those moves. As mentioned earlier, it's usually best to identify the facts, collect evidence, conduct interviews, and then (last or almost last) interview the suspect. Interviewing the suspect first could affect the outcome of the investigation.

War Story 9.2

As a rookie federal agent, I was in the very early stages of investigating a bribery case involving a government contracting official, who had since retired. I briefed one of my higher-ranking supervisors on what was suspected, what had been accomplished to date, and what was planned. There was much work ahead. The supervisor had experience successfully investigating bribery cases so I had a great amount of professional respect for him.

But what he said next baffled me. He suggested an entirely different investigative approach than what I had been using for over a decade before becoming a federal agent. What he suggested went against everything I was ever taught. He said, "Why don't you go ahead an interview the suspect now?"

Had I not known that supervisor's reputation for being successful at working corruption cases, I would have immediately dismissed his suggestion. The supervisor explained that at this point, there was absolutely nothing the retired government employee could do to interfere or impede the investigation, and the suspect might save me a lot of time by just admitting to accepting the bribes.

As much as I respected the supervisor, I did not want to use his strategy. That's not to say that he was wrong. I like finding the evidence first (if at all possible) and then conducting the suspect interviews. In other words, I like to know the answers to most of the questions before I ask them. Plus, my way of investigating usually does not focus on just the original matter being investigated. My belief is that anyone who pays or accepts bribes (especially on a regular basis) has no morals; therefore, during my investigation, I likely will identify much more wrongdoing (perhaps even more serious) by that same individual and perhaps others.

I mention this war story only because even among the best investigators, there will be different opinions on how to approach each case. One of the concerns I have about interviewing a suspect early in the investigation is that he or she might contact other involved parties and/or cause the destruction of evidence.

In the bribery case example, if I interviewed the person who received the bribes, I'd almost expect him to contact the person who paid the bribes (or others), which could complicate the rest of my investigation. A compromise on this strategy might be to have both bribery suspects (the payer and receiver) interviewed simultaneously but separately (or in rapid succession). This might require the two interviews to be conducted by different interviewers, or the same interviewer could conduct the second interview almost immediately after the first. If that was done, you'd definitely get everyone's attention real fast.

War Story 9.3

While serving as a federal agent, a senior agent in my office routinely asked several investigators to help him conduct unannounced early-evening interviews at the homes of a suspect company's employees. The senior agent gave us a detailed briefing of his case, a list of people we were supposed to interview (along with their addresses and telephone numbers), and a list of questions to ask each person.

By conducting separate interviews of different employees on the same night without them knowing in advance about the interviews, we felt pretty confident they wouldn't have a chance to get their stories straight with each other before being questioned. Sometimes the strategy worked pretty well. Other times it didn't because nobody was home or the people wouldn't answer their doors. But there is certainly a lot to be said for hitting hard and hitting fast.

In addition to knowing your own capabilities and resources as an investigator, you must consider what resistance might be encountered when you implement a game plan. You also need to consider both the potential benefits and consequences of your actions. In War Story 9.3, the senior agent knew from experience that once he interviewed one employee of the suspect company, odds are that employee would tell others about the interview, perhaps even company executives and/or the company's legal counsel.

If the company's legal counsel got involved, the agent could be almost certain that the lawyer would announce that he or she represents the company and all employees and that no further interviews should be conducted without coordination through the lawyer. By doing the most important interviews all at the same time before legal counsel got involved, the senior agent increased the likelihood of obtaining useful information without having to jump through any legal hoops set up by the lawyer. Obviously, a well-thought-out investigative strategy is very important.

TIP: If you are going to use other investigators or agents to work overtime (especially uncompensated overtime), you'd better at least buy pizza for everyone that night or the following day for lunch (or both).

During police firearms training, instructors often mention Sir Isaac Newton's Third Law of Motion when discussing what recoil is when firing a weapon: "For every action, there is an opposite and equal reaction." That applies to conducting investigations as well. Rest assured that whatever you do when conducting investigations most probably will cause some type of reaction from others.

War Story 9.4
While serving as a rookie military policeman, I turned on my patrol car's blue lights to pull over the car in front of me. The paranoid driver immediately slammed on his brakes, almost causing my car to rear-end him. When you do something in furtherance of an investigation, something else usually happens immediately after.

I don't know if Sir Isaac Newton had a Law of No Motion, but it's also true that sometimes an investigator's lack of action causes (or contributes to) other actions. Probably the best example of the latter is that if you wait too long to conduct an investigation, crime scenes may get tampered with, evidence might disappear, people will establish alibis, and people might get hurt. But sometimes you can use time to your advantage.

War Story 9.5
While conducting burglary surveillance on a midnight shift as undercover detectives, my partner and I observed three men standing at various nearby locations surrounding a small retail establishment that was closed at night. They seemed to be strategically placed and casing the joint. My partner wanted to stop and frisk the men to see what they were up to. But since the suspects were not aware of our presence, I suggested that we just wait and watch them for a while. Within 30 minutes, one of the suspects began using force to break into the retail establishment. My partner and I quickly approached the three men and had them in search positions against a wall in about 30 seconds. In that case, it was what we didn't do (at first) that allowed us to be catch the suspects in the act.

Plans Change

No matter how good your investigative plan is, usually you'll have to change, tweak, or update it as the investigation progresses. All too often things go wrong or don't work out the way you hoped. Time after time, I've been stung by Murphy's Law ("Whatever can go wrong will go wrong"). However, it's just as likely that things will go so well that you'll have to adjust your plans accordingly. Investigative plans are not and should not be written in stone.

War Story 9.6

While serving as a Military Police investigative supervisor, during a particular 30-day time frame, I received regular and recurring reports that a man wearing an Army fatigue uniform with three sergeant stripes on his collar was entering the new recruit barracks and approaching lower-ranking soldiers (mostly privates). The "sergeant" told the privates that they were not allowed to store large amounts of cash in their lockers and convinced them to hand over their cash to him after he provided receipts.

Of course the receipts were bogus and the "sergeant" wasn't even assigned to their company. When the low-ranking soldiers later went to their company's orderly room with their receipts to get some of their cash, they found out they had been swindled.

Because this was a recurring event, the base commander was jumping all over our chief of police (provost marshal) to catch the crook ASAP!

As previously stated, in the Army, crap rolls downhill, and the pressure was on my office to catch the swindler. I was way ahead of everyone though. I already had all the police reports of theft involving this suspect and had created a detailed profile of him based on information from all of the victims. Besides the usual descriptive information obtained, almost every victim described the crook as charming.

I shared the profile information with all of the patrol officers and investigators. Because of the command pressures, all of the investigators were forced to work nightly surveillance where the previous crimes had occurred until the suspect was captured.

One morning during case briefings an investigator on my team told me that the previous night, he had to handle six different complaints where a corporal (two stripes) in a unit asked to borrow VCR players (this was before DVDs), but the borrower never returned them. A seventh guy said the corporal asked to borrow his VCR, but he refused because he thought the corporal was a con man.

That last word stuck in my head. I asked the investigator to describe the borrowing corporal. Sure enough, he fit the description of the swindler we had been looking for. When we went to the corporal's unit looking for him, we were told that he just went AWOL (absent without leave). I obtained a photograph of the corporal from the unit commander and went back to each of the swindled victims with a photographic lineup, which included photographs of the suspect and similar-looking soldiers. Every victim positively identified the corporal as the man who posed as a sergeant and swindled them out of their cash. I subsequently apprehended the swindler. I'll have to admit, though, that he was just as everyone described him: He was charming as could be.

Not only were the victims happy that we caught the subject, but so were the investigators because they didn't have to keep working extra (uncompensated) overtime conducting evening surveillance. And the base commander got off the chief's back. Oh yeah, I also got the VCRs back. The suspect had pawned them.

Murphy's Law

Earlier I mentioned Murphy's Law: "Whatever can go wrong will go wrong." Every veteran law enforcement officer and investigator knows about Murphy's Law from firsthand experience. When working on undercover drug operations, the drug sellers never seem to show up on time. When shooting surveillance video, the camera sometimes stops working. When electronically recording conversations, the record button sometimes malfunctions. When wearing a disguise, your fake mustache might fall into your bowl of soup. (I just made that last one up, but it's probably happened to someone.)

But knowing about Murphy's Law will help you ensure you are not struck by it. Knowing the drug seller probably won't show up on time, bring a snack and a pee bottle. Knowing the video camera might not work, bring a spare battery and/or second camera. Knowing the audio recorder might not work, wear two recording devices. Knowing your fake mustache might fall in the soup, grow a real mustache (guys only, please) or don't sip soup.

Private Investigations

Before getting into the nitty-gritty of preparing an investigative plan, it's worth mentioning that as a private investigator, I often get tasked to perform mini, partial, and limited investigations. One of the reasons for this is because many clients have limited goals and/or don't want to invest much money in the efforts.

For example, I often get calls from attorneys to only conduct one or two interviews. After I conduct the interviews, write up the reports, and electronically copy the audio recordings onto CDs (separate CDs for each recording), I provide copies of everything to my client, provide a verbal overview, and that's usually the end of it (besides submitting my invoice and getting paid).

Very often I get calls to conduct background investigations on individuals. The requests usually are not because employers want to know about a prospective job applicant; instead, clients want me to dig up dirt on someone. This is especially true in child custody and divorce cases. Much of the "dirt" can be found in public records (e.g., arrest, court, or divorce records). Interviewing neighbors and performing surveillance also often results in obtaining useful information.

Asset checks are another frequent request I get as a private eye. Spouses going through divorce often want to know what their spouse (or not-so-better half) owns, where their bank accounts are, and how much money is in those accounts.

Requests for surveillance are by far the most common calls received by private investigators. Usually clients want surveillance performed for short periods of time, ranging between four hours to three days. Some ask for repeated surveillance on weekends. Of course they don't just want surveillance performed; they also want photographs or video taken that shows targets doing something they are not supposed to be doing or with someone they should not be with (or both). In worker's comp cases, investigators attempt to obtain photographs or video depicting "injured" parties doing things outside their home that they said they could not do.

It's always best to perform vehicular surveillance with at least two investigators in two separate cars. But clients often don't want to pay the cost of having two investigators. Also, sometimes targets are well aware that they are likely to be followed, and they take precautions or they try to catch investigators in the act of following them. Getting burned is not only embarrassing; it's hard to explain to clients.

In short, often private investigators are not tasked with conducting thorough and complete full investigations. However, the limited work that is done should still be thorough and complete. Each investigation should start with a well-thought-out plan.

Administrative Responsibilities

Because investigative organizations, businesses, and individual investigators have their own administrative requirements, I'm not going to go into overkill on the admin stuff. However, it is important to remember that many cases you work might go to court and/or you might have to testify about your investigative activity at some point in the future. Also, the case might not go to court for several months or even years. The verdict might get appealed later. Therefore, you should document all of your work very well and, because we live in the digital age, everything should be backed up. Evidence needs to be secured and must have a documented chain of custody.

I have worked many nationwide, complex, long-term investigations that involved voluminous records and documents (paper and electronic), and know how important it is to plan investigations and to stay organized. Managing (or juggling) a caseload is not always easy. (It's like playing several games of chess at the same time, sometimes with idiotic bosses telling you to do the opposite of what you know should be done.)

NOTE: Although I've worked for some superb bosses, during my law enforcement career, I found that some of the greatest obstacles and hindrances that investigators must sometimes overcome when conducting investigations are created not by the suspects but by the investigator's supervisors.

TIP: Just because an investigator is good at administrative functions does *not* make him or her qualified to lead an investigative team. A person who is not an outstanding investigator should not be put in charge; rather, he or she should remain in the field and become proficient at conducting investigations.

Case Files

In each investigation as a PI, I maintain both paper and electronic files. Perhaps because of my background in the days before computers, I'm still very fond of having paper copies of documents. I do use a computer for most of my administrative work. Having PDF copies of documents has numerous advantages, including the ability to electronically store and quickly share information.

Electronic Case Folder

After assigning a unique case number to an investigation, I usually create a corresponding electronic folder (e-folder) to save all related electronic and digital information. Inside that folder, I create additional separate folders so that I can more easily and quickly store and locate case-related information. Because it's all in one e-folder, I can back up the data easily and make it available elsewhere. Listed next is a sample of the contents of an investigative case e-folder.

- Case planning and miscellaneous investigative notes
- Official reports
- Research and data searches (from information brokers, Internet and public record searches)
- Interview prep and questions (separate lists of questions for each interview)
- Charts, tables, and spreadsheets (PowerPoint and Excel)

- Maps and aerial photos
- Audio recordings
- Photos and video recordings
- Correspondence with any attorney(s) and/or my client(s)
- Labels (for CDs and DVDs)
- Case time and billing log
- Invoices

Working File

Usually I keep paper copies of much of the information stored in the e-file. Sometimes information brokers provide me with backgrounds on individuals that might be as many as 100 pages. In those instances I typically print only the first page and a few other pages to remind me that I have the full electronic file saved as a PDF.

My working file also contains conversational and interview notes. As a PI, I also keep an active time and expense list so I can keep track of my time and expenses for each case, which I later bill the client for. Working files also contain my interview plan sheet, which I make pen-and-ink adjustments to as the investigation progresses.

NOTE: Investigators should always be careful to safeguard individuals' protected identifying information. Investigators need to utilize security precautions to prevent the theft of names, Social Security numbers, and/or dates of birth. Several insurance companies and others have gotten into legal binds because they failed to secure such data (which is often stored on laptop computers), and the information was stolen.

Official File

During the investigation, I also maintain an official file, which contains paper copies of my final reports along their attachments, certified copies of documents, evidence receipts, and any other official documents. I do not include any draft reports in the official file. When the investigation I am tasked to perform is completed (and after I've sent my invoice to my client), I typically place my working file (which is in a separate folder) inside my official file. I also place all interview notes in the official file at the conclusion of the investigation. At that time, I also usually copy the entire electronic case file onto a CD and put the CD inside the official file. It gives me peace of mind that barring an extreme natural disaster, I'll always have access to 100 percent of the case-related information.

By consolidating case-related information in this way, I'm confident that 100 percent of my case is in one central place and available. However, I still secure separately any case evidence and maintain a separate evidence log.

Investigative Plan

As I discussed previously, there are many ways to conduct an investigation. Even experienced investigators often disagree on the best approaches, and they typically base their opinions on their own experiences and training. Therefore, keep in mind that any guidance I provide is simply my suggestions based on what has worked for me.

Since you already have written down your thoughts about how to work the case in a draft plan, the next thing to do is to prioritize what needs to be accomplished. For example, if you are working a theft case, you'd want to review the original preliminary report (and related documents) and if possible interview the victim and/or complainant. In short, you want to get as much information as possible from the best sources as possible regarding the matter you will be investigating. Very often victims or complainants may have their own suspicions as to who the suspect(s) may be and why they suspect them. They may even know where evidence or other useful information can be obtained.

If you have identified a suspect, try to find out as much about that subject as covertly as possible. You want to know if they have a criminal history or any warrants out for their arrest. Their public social media profiles might contain a lot of information about them (including photographs). You also want to verify their address, perhaps their employment, and things like that.

If there are a number of people whom you will want to interview, prioritize which ones you'd like to interview before others. Obviously their location can play a role in your decision. If you are in Memphis, Tennessee, for example, and two witnesses are in Memphis and two are in southern Mississippi, it would be wiser to try to interview the two in Mississippi during the same trip to save time. Therefore, you will have to decide if you should conduct the interviews in Mississippi before the interviews in Memphis. However, if one of the witnesses is the former girlfriend or boyfriend of the suspect, you'd probably want to wait to interview that person because of the likelihood that she or he will inform the suspect about the interview. Even if the girlfriend or boyfriend truly despises the suspect, she or he probably would tell others and perhaps even the suspect about the interview.

In short, before conducting interviews, the investigator will have to decide on their strategic importance as well as the possible benefits and/or consequences of their timing.

The benefit of telephone interviews is that they save time. Telephonic interviews sometimes can be completed in rapid succession, and they also can also be cost effective. As a PI, I usually ask my clients if they want me to conduct in-person interviews or telephone interviews. I also ask if they want recorded interviews, handwritten statements, and/or written summaries. All of this information has a bearing on how I proceed with the case and how much they will have to pay.

Another thing to consider is whether you will be arranging for (scheduling) interviews or just showing up at people's doors. By just showing up, you can waste considerable time if they are not home. But sometimes, *not* notifying interviewees is the better strategy.

NOTE: Make sure you know and follow the laws covering the electronic recording of all conversations. In some states, only one party to the conversation needs to consent to be recorded. That's called a one-party state. Some states require both (or all) parties to provide their consent before being recorded. That's called a two-party state. Anyone conducting telephone recordings without consent of both (all) parties (if one is physically located in a two-party state) could face charges of illegal wiretapping. (That occurred is in the well-publicized investigation of President Bill Clinton when Linda Tripp secretly recorded telephone conversations with Monica Lewinsky.)

I already discussed the use of investigative tools, resources, and techniques. Investigators should consider all of those and others and incorporate the most appropriate ones into their investigative plans. Very often it's wise to conduct an interview (or a few interviews) before using some tools, resources, and techniques. Nothing says that you have to conduct all interviews first and then use tools or the other way around. You can (and probably should) utilize some simultaneously or in rapid succession.

Some investigations (especially preliminary ones) are conducted by first and second responders when there is no time to sit down and create an investigative plan. Very often those investigations are conducted almost in a reactionary mode and based on the investigators' experience and available resources.

Veteran and/or well-trained investigators initiate some investigative activity almost on instinct. In many such cases, investigators are following response activities from training manuals. For example: In a bank robbery, school shooting, or terrorism investigation, you first do "A," followed by "B," followed by "C," and so on. Bystanders at a bomb scene or large fire might be interviewed quickly with no preparation and with no intentions of attempting to complete detailed interviews at that time, but with the knowledge that follow-up interviews are likely.

It's understood that sometimes you have to do what you have to do. Sometimes you need to quickly improvise when initiating an investigation under extreme conditions. Very often, when conducting reactionary investigations, investigators are mentally planning their moves. But at some point, they should be able to slow down the process to assess and evaluate actions already taken or implemented and to consider future investigative activity in more detail. At that point, it is wise to create a written investigative plan utilizing some or all of the information just provided.

Summary

Regardless of the type of investigation being undertaken, whenever possible, investigators should do these things before and during an investigation:

- Plan
- Strategize
- Evaluate
- Implement
- Reassess, reevaluate, and update the plan

One thing to be sure to schedule time for is to professionally document your investigative activity. It can take two hours to document and proofread a 30-minute interview. An audio-recorded interview or videotaped surveillance will have to be downloaded and copied onto CDs or DVDs and/or saved to an e-file. You may have to make copies of any CDs or DVDs for the client, the case file, and perhaps a first copy as evidence. If one copy is considered to be evidence, you'll also have to log in the evidence and secure it. The entire investigative process usually takes a lot longer than many people think. Sometimes the original removable memory card (if applicable) will have to be logged and secured as evidence.

Clients of a PI sometimes hear a 30-minute recorded interview and wonder why they get billed for four or more hours. As I've mentioned, well-planned interviews take time to prepare for. There is drive time (to and from), report writing time, download and copying time, filing time, and delivery time back to the client (and that's assuming Murphy's Law didn't come into play). However, the end result is a quality work product that can be used indefinitely and withstand any attempts to refute the work.

Juggling a Caseload and Time Management

Being responsible for conducting several different individual and unrelated investigations at the same time can be very challenging. Once again, the ability to prioritize is important, as is the ability to manage time. Whenever possible, I try to work only one case at a time. During a four-hour or even an eight-hour stretch, I like to work one case only. When conducting general investigations, sometimes I devote a couple of days at a time to one case (give or take other incoming assignments by my supervisor or others). If I work a first degree murder type case for a criminal defense attorney, I try to set everything else to the side and concentrate just on that case whenever possible. When conducting major fraud investigations, sometimes I focus on one case for weeks or months. I find that I can get more done more quickly and get better results when I focus all or most of my attention to one case—even if it's just for a day.

But you don't want to lose track of all the other investigative work that needs to be completed on other cases. That's where case planning sheets really come in handy. By creating a well-thought-out investigative plan on each case, you can be away from cases for extended periods of time and still know exactly what's been done already and what you need to do next when you return.

Time Management

Typically, I have two lists that I update almost daily, usually at the end of each workday. The first is the short-term list (which includes a daily and a weekly list). The second is the long-term list.

The daily list has at least the top three priorities numbered because I must get them completed next. Actually my daily list usually has about 10 to 15 items on it. I write the weekly list on the same sheet of paper as my daily list, or an attached sheet, so I can easily see what needs to be done in the near future and can add to that list as the day progresses. By the way, my weekly list includes all seven days of the week, not just the five typical business days.

My long-term list includes possible projects or other things that I am considering or things that I must do much later. Examples of long-term things I might want to accomplish or set aside time for might include: attending training conferences, conducting liaison, going to the shooting range, renewing a license, paying dues, or upcoming court dates.

The third item of necessity for me is an at-a-glance calendar where I can see all of the days of any particular month on two fold-out pages. I write deadlines and commitments in the calendar as soon as I know about them. In my opinion, there is no excuse for missing a deadline. You can't be late or forget about anything if you are managing, monitoring, and planning your days and future on a daily basis.

The last thing I keep and regularly review is a case index that lists all of my open cases.

In summary, if you have a case planning sheet for every one of your cases, an open case index sheet, a short-term list, a long-term list, and a calendar, you've got everything covered. By reviewing them at the end of every workday (or no later than first thing when you start your shift), you'll get more completed in a week than some people get completed in a month—with better results!

NOTE: I have one saying that often rubs people the wrong way. That saying is "If you got everything completed that's listed on your daily list, then you did not have enough on your daily list." The reason I say that is because I believe you should try to get the most out of every single day. Therefore, you should plan to get the almost impossible done every single day. Since you know you are going to revise your list at the end of the day (or first thing when you start your shift), whatever you did not get done at the end of the day should get listed at the top (or close to the top) for the next day.

I'm sure that by now you're wondering what I do when someone throws a monkey wrench into my planning. When that happens, I have to decide how to fit the new in with everything else that needs to be accomplished. Sometimes I can't do everything, so I have to decide which is more important. Because I have my lists, I can postpone things and later pick up where I left off.

For the record, stuff happens all the time where I have to adjust my schedule. But the point of my sharing this information is to help you maximize your time where possible.

NOTE: Another quirk about me is that I very seldom go out to lunch. I brown-bag my lunch whenever possible. It takes me about five minutes to eat lunch, then I'm back to work. Ordinarily I add the time I didn't waste going to lunch to my workout time. Since I usually allow for one hour of exercise on most days, by not taking a lunch break, I get an extra 30 minutes to warm up and shower. Sometimes I exercise in the middle of the day and sometimes at the end of the day.

Occasionally potential clients ask to meet me for lunch. I usually tell them that I'd prefer to have an office business meeting. In my mind, dining and work don't mix. I don't golf either so you can imagine my thoughts when people ask to meet them on a golf course.

War Story 9.7

When working undercover as an investigator in the Army, I once had to chase a suspect who was three times as fast as me, and he had a big head start. Rather than initiating the chase on foot, my partner and I drove our small unmarked police car as fast as it would go. But then the suspect ran onto a golf course. He was still so far ahead of us that we continued our pursuit right onto the golf course. Eventually we did capture our suspect, but when we looked back, we saw deep muddy vehicle tire tracks all across the previously well-manicured lawn, especially a putting green. My partner and I just laughed about it, but I suspect the next round of golfers failed to make par.

War Story 9.8

As a federal agent, I was authorized to perform on-duty physical fitness exercise three or four hours each week (one hour a day, three or four days a week). Before you start think that exercising isn't job related, I should mention that federal agents are also required to participate in semiannual physical fitness tests, which are scored. Because I didn't take lunch breaks, I frequently combined my 30-minute lunchtime with my exercise time, which gave me a full hour to work out and 30 minutes to stretch, shower, and get dressed.

One day I came back to my office after exercising, and my boss told me that I was not permitted to combine my workout time with my lunchtime. He said I had to separate the two. According to the supervisor's instructions, I could eat lunch for 30 minutes and then work out or I could work out, return to the office, and then go to lunch. (What a joy he was to work for . . .)

War Story 9.9

When I was a federal agent, one supervisor required agents to provide verbal case briefings every 90 days. I had no qualms with that because supervisors should be on top of things. But as each case was briefed, we'd have to give a description of what we planned to do to complete each case. When you have about a dozen cases to brief, that's a lot to discuss.

At the end of that 90-day period, the supervisor would then read what the agent said had to be done on each case and ask why all of the work had not been done. Even if the agent successfully completed two of the cases resulting in millions of dollars in recoveries and additional criminal convictions, he still wanted to know why the work on the other cases wasn't completed.

That supervisor had no idea how to juggle a caseload. Comparing his strategy to a football game, it was as if his goal was to make first downs and not touchdowns. With that particular supervisor, no matter what we did, it was never good enough. He seldom if ever made any positive comments when we did catch bad guys.

In fact, during my employee performance reviews, the supervisor gave me pretty good job evaluation scores, but, over time, I concluded that he could not say the words "good" and "work" together in the same sentence. Instead he would say, "Keep up the work." The first time I heard him say that, I thought maybe he just forgot to say the word "good." But it was actually a pattern over a couple years.

As you will remember from Chapter 8 on interviewing, the repeated omission of a word is sometimes very telling.

So to all of you investigators and fraud fighters who have been working hard and giving the job your best, let me say loud and clear, "Keep up the good work!"

Chapter 10 provides guidance on conducting large-scale investigations.

Chapter 10

Large-Scale
Investigations

*"You don't know how much weight is enough until you know how much
weight is too much."*

—Weight-lifting coach

Experience gained conducting major fraud investigations combined with my previously developed expanded-effort investigative techniques helped prepare me to conduct large-scale investigations. By large scale, I mean planning and conducting between approximately 50 to a couple thousand interviews on one case where the persons to be interviewed might be located across the United States or perhaps some across the globe. In one jointly worked taskforce investigation that I was part of, approximately 3,000 interviews were conducted! Just being a member of a taskforce that conducted such a large investigation helped prepare me to later lead, plan, and conduct similar investigations in the future. The guidance provided in this chapter can be applied to any investigation in which multiple interviews need to be conducted or travel to different geographical areas is required.

The first large-scale investigation I was part of consisted of a task-force comprised of about 30 federal agents who mostly stayed on the road investigating one case for about a year. The case involved numerous sexually assaults committed by U.S. and other military officers. In that case I was involved from beginning to end but I was not the lead agent; in fact, I was a pretty much a rookie federal agent.

NOTE: Several military officers were identified for criminal prosecution consideration. However, none of them were criminally prosecuted. The decisions about whether to prosecute were completely out of the control of the investigators. I do have an opinion about the matter, which I'll keep to myself (at least in this writing). Almost surprisingly, the investigative agency's final report is actually available on-line for purchase by several bookstores and other outlets.

The next large-scale investigation I participated in involved the September 11, 2001, terrorist attacks on American soil. Many federal, state, and local law enforcements officers around the country pooled their resources and teamed up to conduct one of the most serious (and successful) criminal investigations in U.S. history. I was just one of many law enforcement officers contributing to the investigative effort.

My most recent large-scale investigation involved millions of dollars, numerous suspects and witnesses, allegations of major fraud, and conflicts of interest involving senior U.S. military officials. The investigation lasted approximately 18 months. Because of my prior experience, I was 100 percent confident I could successfully conduct and lead the investigation.

In that case, I was the lead federal agent and worked an average of 70 hours per week almost exclusively on that case. Sometimes I worked for 18 hours straight for several days in a row. I personally reviewed approximately 40,000 e-mails along with numerous boxes of paper records, contracts, and other electronic data and information. Although I flew across the country conducting interviews, other federal agents across the United States also conducted additional interviews on the case. In those instances, I personally drafted the questions for every interview.

The case was considered a top priority by my agency, and the national news media followed it closely. I often received telephone calls from reporters asking for updates. In keeping with my agency's policy, I never gave the reporters anything they could hang their hat on while the investigation was ongoing.

NOTE: Once again, several military officers were identified for criminal prosecution consideration. However, none of them were criminally prosecuted. I also have an opinion about this matter, which I'll also keep to myself (at least in this writing). Now that the case is closed, much of the information has been made publicly available and the final (partially redacted) investigative report can be reviewed at no cost on the Internet.

You'll recall that I prefer to concentrate fully on only one investigation for short (or extended) periods of time whenever possible. When conducting a large-scale investigation, focusing solely on that one case is extremely important. At a minimum, the lead agent/investigator must fully commit to the investigation; otherwise it likely will fall apart. In larger investigations, a full-time task force (comprised of nonrotating members) should be considered to assist in the investigation if at all possible.

Very often it's the collection and recollection of small details that make a difference as to whether the investigation will be completed thoroughly and successfully. The responsible investigator(s) must be able to dissect, scrutinize, and retain all facts and information and find inconsistencies, consistencies, and patterns while also drawing logical conclusions. The investigative plan also must be updated regularly.

NOTE: If the investigation is high profile, the lead investigator can expect several rounds of "Brief-o-rama." That's a term a coworker shared with me when she had to constantly brief her supervisors on a high-profile case she worked. If briefings are mandatory, the lead investigator should try to limit and control those briefings (perhaps scheduling them for every Monday morning).

In my last large-scale investigation, supervisors kept asking questions like "How many interviews have been conducted?" and "How many of them were military generals?"

NOTE: An American combat veteran told me that during the Vietnam War, they called similar inquiries, "body counts". Some leaders would determine if they were winning the war by the number of fatalities caused.

In large paramilitary organizations, there are a lot of "supervisors." Sometimes my superiors asked me for the names of the people I was going to interview in advance, and they wanted to know what questions I was going to ask during the interviews. When I inquired why they needed that information, I was told that senior leaders in our agency wanted to know.

It was and is my opinion that the people (who were not in my chain of command) who were asking for that information did not have a need to know so I tried to throw them off track whenever possible. One time I refused to tell my superiors whom I planned to interview out of concern that my superiors would leak the information. (I later found evidence indicating that I had a right to be concerned.)

I did offer to provide those superiors with the names of individuals who had already been interviewed, but they said that was not good enough. (Think about that: Since my supervisors could read my reports of interviews after the interviews were completed, what possible reason would they have for wanting to know in advance who was going to be interviewed and what questions would be asked?)

TIP: In large-scale high profile investigations, expect to have many distractions from your chain-of-command. Even well-meaning supervisors can cause considerable amounts of unnecessary stress on the lead investigator(s) and cause valuable time to be wasted.

Large-scale investigations must be extremely well planned and coordinated and kept very well organized. The ability to manage time and resources (including travel costs) is also critical. If several others are assisting in the investigation, then the ability to communicate with one another and share information on a timely basis is also important.

When leading these types of investigations, there is no substitute for experience. In professional sports, commentators often remark on the number of members on each team who have (or don't have) playoff experience. We all know the game itself is exactly the same. But when you're playing for something big and pressure filled, experience matters. The same is true of conducting large-scale investigations. Such investigations are not easy, but participating in one is a great experience. Upon completion, all other cases seem very small.

War Story 10.1

While preparing this chapter, I recalled younger days when assigned KP (kitchen police) duties while in the U.S. Army. In the kitchen located in the back of the dining facility (also called mess hall or chow hall), I got to watch the cooks firsthand make meals on a large scale. Potatoes were peeled by the sacksful just to prepare for one meal (I know because I peeled bags full of them). Spaghetti noodles were cooked in pots as big as small economy cars. Spices weren't measured by spoons but by the cups or even boxes. Everything used in the Army kitchen is just like what is used in anyone else's kitchen but the scale seems to be a zillion times larger. Cleanup is also a zillion times worse because all those pots, pans, utensils, plates, bowls, glasses, coffee cups, and trays all have to be cleaned before the next meal. (Yes, I know firsthand about that too.) Conducting large-scale investigations is kind of like preparing those mess hall meals; until you've been part of the process, you don't really have a full appreciation for what it takes to get the job done.

NOTE: I've known some federal agents who participated in long-term undercover operations including fake storefronts and legally listening to other people's telephone calls at all hours of the day and night as well as conducting long term surveillance. Every one of the agents said it was a great experience but added they never wanted to do it again. Extreme large-scale investigations might fall into that same category, but conducting one every five to seven years only would be more palatable.

Communication

As briefly mentioned, if others are working jointly with or assisting in the investigation, it is imperative that they all be able to communicate with each other, especially with the lead investigator. Today, just about everyone has a cell phone and/or a smartphone and an e-mail address.

A list of all telephone numbers and e-mail addresses of all participating investigators (and supervisors) should be created and circulated to each full-time member. Contact information for the support staff and other professionals on the team should also be shared with all members.

If investigators are sent leads to complete assignments on a single or infrequent basis, the assigned investigators should be able to reach a knowledgeable participant on the investigative team in the event they have any questions. Make sure your instructions for others are crystal clear as to what you want them to do. If you want them to conduct extremely detailed interviews, provide them with sufficient background information. I also suggest you include all the questions you want asked if at all possible.

During the most recent large-scale investigation I led, a few investigators elected to not ask all of the questions they were tasked with and/or they provided insufficient details in their written summary reports. In those instances, I sent the investigators back to conduct follow-up interviews and/or told them to rewrite their reports.

TIP: Some investigators avoid assisting others or do poorer-quality work when tasked to assist others. Do not accept inferior work from them; make them do it over until they get it right. If they are full-time task force members and fail to commit to the cause, kick them off the team.

The team's information technology personnel should ensure that case-related information (especially completed reports) can be quickly and safely imported, saved, stored, shared, and available to all members of the team on demand. It goes without saying that all case-related information must be secured from unauthorized access or intrusions and shared only with personnel who have a need to know. All parties involved should abide by their internal policies concerning any case-related documentation, storage, correspondence, and communication.

TIP: If you have no control over the selection of places to work and/or to conduct the majority of your work, consider having the area(s) swept for electronic bugs, cameras, and/or eavesdropping devices. Even if professionals cannot conduct the search for such devices, at least do a careful visual inspection for such items.

Planning

The only thing that's really different about conducting a large-scale investigation as compared to any other investigation is its sheer volume, the logistics, and expense. All of the same investigative planning skills and other considerations described in the previous chapters also apply to conducting larger investigations. In a large-scale investigation, there should be one final decision maker. The ability to delegate is important but in the end, the lead investigator should make the final key investigative decisions. (Obviously the assisting investigators in the field need to be permitted to use their usual discretion when completing their assignments; the lead investigator does not need to be a complete micromanager.)

TIP: It's often good to have a secondary lead investigator assigned to the case in the event that the primary lead investigator is unable to be present for critical events. Just make sure that the primary and secondary investigator have no qualms about working together in such roles.

Interview Log

When planning and conducting interviews of numerous individuals, I find Microsoft Excel to be a great tool. Some of the suggested fields (columns) to use when creating your interview log are discussed next. You can add additional fields as you desire. Using different color font and cell colors will allow for important information to stand out visually. If you use different colors on the log sheet (at least the master log), the log can serve as a useful at-a-glance reference. (See Exhibit 10.1 for a sample interview log.)

Keep in mind that as the investigation proceeds, you probably will sort the fields to more easily identify or obtain information. For example, later you might want to know all interviews that will take place in certain states so that you can maximize the use of investigative time and minimize travel expenses. Therefore, make sure the entries are entered uniformly. For example, don't enter "VA" for Virginia once and then later enter "Virg" because it will complicate things when sorting.

CASE ASSIGNED TO: Investigator Charles Piper - Memphis, TN   **Last Updated: 7/1/2013**

INTERVIEW ORDER	NAME OF INTERVIEWER	INTERVIEWER'S OFFICE	LAST NAME	FIRST NAME	STATUS	POSITION	State or Country	City	Interview Folder Created	Background Info Obtained	Questions Drafted	Lead Sent	INTERVIEW Completed	Interview Report Completed	Remarks
	2 PIPER	Memphis, TN	Patterson	Ken	Witness	Contracting Officer (Awarded Contract)	TN	Memphis	Yes	Yes	Yes		6/1/2013	6/3/2013	Thinks something's wrong
DONE	Son	Japan	Young	Wendy	OTHER	Losing bidder	Japan	Tokyo	Yes	Yes	Yes		6/3/2013	6/7/2013	Believes there were bribes
DONE	Von Clark	Germany	Kruder	Carl	OTHER	Losing bidder	Germany	Mannheim	Yes	Yes	Yes				
DONE	1 B. Franklin	Richmond, VA	Sorsby	Jerry	OTHER	Losing bidder	VA	Richmond	Yes	Yes	Yes				
DONE	PIPER	Memphis, TN	Whistle	Wendy	COMPLAINANT	Bid Evaluator	AL	Huntsville	Yes	Yes	Yes		5/27/2013	5/28/2013	Was actual LOW BIDDER
	PIPER	Memphis, TN	Collins	Joseph	Suspect	Bid Evaluator	TN	Memphis	Yes	Yes	Yes				
	PIPER	Memphis, TN	Brownoser	Bill	Suspect	Bid Evaluator	TN	Memphis	Yes	Yes	Yes				
	PIPER	Memphis, TN	King	Brenda	Suspect	Bid Evaluator	TN	Memphis	Yes	Some					
	PIPER	Memphis, TN	Laziest	Lucy	Suspect	Bid Evaluator	TN	Memphis	Yes						Friend w/ Winning Bidder
Last	PIPER	Memphis, TN	Mean	Michael	Suspect #1	Advisor	TN	Memphis							
	PIPER	Memphis, TN	Morrison	Melvin	Suspect	Advisor	TN	Memphis							
2nd to Last	PIPER	Memphis, TN	Goalong	Gus	Suspect #2	Source Selection Officer	TN	Memphis		Some					
	PIPER	Memphis, TN	Patera	Priscilla	Witness	Former Employee	TN	Memphis							
	PIPER	Memphis, TN	Ditmer	Danny	Witness	Former Employee	TN	Memphis							
	PIPER	Memphis, TN	Winfield	Raymond	Witness	Former Employee	TN	Memphis							
	PIPER	Memphis, TN	Stern	Eugene	Witness	Former Employee	TN	Memphis							
	PIPER	Memphis, TN	Loveday	Mickey	Witness	Former Employee	MS	Jackson							
	PIPER	Memphis, TN	Hartnett	Jerry	Witness	Former Employee	AR	Little Rock							
	PIPER	Memphis, TN	Bansley	Alissa	Witness	Former Employee	TN	Nashville							
	PIPER	Memphis, TN	Fey	Doug	Witness	Former Employee	TN	Germantown							
LA 1	Magnum	Los Angeles, CA	Melton	George	Other	Contractor	CA	Long Beach	Yes	Yes	Yes	6/5/2013			Bid on Project Before
LA 2	Magnum	Los Angeles, CA	McCarthy	Melvin	Other	Contractor	CA	Los Angeles	Yes	Yes	Yes	6/5/2013			Bid on Project Before
LA 3	Magnum	Los Angeles, CA	Jones	Vance	Other	Contractor	CA	San Diego	Yes	Yes	Yes	6/5/2013			Bid on Project Before
NY1	Jeter	New York, NY	Magic	Dave	Other	Contractor	NY	New York	Yes	Yes	Yes	6/12/2013			Bid on Project Before
NY2	Jeter	New York, NY	Drews	Bertha	Other	Contractor	NY	Brooklyn	Yes	Yes	Yes	6/12/2013			Bid on Project Before
Balt 1	Robinson	Baltimore, MD	Sobscy	Cathy	Other	Contractor	MD	Baltimore	Yes	Yes	Yes	6/14/2013			Bid on Project Before
Balt 2	Robinson	Baltimore, MD	Gage	Jerry	Other	Contractor	MD	Aberdeen	Yes	Yes	Yes	6/14/2013			Bid on Project Before
	Piper		Gill	Terry	Possible Witness	Contracting Officer	TN	Memphis							Works at Contract Office
	Piper		Macy	Adam	Possible Witness	Contracting Officer	TN	Memphis							Works at Contract Office
	Piper		Payton	Diane	Possible Witness	Contracting Officer	TN	Memphis							Works at Contract Office
	Piper		Rose	Paul	Possible Witness	Contracting Officer	TN	Memphis							Works at Contract Office
	Piper		Sayers	Dick	Possible Witness	Contracting Officer	TN	Memphis							Works at Contract Office
	Piper		Carey	Chris	Possible Witness	Contracting Officer	TN	Memphis							Works at Contract Office
	Piper		Brickhouse	Elizabeth	Possible Witness	Contracting Officer	TN	Memphis							Works at Contract Office
	Piper		Santo	Edward	Possible Witness	Contracting Officer	TN	Memphis							Works at Contract Office

SAMPLE ONLY

Fictitious Illustration Intended for Demonstration Purposes Only

Prepared by Charles E. Piper, CFE, CRT

Exhibit 10.1   Large-Scale Investigation Interview Log Sheet Example for Possible Corrupt Procurement Case

Interview Log Fields

These fields, sometimes called column headings, begin on the left side of the spreadsheet.

Order

This field contains the projected planned numeric order of conducting the interviews. The numbers are subject to change. In large-scale investigations, I usually number only the first few because I know the order will change and additional interviews probably will be added later. After each interview is completed, write the word "COMPLETED" (or "DONE") and color code the cell yellow (or some other color of your choice).

Interviewer

In this field list the name(s) (if known) and/or office(s) of the interviewer who is assigned (or will be assigned) to conduct each interview. After the interview is completed, ensure that the actual interviewer's name is written in this block. If the investigator is located in a different geographical office, include that location in a field.

NOTE: Sometimes more than one person conducts the interview, and usually only one person writes the summary report. If there were two interviewers you'll have to decide if you want to create a subfield to include both names. Also, sometimes the same person is interviewed more than once on different dates and sometimes by different investigators. When that happens, you'll need to create some subentries.

Name

This field contains the name of the person to be interviewed. The last name goes first.

Status

In this field list the person to be interviewed (or already interviewed) as a complainant, victim, witness, suspect, subject, or other. Suspects and subjects are obviously very important, and the lead investigator might consider personally conducting those interviews. Subjects are people who will or will most probably be charged with a violation(s). Suspects have not quite made it to that level. You might want to color code the cells for subjects as red and suspects as pink or something like that.

Rank
If applicable, in this field include the person's rank if the interviewee is a military, police, or government employee.

Position
This field includes the person's job or position. Example: CEO, janitor, contractor, company commander, and so on.

Assignment
If military, in this field list the unit the person is assigned to. If a large organization, include the person's section or division. Keep in mind that one of the purposes of the log is to make conducting future interviews easier. The more helpful information you can list, the more time you can save.

Country
If the persons to be interviewed are located in different countries, you'll need to create a separate field for this. If possible, use standard abbreviations rather than spelling out because the field's width will be smaller and you'll be less likely to make spelling errors.

NOTE: The fields might be sorted later so you'll want to keep entries consistent.

State
If the country calls its states different things (e.g., provinces), you'll have to make the adjustment. In the United States, just use the standard two-letter state abbreviation. Remember, you might sort this data later.

Interview Folder Created
There should be a separate interview folder (I prefer both hard-copy and electronic) for each person to be interviewed. After the interview folder is created, enter "YES" in the cell.

NOTE: There is no reason to enter "NO"; just leave the cell blank/empty if the folder is not created yet. This is true with all of the following fields.

NOTE: The investigator(s) who conduct the interviews will use the interview folders later. When the interviews are completed, the interviewer(s) can place their notes (in envelopes) in the appropriate hard-copy folders along with copies of the final summary interview reports. If the interviews were electronically recorded, consider having copies made onto CDs, marked, and placed in the interview folders.

Background Obtained

If background information has been obtained about the person to be interviewed and it has been placed in the interview folder, enter "OBTAINED" (or "YES"). You could enter "SOME" if you have not completed obtaining the background information you want. Background information might include verification of address, phone number, employment, criminal history, photograph, social media, and/or Internet search. Color coding this field may prove beneficial, especially if you delegated responsibility for obtaining background information.

Questions Drafted

If the interview questions have been drafted, enter "COMPLETED" (or "YES").

NOTE: The interview questions and other interview-related documents should be printed and placed in the person's interview folder.

Map Obtained

If a map and/or directions have been printed or obtained and placed in the interview folder, enter "YES." The map is used to help the interviewer find the location and/or to plan out their trip(s) if several interviews are to be conducted during the same time frame.

Interviewed

Enter the date the interview was completed.

Report

Enter the date the interview report was approved or finalized.

NOTE: If no date is entered, that should/could mean that you do not yet have the report. Sometimes assisting agents or investigators are good about getting the interviews done but terrible about completing the reports in a timely fashion.

NOTE: You can opt to hyperlink each report to the applicable cell. Doing so would take a little more administrative time but could save valuable time later. Place a hard copy of the report inside the individual's interview folder and the original in the official file.

Remark #1
If there is something worth noting about the person interviewed (or to be interviewed), make a note about it in one of the remarks fields. Use a different-color font to make the information stand out. I use the red as a danger/warning/alert color. Examples may include "Needs to Be Reinterviewed" or "Violent History."

Remark #2
Same as Remark #1. Other examples might be: "Roommate of Suspect John Smith," "In Hospital," "Out of Country until June 16," "See John Smith's Report of Interview before Interviewing," or "Interview Scheduled for December 22."

Remark #3
Same as Remark #1. Other examples might be postinterview notes: "Confessed," "Provided Evidence," or "Denied but have proof."

The lead investigator can add additional fields as appropriate, including addresses and telephone numbers.

Re: Strategy

When conducting large-scale investigations, it's usually best to delay conducting most interviews until you've created and completed the interview folders for at least most of the first several interviews you intend to conduct. You can complete the other interview folders as the investigation progresses. Sometimes you can delegate to less experienced investigators or support staff the obtaining of some of the information needed (maps, background information, etc.). As you can tell from the text, the pre-interview work is like an assembly-line process.

As the investigation progresses, often you will think of additional questions for people who have not yet been interviewed based on information received from others interviewed or from e-mails reviewed, and so on. In fact, if you identify a key e-mail or other document that could come in handy during an interview, photocopy it and put it in the interview folder. Sometimes, as new information is received, you'll decide that some people need to be interviewed again. If you make sure to keep the interview log updated, it will also serve as a guide through the completion of the investigation.

If conducting interviews in person and by telephone, you should create additional fields reflecting the method conducted. Telephone interviews can be completed much more quickly and at less cost than in-person interviews. However, there are some disadvantages to conducting telephone interviews. You may elect to conduct telephone interviews first with an option to interview those same individuals in person if they possess or are likely to possess useful information.

If there are language barriers to consider, you might need to create separate fields for that too. For example, if many of the persons to be interviewed speak Spanish only, that fact would be good to know in advance so you can assign a Spanish-speaking interviewer to those leads (or have an interpreter available).

Because the information in the fields can be sorted, you can easily maximize your time, money, and resources by conducting all or most interviews in certain geographical areas during the same trips. That's another reason why on large-scale investigations, it's usually better not to start conducting many interviews until after you have fully grasped and identified who needs to be interviewed and where they are located. Trust me, your boss will go through the roof if you fly from Los Angeles to Washington, DC, and return and then tell your boss a few days later you have to fly back to DC to conduct another interview that could have been completed earlier.

If you don't plan well, the investigation can drag on two to three times longer than necessary and can cost two to three times more than it should. Also, by planning the order of interviews, you are (I hope) strategizing about the benefits and possible consequences of conducting some interviews before others and some after others. Remember: The objective is to complete the investigation successfully, not just save time and travel funds.

At some point during this type of investigation, some interviews will have to take place in a certain order regardless of where the people are located or the costs that might be incurred. That might mean traveling back and forth to the same or different locations even though doing so is expensive and time consuming. As long as you've been cost conscious earlier in the investigation, most supervisors/clients won't get too upset when you later make strategic (more expensive) and more time-consuming decisions.

For example: Let's say your investigative home office is in Memphis, Tennessee, and you've already completed 65 interviews but now it's time to confront the suspects. Let's say the suspect chief executive officer (CEO) Edward is located in Falls Church, Virginia, and the co-suspect is chief financial officer (CFO) Frank located in Chicago, Illinois. You decided to interview CEO Edward and then fly to Chicago to interview CFO Frank. But after interviewing CFO Frank, you realize you need to reinterview shift supervisor Susan in Savannah, Georgia. After doing so, you fly back to Chicago and reinterview CFO Frank, then return to your office in Memphis to digest everything and write up your reports. Then you fly back to Falls Church to reinterview CEO Edward.

Under this scenario, this may be the only way to conduct the investigation properly. As long as this type of travel is the exception and not the norm, you can justify this amount of travel (and expense). In short, the lead investigator always needs to keep in mind the most economical, practical yet still productive ways to accomplish the objectives in the timeliest manner.

Some might suggest that any trained investigator could conduct any interview, but in complex cases, key interviews should be conducted by the investigator(s) with the most case knowledge who is best prepared to conduct those interviews. The bottom line is, some interviews can be assigned to others and some should be conducted by the lead investigator(s).

CAUTION: Private investigators and others must ensure they are authorized/allowed to conduct interviews outside of their own licensed or approved areas. In some cases, interviews outside the area where the private investigator is licensed might have to be assigned to others to comply with rules, laws, and regulations.

Final Summary Report

From the time the investigation is initiated, the lead investigator should be thinking about the possible content and format that will be used for the final report. To that end, the lead investigator should implement measures so that all information that will (or might) go into the final report is readily available. Requiring that all of the reports prepared during the investigation are saved and stored in digital format (perhaps a PDF) in a central system/location will pay huge dividends when completing the final summary report. Mandate this before the first investigative report is even written.

TIP: Before you start typing your final summary investigative report, it is imperative that you start by creating an outline.

TIP: Information contained in previously written (and approved) case-related reports can be copied and pasted into the final report. This can save an incredible amount of time when drafting the final report.

Attachments and Exhibits

Very often, investigators include attachments and/or exhibits to their final reports. They may include actual copies of other investigative reports, copies of photographs, illustrative graphics, or visual aids and perhaps even copies of CDs or DVDs. As each attachment or exhibit is referenced in the narrative of the final report, it should be numerically listed (e.g., See Attachment 1; See Attachment 2; See Attachment 3, etc.)

At the end of the final summary report, a descriptive listing of each attachment and exhibit should be included. An example follows.

ATTACHMENTS:

(1) Report of Interview of John Smith, January 26, 2013
(2) Report of Interview of Martin Jones, January 27, 2013
(3) Photograph of Mary Smith
(4) Chicago Police Report, Incident # 1234567, March 12, 2011

EXHIBITS:

(A) CD, Audio Interview of John Smith, January 26, 2013

(B) DVD, Video of Surveillance on Mary Smith, January 28, 2013.

In summary, authoring the final summary report can be a herculean task in itself. But if you prepare to write it from Day 1, it will not be as difficult. There's nothing that says the report has to be completely written by one person. Depending on the magnitude of the case, some sections can be written by other knowledgeable investigators and combined to make one final work product. Of course, one person has to make the final decision as to the format on how the report will be written. The lead investigator should review the final report for accuracy and completeness.

War Story 10.2

In the first large-scale investigation I worked, the format used to prepare the final report was completely different from our usual template-like investigative reports, which were intended for smaller cases. Instead, a format was used that allowed readers to more easily comprehend the case facts obtained during the investigation. Photographs were included right between narrative paragraphs (just like in a book). A fold-out graphic illustration was also included in the report.

However, in the last large-scale investigation I worked, my supervisors would not allow me to deviate from the standard template format, which made it very difficult for the readers to comprehend all the facts. Because of the complexity of the investigation, the standard report format was inadequate. Although I had prepared a timeline, link charts, and graphs to help illustrate the complex case facts, I could not incorporate them in the report format I was forced to use.

TIP: Although format uniformity is important for investigative reports, investigators on large-scale investigations sometimes need more latitude when completing the final summary reports so they can best communicate and illustrate the case facts.

Postdraft Report

Obviously the final report must also be proofread for grammar, punctuation, and spelling. The report must also be fact checked and checked to ensure that everything is included that is supposed to be included. Having several different people assist in these tasks certainly helps, if that's possible.

TIP: When conducting investigations that involve previous years, be careful when typing and reviewing to ensure you typed correct years. Fingers seem to want to automatically type the current year no matter what.

Report Distribution

It's good idea to write and maintain a distribution list for the final report. If you include the list in the final report (on the first page or last page), all those who received copies will know who else received copies. You'll also be certain that those who should receive a copy of the final report receive one. (Just make sure you do provide them all with copies.)

TIP: Make an electronic backup and printed copy for the case file. After all that hard work, you don't want to lose everything.

Investigative Notes and Evidence

Also from the day the investigation is initiated, the lead investigator should make arrangements to ensure that all original case notes (especially interview notes) are sent to his or her office for inclusion in the working file or wherever your investigative policy dictates. If the case later goes to court, it will be good to know that everything is in one central location.

The same is true of evidence. By the time the investigation is concluded, the lead investigator must be assured that all evidence is documented, secured, and accounted for.

In summary, when planning and conducting a large-scale investigation, you will want to incorporate, or at least consider, everything discussed in this and the previous chapters as well as things you've learned from your own experiences and training. By thinking about the case's conclusion when you initiate the investigation, you will ensure that you complete a great-quality investigation and produce a great final work product.

TIP: During large-scale investigations it's important that all of the team members try to eat well and make time to exercise regularly. Working long hours for extended periods can take a toll on even the most dedicated individuals.

Chapter 11 details ways to best present your case to others.

Chapter 11

Making Presentations

"First impressions are not just lasting impressions; first impressions are the only impressions."

—Trial attorney

The only thing worse than trying to explain the results of a complex fraud investigation verbally is having to listen to someone else trying to explain the results of a complex fraud investigation.

Listeners often experience droopy eyelids, unsuccessful attempts to hold back yawns, or sudden urges to respond to every text message they ever received. All of these are red flags that you are losing your audience. If you see all three, you're really in trouble. Even when you do an outstanding job of conducting an investigation, if you can't hold the interest of others while briefing them, it's game over.

Let's think about some of those case presentations from the perspective of a criminal or civil prosecuting attorney who is listening to an investigator's or fraud fighter's boring/dry verbal summary. The prosecutor probably has many thoughts going on in his or her head during the briefing. Some examples might be:

- How can I get out of this meeting?
- Is this investigator ever going to shut up?
- I have to stop drinking decaf.
- Why did I ever say I wanted to prosecute fraud cases?
- When is my next meeting?
- Maybe the fire alarm will go off.
- Ring phone! Ring!
- I hope this investigator does not ask me if I understand what he is talking about.
- Should I say I decline to prosecute now, or wait a few more minutes?
- Does this investigator really think I can hold a jury's attention with this boring case?

Because I've also conducted general crime investigations (burglaries, thefts, assaults, illegal drugs, etc.), I know how smoothly case presentations can go. You can finish briefing one of those cases in about 15 minutes, which includes time for questions and answers. Plus, the prosecutors know that those kinds of cases already have jury appeal, and the facts can be presented easily in court. If the evidence is strong enough, those kinds of cases will result in slam-dunk convictions. In fact, the suspects often just plead guilty. In reality, a prosecutor usually can get convictions, settlements, guilty pleas, and/or guilty verdicts on several small cases in the time it takes to prepare for and prosecute one complex major fraud case.

Over the years, I've learned that investigators must present their cases (especially fraud cases) to others in a way that keeps their interest and, it is hoped, inspire them to accept the case or want to hear more. There are three steps to effective verbal communication:

1. Tell listeners what you are going to tell them.
2. Tell them.
3. Tell them what you just told them.

In other words, give listeners an overview of what the case is about, tell them the case facts, and then summarize. Next is a fictional example of a verbal presentation to a federal criminal prosecutor in the Western District of Tennessee on a very simple fraud case.

1. Tell them what you're going to tell them.
   - This is an Entitlement Fraud case involving a 36-year-old male suspect.
   - It appears there are violations of Title 18 USC 641 (Theft of Public Money) and Title 18 USC 1344 (Bank Fraud) involving the theft of $17,100
2. Tell them.
   - A military retiree named John Smith who lived in Memphis, TN, died on January 2, 2011, at the age of 82. He was widowed and had an individual (not joint) savings account at the ABC Bank in Memphis, Tennessee.
   - Each month the federal government electronically deposited Smith's military retirement payments into his savings account in the amount of $950 per month.
   - The government was never told that Smith died so the checks kept getting electronically deposited into his savings account for an additional 19 months after he died. A total of $18,050 was deposited into Smith's bank account by the government after Smith died.
   - Smith had a caretaker named Carl Crook who is currently 36 years old.
   - After Smith died, Crook obtained and used Smith's ATM card and PIN to access Smith's savings account.
   - For 19 straight months, Crook withdrew $900 from the account each month totaling $17,100
   - We already obtained Smith's bank account statements for the 19 months, which show the dates and locations of the pension deposits and ATM withdrawals.
   - There were no other deposits (besides the pension checks) made into the account after Smith died.
   - Crook was not authorized by Smith or the bank to make the withdrawals.
   - The ATM machine Crook routinely used to make the withdrawals is located in the drive-through at ABC's Bank in Memphis, Tennessee, on Poplar Avenue.

- The evidence that we have includes several security videotapes from the bank's exterior that show Crook driving his car to use the ATM machine on the same date and times that the ATM withdrawals were made.
- The videos show the car, the license plate, and close-ups of Smith pushing the buttons on the ATM machine.
- Last week, Investigator Joe Cool and I interviewed Crook at Crook's apartment in Memphis. Crook told us he knew that he was not entitled to Smith's money but needed it to pay bills.
- Crook voluntarily wrote a statement in which he admitted to taking the money and that Crook knew he was not entitled to the money.
- Crook told me he'd be glad to pay the money back but he has not yet found a new job.
- Records indicate that Crook has no prior arrests.
3. Tell them what you told them.
    - So it looks like we have a pretty strong case against Carl Crook for stealing $17,100 of government money that he was not entitled to and for fraudulently using the bank's ATM machine.

Granted, this sample was not very complex. But it does illustrate a good approach to providing a case briefing to a prosecutor. A common mistake I made in earlier years when briefing prosecutors is that I would not tell them the meaty details until the very end (almost like telling them a story). I think that contributed greatly to the droopy eyes and yawns. You'll notice in the example, the prosecutor was told right from the onset what type of case it was, the possible statutes violated, and the money involved.

You'll also notice that in Step 2 ("Tell them"), the facts provided were basically broken into three separate parts. First, the investigator described the deceased and the money situation. Second, the investigator described Crook, how Crook took the money and the dollar loss. Third, the investigator described the evidence against Crook.

In Step 3 ("Tell them what you told them"), the investigator provided a very short summary.

NOTE: Your presentation doesn't have to be exactly like the one provided, but it should follow an organized format.

Graphics, Charts, Visual Aids, Photos, and Videos

Keep in mind that prosecutors often wonder how a case will play out in court. Before even meeting the prosecutor, the investigator should prepare some visual aids that will assist in presenting the facts as well as keep the presentation interesting. (See the appendix for samples of case presentation visual aids.)

For example, in this case, security video footage was obtained as evidence. At a minimum, the investigator should present a few clips to the prosecutor (assuming the film quality actually clearly depicts the suspect at the ATM machine). An alternative might be to get some clear still photo shots from the video depicting the suspect at the ATM machine and/or his vehicle and the license plate. At least give the prosecutor a taste of what he or she could later present in court.

If possible, try to obtain a couple of photographs of the military retiree taken back in the days when the man was a fit-to-fight soldier and another photo of him taken during his older years. The prosecutor can determine if the photos are useful. You might also want to bring a photograph of the suspect to the meeting. Also bring a copy of the signed confession (if one was obtained). I'll bet the prosecutor actually will want to read that.

Bring copies of the bank statements in case the prosecutor asks for them. If you're like me, you will already have written a report describing your review of the bank statements that reflects the dates and dollar amounts the retirement checks were deposited as well as the dates and amounts of the ATM withdrawals. That report would include copies of all 19 months of bank statements. As a matter of fact, it would be wise to also include one or more bank statements from the month(s) before the retiree died. Those might show that similar ATM withdrawals were or were not made before the retiree died. The previous bank statement(s) would also show the retirement checks being regularly electronically deposited before the military retiree died.

You also could create a graphic timeline showing the dates of the deposits and the withdrawals.

Obtain photographs of the exterior of the bank where the ATM machine was used. Also include a close-up photograph of the ATM machine.

You could even create a double-bar graph. One bar could show the amount of money the government deposited into Smith's bank account after Smith died and the next bar could show how much money Crook withdrew from the account. The bar graph would basically show that Crook stole almost all of the money deposited into the account after Smith died.

With a little creativity, oral, visual, and written presentations can make your case very easy to understand. You can almost make a case presentation come to life! Just because a case might be filled with facts and figures doesn't mean it has to be boring when presented.

NOTE: So now you have another thing to be thinking about while conducting your investigation. By thinking about your future case briefings during the investigation, you'll save time in the long run. For example, you could take those exterior photographs of the bank after you conduct the interview(s) of the bank employees and/or when you obtain the bank records.

TIP: Take photographs of the bank *after* the interviews or after you receive the records. If you stand outside taking photos of the bank before going inside, you will draw unwanted attention to yourself. (Someone might even call the cops on you.)

TIP: To illustrate quantity, you might want to show a comparable photograph. For example, once I had to brief a prosecutor about a case involving 50,000 defective shirts. To illustrate how many shirts that was, I brought an aerial photograph of a filled professional baseball stadium that held about the same number of people.

TIP: When presenting investigative results on a case involving defective widgets, also show the end items that the widgets go into. In one case I worked, I had photographs of defective electric cable (which were pretty boring). But then I added next to it a photograph of a nuclear aircraft carrier that the cable was supposed to be installed in, and the case suddenly got more interesting.

Investigator's Appearance and Voice

Prosecutors often try to envision how the case might play out in court. They might also wonder what type of impression the investigator might make in court. If the investigator is dressed in professional attire during the presentation, the attire part is taken care of.

If you want to make a good impression, your demeanor and bearing during the presentation can help your cause (especially if it's your first time making a presentation to that attorney). So save your street talk for the streets and sit up straight.

Your voice can also be a selling point. Speaking loudly and clearly and pausing when appropriate could help your cause (rather than speaking softly and/or rattling your words off a mile a minute). Usually by the time investigators have completed their cases, they know them like the back of their hands. But sometimes when providing a first-time case presentation, they make the mistake of briefing the case facts rapidly and never give the listeners a chance to digest the information.

TIP: If you want to watch some experts speak effectively about a lot of different areas, watch the Weather Channel. They take their time and pause appropriately and give you time to grasp what they said. In comparison, many local news station weathermen and women often speak very fast and flip through slides at a pace where you have no idea what they just said.

A Copy for the Prosecutor

When briefing prosecutors with hopes that they accept your case for prosecution, bring them their very own copies of reports, attachments, bank records, photos, graphics, and whatever else for their own files. You don't have to give them everything up front, but at least give them a copy of the summary report. If they accept the case, eventually they will need copies of much of what you have in your files. Make sure you provide a professionally written and packaged product. If there are a lot of attachments to the report, tab and number the attachments.

NOTE: Whenever I make a presentation to attorneys on cases that I believe they'll accept (or for work they asked me to do), I provide them with a folder or binder that includes everything I want them to reference during the presentation or later. When I leave the meeting, I want them to have everything they need. If it's a case that is not worth their time and you know they will not accept it for prosecution, there's no reason to go overboard copying and binding things. Save the paper and ink for next time.

TIP: Whenever you provide someone with a folder or binder, expect that they will start flipping through the pages immediately while you are talking to them. You can control that, if you so desire, by not giving them the folder until you've finished your presentation or by having them turn to specific pages during your presentation.

In summary, impress on prosecutors (or others you are briefing) that you are a thorough and articulate investigator who is prepared, makes a good impression, and is able to communicate case facts both orally and in writing. What more could any attorney want?

As time progresses and you present additional cases in the same fashion, you'll find that prosecutors and other attorneys are eager to receive and accept your cases. You will then have established a solid reputation.

War Story 11.1

I once went a bit overboard with the visual aids on a presentation involving a case where the government kept depositing money into a deceased retiree's bank account. I went to a graveyard and threw a couple of dollar bills on the ground by the unmarked side of a headstone. Most people bring flowers to the cemetery; I brought cash. Then I photographed the cash on the ground next to the headstone. I have to admit, it looked pretty bizarre. But it's pretty bizarre to keep using taxpayer money to pay dead people. After taking the photo and retrieving my cash, I couldn't help but feel like the ghosts were going to get me. Maybe the ghosts were laughing too.

I showed the headstone-cash photo to the assigned federal prosecutor. We had already successfully worked several cases together before and we got along very well. (Yes, he thought I was nuts too.)

But I also included a typed caption under the photograph of the headstone and money that was a partial quote from General Doulas MacArthur and I added a second line:

General MacArthur once said, "Old soldiers never die; they just fade away."

(I added)

"And the Government keeps paying some of them, just in case they decide to come back."

No, we did not use any of that stuff in court. I actually created the photo with the caption for future fraud awareness training briefings to help retain the attention of my audiences. (They probably thought I was a sicko too.)

Presentations to Supervisors

You also can provide similar presentations to your supervisors. But first-line supervisory reviews are usually very informal. When the big bosses come to town for case briefings, you certainly might want to show some visual aids. However, some supervisors can never be pleased, no matter what you present. (If you haven't already had supervisors like that, you will one day, unfortunately.)

War Story 11.2
When I was a young federal agent, one of my supervisors insisted that "his agents" always wear long-sleeve white dress shirts with ties. Dress-casual-Fridays must have driven him nuts! That same supervisor was real anal about knowing the exact dates that we used investigative tools. For example, during one case briefing, I told the supervisor that I served a subpoena on a bank to get financial records on a bribery case. The supervisor immediately yelled, "When!?"

I replied, "A couple of weeks ago." He then pounded the desk and yelled again, even louder, "WHEN?!" The supervisor said he wanted the exact date. Since I knew I had also served a few other subpoenas on the same case and didn't know the exact dates they were served, I wasn't about to tell the supervisor about them because then he would have gotten real angry.

Next he asked me for the federal criminal statute numbers of the possible violations. I told him it was a bribery case, but he wanted the statute number (Title 18 USC 201). I didn't know the statute number off the top of my head, and that angered the supervisor even more.

Here I was doing all this great work on the bribery case as a rookie agent and was getting chastised because I didn't know specific dates and statute numbers during a case briefing. The supervisor was making me out to be incompetent. As the years passed, I learned that no matter what I did, I was never going to please him. Just about every other agent thought that the supervisor was completely nuts. He was even more anal when reviewing investigative reports, measuring margins as well as spaces between sentences.

Another federal agent in my office wrote a report and used a sentence like "The man was pronounced dead at the hospital. . . ." The supervisor verbally scolded the agent and sent the report back with red pen marks all over it. The reason? The agent used four periods at the end of the sentence instead of three.

As I mentioned earlier, conducting major fraud investigations takes a long time. After a few years serving as a federal agent, I realized that during case briefings, supervisors usually asked what investigative tools were used. I've always been a believer that you should use the tools that you need to get the job done. But many of my supervisors seemed to think they could gauge whether agents/investigators were doing their jobs by the number and types of investigative tools that were used on each case. (And you'd better know the dates those tools were used too!)

To get the supervisors off my back, I made a separate list of all the possible investigative tools I could use on any case and tacked the list on my wall next to my desk. The list included these things:

- Search warrants
- Grand jury subpoenas
- Administrative subpoenas
- Mail covers
- Trash covers
- Surveillance

- Photography
- Polygraphs
- Undercover operations
- Laboratory analysis
- Computer analysis
- Informants
- Arrests
- Task forces
- Investigative project
- Management control deficiency report
- Fraud vulnerability report

The supervisory mentality of thinking that tool use meant that investigators were doing their jobs was kind of like judging the effectiveness of a quarterback by the number of times he threw the ball to different receivers instead of the number of times he completed thrown passes.

War Story 11.3
Due to the pressures from management, I came to realize that while preparing my investigative plans, I also had to find ways to incorporate as many investigative tools as possible. On major fraud cases, the first thing I often did was obtain mail covers. Depending on how the request was written, the results could identify alias names, others (including other company names) receiving mail at the same address, possible financial institutions, and so on.

One of the next things I did was covertly drive by the business entity or suspect's address, surveil it for a short while, and then take a photograph of the exterior. I got two points on the scoreboard for that: surveillance and photography.

As soon as I got some documents to review, I usually entered at least some of the data in my computer and analyzed it. Instant stat: computer analysis. I wasn't just doing this to claim the stat; I was just making sure I got credit for it.

We had to use a few subpoenas on almost every case, so those numbers always took care of themselves.

Once I learned how to play the "tools game" combined with getting lots of indictments, convictions, and dollar recoveries, I started being treated more favorably and received better evaluations from those supervisors—except from the supervisor who could not say the words "good" and "work" in the same sentence.

Indictments, Convictions, and Dollar Recoveries

For the first approximately 15 years I served as a federal agent, supervisors put enormous pressures on every investigator and every office to obtain indictments, convictions, and dollar recoveries. They also liked to see that people or companies (suspects) that did wrong were suspended or debarred from doing business with the government. Almost all of those things were completely out of the investigator's control. The investigator's job was to investigate; it was up to the attorneys to decide if they wanted to accept the cases and prosecute the suspects or to suspend or debar others. Granted, sometimes we could obtain guilty pleas and civil settlements rather than risking losing our stats completely in trials.

There's an obvious danger in the push to get indictments and convictions because it can cause agents to dismiss exculpatory evidence and/or only report evidence that could result in convictions. I never played that game. To me, the facts were the facts, and I documented everything. But I could see how others might get caught up in the win-at-all-cost mentality.

After about my 15-year anniversary, there was a shift in my agency's approach: No longer were agents officially evaluated on the numbers of indictments, convictions, and recoveries our cases obtained. However, we all noticed that the agents/investigators who got the most indictments, convictions, and/or recoveries also got the highest evaluations and bonuses. But if we were ever asked officially (especially under oath at a trial) whether our job performance was measured by indictments, convictions, or recoveries, we could truthfully answer no. But unofficially, all the agents/investigators knew that was still the case.

The number of war stories that could be told about ridiculous policies, procedures, and decisions in existence within the criminal justice system and/or the investigative agencies is endless. I'll provide a few more before moving on.

War Story 11.4

While serving as a MP investigator, a male second lieutenant was in charge of our investigative section for about six months. Second lieutenant is the lowest-ranking commissioned officer grade in the Army. Like most commissioned officers in the U.S. Army, the lieutenant had never conducted a criminal investigation or made an arrest in his life. He was a, "supervisor."

The investigators in our section were required to brief the lieutenant on each of their cases. In my opinion, the lieutenant had no idea what he was doing. His idea of leadership was to yell at us all the time! But we were stuck with him.

One day I briefed the lieutenant on a barracks theft case (larceny) and pointed out that the evidence was very weak against the suspect. I told the lieutenant that I did not want to charge the suspect with any crimes because the proof was not strong enough. The lieutenant was in a position to agree or disagree with me. He could even have told me to keep investigating the case. But after my briefing, I asked if he agreed that we should not charge the suspect with any crime. The lieutenant, who was a black male, looked at me and asked, "What color is the suspect?"

I didn't give the question much thought and accurately answered that the suspect was black. The lieutenant then told me not to charge the suspect. I didn't think anything about his decision until I was halfway back to my office, and then I realized how out of place the lieutenant's question was.

In police work, cops often have to reference people's race because it's relevant as an identifier. For example, witnesses might report they saw an unknown white, black, or Hispanic male in his mid-20s wearing blue jeans and a white T-shirt in the area of a crime. Descriptions are relevant and important. So the question "What color is the suspect?" is asked fairly often. That's why the lieutenant's question didn't hit me as being out of place right away. In fact, I just chalked it off to being a reactionary police question.

But a few months later, the same exact thing happened involving a different suspect. This time when the lieutenant asked me what the suspect's race was, I hesitated for a long time before answering him.

In fact, I looked in the lieutenant's eyes and intentionally delayed answering him because I wanted him to realize he was asking an irrelevant question. As soon as I told him that the suspect was black, the lieutenant immediately replied, "Then don't charge him."

You can take away from that story whatever you want. But investigators and supervisors must remove their personal likes and dislikes when making decisions and must think and react objectively. I've known cops who were not particularly fond of particular races, but I only knew of one who actually acted in bad faith while on the job because of that dislike. (He was subsequently fired, thank goodness.) There's no need for me to preach about any of this. But if you are new to the investigative, law enforcement, or fraud-fighting profession, be aware that you can and probably will encounter such issues during your career.

What happened to that second lieutenant? I know he later got promoted twice and was up to the rank of captain when I last saw him. I hope he had a wakeup call along the way. The other investigators and I were just glad to see him and his yelling ways leave our office for good. (PS: You've read enough war stories in this book to realize that complaining about a military officer wouldn't have done much good.)

War Story 11.5
While serving as a patrol supervisor on a military installation, I was dispatched to assist two young MPs on a domestic disturbance call. One of the MPs was a female and one was a male. Upon my arrival inside of the house, the husband and wife were still arguing with each other and the MPs were just standing around.

I asked the wife to take a few steps away and asked the female MP to come with us (as a witness). During my conversation with the woman, I politely said a few things to help defuse the situation. Then I asked the husband to step away and asked the male MP to come with us as I had a similar conversation with the husband. In those days we were not forced take anyone into custody or make one party leave on domestic calls just to keep the peace. When all was said and done, the couple calmed down and thanked us for our time.

When the two MPs and I approached our patrol cars, the female MP said to me, "I'm going to have to make a complaint against you for the way you talked to that lady. You only said those things to her because she's a female."

I was shocked at the female MP's assertion because I didn't say anything wrong. I quickly asked what I had said that was out of line. Then she repeated what I had said earlier to the wife. I still didn't see anything wrong with what I said. But then the male MP interjected, "That's the same exact thing he said to the husband." What a relief that was. I knew I didn't say anything wrong to either one of them.

But this particular female MP had a reputation for constantly complaining that females were being treated unfairly. It came up in almost every conversation I ever had with her before that incident and after. Of course, after she set her sights on complaining about me, I avoided her as much as possible.

Maybe she said this as a scare tactic to throw me off. After all, if anyone had a right to complain it was me, because both MPs were standing inside a house on a domestic disturbance call doing absolutely nothing. Maybe this was her way to protect herself from getting in trouble for not knowing how to do her job.

By the way, I had no intentions of complaining about her failure to act. I knew she was inexperienced and hoped she learned a few things.

The point of this story is to remind you that sometimes you have to be cautious around some of the people you work with. Some will have issues that are hard to work around. But be careful you don't get burned by them. In this scenario, the male MP also served as a truthful witness, and his testimony would have nullified her complaint. If you have to be around someone that has issues, bring witnesses (even if they don't know that's why you are bringing them with you).

War Story 11.6

One night while I was serving as a civilian supervisory detective on an Army base, a group of young soldiers made a complaint against one of the MP investigators who had been working a one-night undercover assignment. The complainants said they were walking in a park and the undercover investigator insisted that they sell him illegal drugs. When they refused (because they didn't have any drugs), the investigator pulled out his badge and pistol, aimed his pistol at them, and ordered them to the ground.

Since the allegations were serious, I interviewed the complainants in detail and had them each write statements describing what happened. One thing that seemed unusual was that each of the complainants said that the investigator pointed his pistol at one of their friends; nobody said that a pistol was pointed directly at them.

Next, I separately interviewed the investigator and asked what transpired that night. As the investigator's supervisor, I knew he was on an undercover assignment and was supposed to be searching for drug sellers. The investigator was even given government funds to make drug purchases during his assignment.

During the interviews, I learned that the investigator was over-zealous in his attempt to purchase illegal drugs. When the group of men challenged and threatened the undercover investigator (because they didn't use drugs), the investigator ordered them to the ground and searched them. The investigator admitted that he removed his pistol from his holster but said he never aimed it at anyone. In a separate interview, his partner later corroborated this information.

My own supervisor, who was an Army Lieutenant Colonel, wanted the investigator kicked off the investigative team and assigned back to a uniformed patrol position. But I took full responsibility for what happened. I explained that the investigator was one of the best general crimes investigators I had ever worked with but had not been trained on how to work undercover or buy illegal drugs. I said it was my fault for assuming he knew how to work undercover.

I wrote a final report detailing everything learned during the investigation and personally apologize to the men who had been mistreated. The investigator went on to solve many more crimes. Before any similar missions were conducted, I made sure the investigators had received proper instructions and training to complete their assignments.

War Story 11.7

While serving in that same office as a supervisory detective, very often, people would call the investigative section on the telephone and I would answer, *"MPI, Piper."* I don't know where I picked up that habit because Army policy was to answer the phone more formerly by saying something like, *"Military Police Investigations; Detective Piper; May I help you, Sir or Ma'am?"*

I think I shortened my answer because after saying all those words, people would sometimes hang up. And whenever they hung up, I'd start swearing up a storm! That was another habit I picked up—as soon as callers hung up before saying anything, I'd start swearing out loud.

One day, my desk phone rang three times in a row and each time, the callers hung up after I answered. Each time they hung up on me, I started swearing out loud. After the third hang-up, I was screaming swear words all over the place! Then I heard a bunch of laughter coming from one of the investigator's offices down the hall. I walked in to see what was so funny and saw a bunch of the investigators sitting around and shooting the bull. But as soon as I walked in, they all got quiet.

I looked at the more senior investigator who seemed to have a half smile on his face and asked him, *"Did you just call me and hang up the phone!?"* All of the investigators in the room immediately burst out laughing! I then asked, *"Did you do it three times in a row?!"* They laughed even harder.

I started laughing myself and then asked, *"How often have you been doing that to me?!* One of the other investigators replied, *"Only when we needed a laugh!"* We all then burst out laughing.

Chapter 12 provides some tips about testifying.

Chapter 12

Providing Testimony

"Do you swear to tell the truth . . . and nothing but the truth?"
—Question asked before testifying in court

When in court, investigators and fraud fighters should present a professional appearance with good bearing and be mindful of their own personal conduct. Remember that some of the same people you might speak to in the courtroom might see you before or after you enter the courtroom. So stay in "professional mode" at all times, even in the building's parking lot, hallways, or other nearby areas.

Be prepared to testify by reviewing the case facts before showing up. If the facts are fresh in your memory you should do fine when testifying. It can't hurt to mentally rehearse before going inside the building.

TIP: In some of the training classes I've attended, the instructors filmed the students' participation in certain exercises, including testifying in mock courtroom trials and while conducting mock interviews and interrogations. It's amazing how much you can learn to improve by watching yourself (and others) on tape. As a PI, I usually critique the audio-recorded interviews I conduct when playing them. Professional athletes, coaches, and trainers also use videotape to analyze athletes' movements to ensure they are using proper techniques. Sometimes slight adjustments make a huge difference in performance. Be your own best critic.

If you've never been in a courtroom, do yourself a favor and go into one—preferably while some form of hearing is going on. If you are scheduled to testify, try to see the actual courtroom you'll be testifying in. Being familiar with your surroundings will help make you feel more relaxed.

If you've never testified before, ask the attorney on your side what you should expect. If that's not possible, ask a peer who has courtroom testimony experience. You are better off feeling a little uncomfortable asking those type questions of people you know than going into the courtroom unprepared in front of a bunch of people you don't know.

War Story 12.1

In my early 20s, I was serving as a hotshot plainclothes MP investigator. I was good at my job and always conducted thorough investigations. Most of the time, the military commanders took disciplinary action against the suspects that I found evidence of wrongdoing against and the cases never went to trial. But one day that changed and the staff judge advocate (SJA) attorney I often worked with told me one of my cases was going to be tried at a military court martial.

I prepared to provide testimony by reviewing my summary investigative report the day before going to court. The next day, after sitting in the courthouse hallway for about an hour, I was finally called in to raise my right hand, take the oath, and answer questions.

As soon as I walked into the courtroom, I felt tense. There were a bunch of military officers serving as jurors wearing their full dress uniforms and staring at me. I kind of lost my breath. After taking the oath, the prosecutor asked me some questions. I immediately went from hotshot investigator to scared puppy. I stumbled over my words and my voice sounded like a high school kid going through puberty. The only thing I could think of was getting the heck out of there!

When finished, I walked into the hallway and asked myself, "What the heck happened in there!?" I felt ashamed of myself. I don't recall the prosecutor giving me a hard time about it later. He probably was accustomed to seeing young guys melt on the stand. Today I have no recollection of the outcome of the case.

Over the next few decades, I've testified at numerous military court martials, grand jury proceedings, preliminary hearings, and trials from coast to coast. I learned a great deal from that first time testifying, which helped improve my testimony skills. The more you testify, the more comfortable you become doing so.

Dealing with Opposing Counsel

If you are testifying for the prosecution, the prosecutor will be the first one to ask you questions. You'll usually know in advance what's coming. The prosecutor isn't going to ask you any trick questions. However, once the opposition's attorney starts asking you questions, he or she might very well try to trip you up.

Keep in mind that cross-examination is what they do for a living. Just like you have techniques to do your job, the attorneys have theirs. The attorneys have a purpose (or dual purpose) for asking questions in a certain order, using a certain wording, and even their voice tone. They may have crafted every question carefully, and you will be on stage for the performance. They probably have already rehearsed their lines. So be prepared.

War Story 12.2

While serving as a MP investigator, I responded to a report of theft at a business. It was reported that a soldier walked into the on-base dry cleaners, stole a bag full of cash that was on the counter, and then left the area. I later located the soldier, received consent to search his car, and found all the stolen cash spread out under the car's front seat floor mats.

The case later went to a court martial, and the defense attorney asked me if I was wearing a suit jacket that day. I told him I was not. He then asked if my weapon (pistol) was exposed when I spoke to the suspect. I truthfully told him that I did not have my weapon on that day because I had just finished my shift. He then asked with a lot of emotion in his voice, "Weren't you scared being out there by yourself searching the man's car?"

I kind of laughed and answered, "No, I wasn't scared." He continued asking me if I was scared or afraid while I was searching the suspect's car and I kept telling him I was not. Quite frankly, I started thinking the defense attorney must be a wimp!

After the trial, I replayed the defense attorney's questions in my mind. It wasn't until then that I realized that the reason he was trying to get me to elaborate on why I was not in fear was so he could twist my reasons to show that his client (the suspect) was coerced (or in fear) when he gave consent to have his vehicle searched.

If I testified that my weapon was exposed when I asked the suspect for consent to search, the attorney probably would have argued that the exposed weapon caused his client to be fearful. If I had said that I wasn't afraid because there were several (a large number of) uniformed MPs (carrying weapons and batons) surrounding the suspect (his client), the attorney probably would have argued that the suspect felt intimidated into giving consent to have his car searched because of the large number of police officers present.

I believe that the defense attorney was trying to get the legality of the search thrown out of court. If he had succeeded in showing that coercion was used to gain permission to search, then the evidence (the stolen cash) would not have been admissible in the trial. If the evidence was not admissible, the case would have been dismissed.

But the truth was that I didn't have my weapon on that day, there were not a lot of uniformed MPs in the area, and there was no reason his client (the suspect) should have felt intimidated into giving voluntary consent to search his own car.

It's not that the defense attorney was mean; he was doing his job to the best of his ability. But as an investigator or fraud fighter, you must be mindful that attorneys are often just as good at their jobs as you are at yours (maybe even better).

NOTE: I should have been wearing my weapon before going out and searching for the suspect. However, the Army unit I was in made the off-duty investigators secure their weapons in a completely different building several blocks away from our office. (Yes, that was stupid.) Because my shift was over, I turned in my weapon and had no intentions of doing any more investigative work outside of the office that day. Since the on-call investigator was tied up on another case, I volunteered to respond to the dry cleaning store incident.

TIP: If you are armed when conducting investigations, don't have your weapon exposed unless it serves a real purpose, especially when conducting interviews, interrogations, and/or asking someone for consent to search.

TIP: Another bit of advice when testifying is to just answer the attorneys' questions. Don't volunteer extra stuff. Do you remember the attorney who told me, "The more you write in your reports, the more you have to defend in court"? Well, one thing he certainly would have been right about is the more you say in court, the more the opposition can twist your words around or use them against you. There's nothing that says you have to answer more than the question you are asked. Don't elaborate unless your response warrants an elaboration. Another thing you want to do while testifying is to keep your emotions in check.

War Story 12.3
While serving as a federal agent, I had to testify at several trials. Over the years, I came to dislike the way some defense attorneys kept trying to twist my words around. During one particular trial, I politely and professionally answered all of the prosecutor's questions, as usual. I even made it a point to look at the jurors on occasion. I was comfortable and knew how to handle myself.

But then the defense counsel started asking me questions. He kept insinuating that I couldn't possibly remember everything I was testifying about. He was really starting to tick me off. My tone of voice became angry while answering the defense attorney's questions. I knew what he was trying to do and I didn't appreciate it.

As a seasoned investigator, I've learned to frequently critique myself. I didn't like the way I handled myself on the stand that day. I showed emotion that I should not have, and I'm quite certain the jurors picked up on it. I should have remained calm no matter what anyone asked me. Perhaps my display of anger and resentment was exactly what the defense counsel was trying to get me to show! I do recall that the suspect was found guilty. But I learned that day that no matter who asks the questions in a court setting, the investigator should stay calm and professional. I never made that mistake again and, having read this hopefully you never will either.

War Story 12.4
Since serving as a PI, I've had the pleasure of working with some excellent criminal defense attorneys. I have to admit: Learning how to investigate from "the other side" has been an interesting experience. As I mentioned earlier, one defense attorney told me, "If it's not in the police report, it didn't happen." In other words, it's going to be difficult for you to testify that you did or saw things that you never wrote down in any of your reports. This is another reason why I am a proponent of writing detailed investigative reports.

I've also attended training sessions with defense attorneys and can tell you that they look at things from a completely different angle then prosecutors. They will attack or point out what you did, what you didn't do, what you didn't do in accordance with policies and procedures or your training, and what you didn't do historically or consistently.

For example, a uniformed police officer might report something(s) a driver did wrong that gave her probable cause to pull over a vehicle. But the defense attorney will point out the things the driver did not do wrong prior to getting pulled over in an effort to show that the police officer did not have probable cause to pull the vehicle over.

It could be that the driver did several things wrong, but the police officer documented or issued a citation for only one. Remember, "If it's not in the police report, it didn't happen." You might think you did a good job, but the defense attorney's job includes showing that you did not do such a good job. Document your actions and pertinent observations and be prepared for your investigative activity and reports to be dissected by the opposition.

TIP: One attorney provided an example of only answering the question you are asked while testifying. He suggested that if the opposing counsel asks you if you know what time it is, just answer by saying "Yes." Don't say what time it is; that's not what you were asked.

Visual Aids in Court

In the last chapter, I mentioned the use of visual aids when making presentations. Visual aids are also frequently used in courtrooms and can make or break a case. As a PI, I often obtain surveillance video and take case-related photographs. Patrol officers often film their traffic stops. Cameras are just about everywhere these days. But evidence can be used both to prove and to disprove points. If charging someone with a crime, the evidence presented should actually prove the intended points. Sometimes the evidence can be used against the ones presenting it.

War Story 12.5

While serving as a federal agent, I assisted some other agents execute a search warrant on a company that was not providing a required deicer fluid in the fuel it put in military aircraft. Not adding the liquid deicer fluid could cause the fuel to freeze at high altitudes. (That would not be a good thing.) The case later went to trial and, in preparation, the case agent had an enlarged professionally printed graph chart made to show the jury that the contractor had not purchased enough deicer fluid to service all the military aircraft it had provided fuel to.

The graph had two columns. One showed the amount of gallons of fuel pumped into military aircraft, and the other showed a much smaller amount of deicer fluid purchased. Utilizing a ratio and some basic math skills along with the at-a-glance chart, the investigator was able to demonstrate that the business never purchased or possessed enough deicer fluid to provide the amount of acceptable fuel it billed the military for. The graph was great except for one problem: It was inaccurate!

While the trial was going on, the investigator who was going to testify about the information on the chart started recalculating the formulas and numbers just to verify his math. But to his dismay, he found that the math answers he previously came up with were wrong. They weren't off by much, but he knew the defense counsel might be able to discredit his testimony because of some simple math errors. Finding the mistakes also meant that the fancy chart was an inaccurate representation and there was no time to run to the local printer to get a new chart made.

Luckily for the investigator, the adjustment that had to be made required increases to both columns (not decreases), and the two columns were printed in dark black ink. Ingeniously, the investigator went to a local drugstore, purchased a role of black electrical tape, and placed small pieces of the black tape on the top of each of the black columns. The black tape blended perfectly with the black ink used on the columns and no one could tell that graphic numeric increases had been made to both columns.

The chart was subsequently used in the trial, and the suspects were found guilty. After the trial, many of the jurors said that the chart greatly influenced their decisions to find the suspects guilty. That day, we all relearned the importance of being 100 percent prepared before going to trial (and the benefits of black electrical tape).

Make Sure You Understand the Question

While you are testifying, it's very important that you understand each question before you provide a response. Depending on the setting, sometimes the jurors or judge may also ask questions while you are under oath.

War Story 12.6
While serving as a patrol officer specializing in vehicular traffic accidents and other related matters, I made a traffic stop on a vehicle and charged the woman driver with driving while intoxicated (DWI). To this day I remember that arrest clearly because the woman was extremely disorderly and combative. Later the case went to court and I had to testify in front of a magistrate judge. I had just finished working the midnight shift and had attended college classes before that. Needless to say I was dog-tired. Luckily my case was one of the first ones heard.

At this point in my career, I had testified numerous times in courtroom settings and dozens of times in front of that particular magistrate judge. He was a very old man, and I knew he had some quirks including being a bit hard of hearing. So I always made sure I spoke loudly and clearly when testifying.

On the date of this hearing, both I and the woman I arrested for DWI were standing directly in front of the judge while I provided my testimony. The courtroom was jam-packed with people, and everyone was eager to get out of there.

Standing off to the side adjacent to me were about two dozen other police officers who were waiting their turn to testify about their own cases.

After testifying about how I observed the woman driving erratically and swerving from lane to lane, my detection of the strong smell of alcohol on her breath, and her flunking the Breathalyzer test, the judge asked me a question that seemed totally unnecessary, given the facts I presented. He asked me a question I will never forget:

"Would she not have been driving better, had she not been drinking?"

I thought deeply about his question. Maybe I thought too deeply because I didn't know how to answer it. I had flashbacks to taking my college algebra course and remembered that two negatives equal a positive. The judge asked, "Would she *not* have been driving better, had she *not* been drinking?" There were two negatives so I answered, "Yes, your honor."

The judge leaned down from his elevated platform and yelled at me, "Yes?!"

Realizing that I might have read too deeply into his question, I quickly responded, "No, your honor." Then the judge again leaned down from his elevated platform and yelled at me, "No?!"

People in the courtroom started laughing, and I felt sweat starting to drip down my back. Being confused, I said, "Your honor, I'm not sure that I understand your question. But the woman was driving erratically and was intoxicated and in no condition to be driving." I figured I answered his question in better detail than he could have asked for.

But the judge looked a bit angry. He then looked down at me firmly and said in an even louder tone, "I'm asking you, would she not have been driving better, had she not been drinking?!"

Now the sweat was really pouring down my back. Almost pleading for someone to tell me how to answer, I looked over at the other police officers nearby. All the cops were smiling and some of them were laughing. Worse yet, half of them were shaking their heads yes and the other half was shaking their heads no.

Knowing I got the question wrong the first time, I replied, "No, your honor."

Then the judge again leaned down from his elevated platform and yelled at me, "No?!"

So I again quickly changed my answer again and replied, "Yes, your honor."

Then the judge actually stood up and yelled at me, "Yes?!"

At this point, everyone in the courtroom was laughing out loud. Even the woman accused of DWI was bent over laughing!

Finally someone came over to assist me. The assigned prosecutor stepped up to me, and I quietly told him that I didn't know how to answer the question. Then the prosecutor decided to offer me some assistance. He whispered into my ear, "The judge is asking you, Would she not have been driving better, had she not been drinking?"

Of all the things the prosecutor could have said, he decided to repeat the exact same question to me! So now I stood there feeling like a man alone on stage with the whole world laughing at him, but I wasn't trying to do a comedy act.

I don't remember if the woman was found guilty or not. I just remember that I felt like a fool and couldn't wait to get out of that courtroom. To this day I have no idea what the correct answer to the judge's question would have been. Whenever I hear a double-negative question, I always have flashbacks to that day testifying.

In closing this chapter, my best advice for anyone being asked a question under oath is to tell the truth. You might want to consider why the person is asking the question. Stay calm and act professionally while on the stand. Also, make sure you understand the question before providing an answer. If you don't understand the question, ask the person to rephrase it. If that doesn't work, pray for rain. (That's a baseball adage; baseball games get rained out.)

Chapter 13 provides tips on what should be done after the investigation and adjudication are complete.

Chapter 13

Closing the Case

"2 Good 2 Be 4 Gotten"

—Graduation yearbook signature

One of best feelings an investigator or fraud fighter can have besides solving cases is closing or "getting rid of" cases that are either completed or have no merit in pursuing. But the work is really not completed just because the investigation is finished. First, the completed case file with the final report has to be filed somewhere, and keep in mind that sometimes old closed investigations come in handy later. Second, after the investigation has been completed, sometimes the investigator can initiate or request consideration for other nonjudicial actions and/or make suggestions to improve crime prevention and detection measures.

Old Case Files

Sometimes new evidence or fresh leads are developed that warrant reopening cases and sometimes cases are appealed. I've frequently requested and/or obtained old case files because they contain information in them that is useful to complete open investigations.

Useful information in closed cases may include:

- Templates (or go-bys) of other reports, graphs, or charts to replicate for use on current cases
- Individuals' names or contact information
- Transcripts from previous interviews or Title III telephone intercepts
- Laboratory reports
- Descriptions of stolen property
- Mug shots
- Audio interview recordings
- Written statements
- Other information

These reasons are enough to realize that the proper administrative closing of cases is important. In Government investigations, once cases are closed, Freedom of Information Act (FOIA) or similar requests made by the media and/or general public are likely to be approved. Most will agree that transparency should play an important part in our judicial system. In fact, countless times DNA evidence has proven that individuals have been convicted and imprisoned for crimes they never committed; so old case files can be useful to a lot of people.

Most large investigative organizations have strict policies and procedures on the filing and archiving of closed investigative files. Here I just want to emphasize that such policies and procedures should exist to ensure that closed case files are maintained in an appropriate manner for an adequate amount of time.

As previously suggested, working files, investigator notes, and other related items should be stored in the official investigative file when the case is closed. By keeping everything together in one place, everyone will be assured that all of the case-related information can be easily located and recovered if needed.

Evidence

Physical evidence on closed cases must be maintained and/or disposed of in accordance with your agency's policy. Some agencies require that evidence be maintained for five or more years after the case is closed. However, often evidence can be released, destroyed, and/or returned to owners upon written approval of designated individuals. (For law enforcement, this is often approval by the prosecuting attorney.)

Recommendations for Improvement

As part of their thorough and complete investigation, an investigator or fraud fighter should inquire into the cause or contributing factors that led to the matter that was investigated. Perhaps there are systemic weaknesses or management deficiencies that need to be addressed. Chapter 5 described my recommendations for improvement in cases involving improper contract award procedures, purchases of defective electric cable, quality assurance procedures, and sale and distribution of prescription medications.

War Story 13.1

While serving as a federal agent, I was asked to provide some minor investigative assistance to an agent from another state. Essentially all I had to do was make an inquiry with the shipping and receiving (S&R) warehouse on a nearby military installation to track the location of some items that were shipped to a unit on the base. I anticipated this assignment would last a couple of hours, including writing a summary report describing my actions.

But within 30 minutes, I discovered there existed systemic weakness within the base's S&R procedures that resulted in large dollar losses and the failures of military units to receive supplies already paid for.

To avoid having delivery trucks travel separately to individual units when making deliveries, the base arranged to have all shipments of goods delivered to the on-base S&R warehouse. It was assumed that having one location serve all the units would reduce costs for the units on-base and for the delivery carriers. It would also save the delivery carriers' time.

There was no question it worked well for the delivery truck drivers. Everything was delivered to one location. All the bulk items and crates had the same delivery address: the S&R warehouse.

The problem was that many of the vendors that sold the goods to the military units didn't realize that the address they were shipping to wasn't the precise location of the purchaser. Both vendors and purchasers were following the base's instructions of listing the on-base S&R warehouse as the final destination.

The deliveries were made to the warehouse (often in large crates) with generic shipping and receiving addresses. Warehouse employees sometimes didn't know which military units to call to have the items picked up. Keep in mind that the understaffed laborers were responsible for lifting and hauling, not making phone calls to supply vendors to figure out who paid for what. So when the shipments received did not have the units' names on them, the goods were placed in temporary storage in the warehouse.

After about 90 days, if no units came to claim the deliveries, the warehouse shipped the items to another facility that was responsible for "reutilizing" excess military items. This was the same place where units brought their old computers, printers, desks, and chairs after they purchased new ones.

Upon receipt, the items were inventoried, and the inventory was placed online so that U.S. military units across the country (perhaps the world) could see what was available and ask for those items free of charge. (They probably had to pay for shipping.)

After a set amount of time (perhaps 30 to 90 days), nonprofit organizations, including police departments, could request whatever items remained.

After another set amount of time (perhaps another 30 to 90 days), the remaining items were auctioned off to the general public, usually for pennies on the dollar. I witnessed some of those auctions, and it was like watching your tax dollars getting flushed down the toilet.

NOTE: Items of a sensitive nature were not made available to non-U.S. military organizations. For safety and national security reasons, some excess items had to be destroyed or rendered useless if not claimed by U.S. military units.

You'd think that all of the police departments that obtained the surplus property (at no cost) would do the right thing with the property. But in the early 1990s I investigated several incidents where some small-town police departments were obtaining military surplus property they couldn't possibly have a use for. For example, some departments with just a few officers obtained several surplus government cars—more cars than they had police officers! Some obtained backpacks, shovels, fatigue uniforms, and other items by the lots full even though they only had a few officers.

I also learned that some of the higher-ups in the reutilization branch were evaluated on how much money they made from sales (not reutilization). I found indicators that many items that could have been reutilized by military organizations were being hidden in separate storage facilities so they could later be sold at auction.

Although I wrote a management control deficiency report detailing my findings, it doesn't look like much has changed over the years. In fact, in early August 2013, the Associated Press published an article titled "Military Surplus Program Abused— Agencies Grab Stuff They Don't Use."

The article highlighted some of the various discrepancies in the 1033 Program, which permits transfer of excess military items to police departments, and how many small police departments obtain a disproportionate amount of surplus military property. The article said one small police department (which had no deep-water areas) obtained boats, scuba gear, rescue rafts, life preservers, and the like.

These cases are classic examples of a broken system where perhaps no one did anything wrong criminally or civilly; it was/

is just another government program created with good intentions but lacking in oversight and overreliance on trust.

Regarding the shipping and receiving arrangement on the military base I encountered, you can't convince me that the warehouse employees didn't realize that what was going on was wasteful. But it always came down to "It's not my job" (and they probably didn't have the space to store stuff on a long-term basis). In all probability, at least some of the units complained after ordering items that they never received. But the shipping vendor probably showed proof of delivery to the base S&H warehouse, and the warehouse probably said it didn't have the items. My guess is the unit probably just ordered some more.

In response to that small lead work I started for the other agent, I learned that the items he was trying to locate were sent to the on-base reutilization office and subsequently given away for free to about six different organizations around the world.

The sad thing was that the base I was on had many investigators but only one worked fraud investigations. Everyone else concentrated on investigating burglaries, thefts, assaults, drugs, and similar cases. In my opinion, the organization's anti-fraud, waste, and abuse program pretty much consisted of posters on walls. (It was a joke.)

The point of this and other related stories is to remind investigators and fraud fighters that at the conclusion of their investigations, they should document any causes, systemic weaknesses, contributing factors, or management deficiencies found and then make recommendations for improvement. The reports can be called management control deficiency reports, fraud vulnerability reports, waste and abuse reports, or even suggestions for improvement. The names don't matter as long as the problems are addressed. But as demonstrated, sometimes nothing happens until the media gets a hold of the information.

My suggestion is that investigators or fraud fighters who author a deficiency report with recommendations give copies to the top leaders of the affected organizations and make sure the distribution is written on the report.

Depending on the amount of leverage you have, you can even request or demand that they respond with a corrective action report or something similar within 90 days. Then monitor the response time to ensure they follow through.

NOTE: If you title your report "Management Control Deficiency Report" or use any accusatory verbiage, you'd better be sure you are right. The "accused" will probably get pretty defensive so be careful of your choice of words. Also keep in mind that there's a chance you don't really know everything about the situation and it's not as out of control as it seems. In the scenario just given, it was definitely out of control. Consider using words like "appears" and "possible" but don't water down the facts. If you have real examples, reference them in detail.

War Story 13.2
During a healthcare fraud investigation, I pulled about 20 random files from a particular medical facility for an audit and found major fraud in 18 of them. Based on that random sample, I was of the opinion that reviewing all of the patient files from the past year would identify huge amounts of fraud. Believe it or not, after reviewing about a year's worth of files, I found no other fraud. It just so happened that I pulled the only 18 files that had evidence of fraud.

That's why I'm not a big proponent of using extrapolation formulas to determine dollar losses based on statistically random samplings (unless all parties agree with their use). I saw with my very own eyes that sometimes a sample is not a true representative of the whole.

Suspensions, Debarment, and Improvement Plans

Depending on the type of investigation conducted and the organization conducting it, after any criminal or civil action is completed, recommendations can sometimes be made to initiate suspensions, debarments, improvement plans, or other administrative action against the person(s) or business entities that were the subject of the investigation if evidence was found that they violated the law. If these types of actions are available, as they are with many government programs, the investigator should be aware of them and should be sure to forward the necessary information to the appropriate personnel for consideration.

Large agencies and organizations often have complete instructions and manuals covering these topics. Obviously, this chapter cannot condense everything into a few pages.

In summary, investigators and fraud fighters who are attempting to conduct thorough and complete investigations should ensure that they become aware of all postcase closing procedures before putting the case file in its final resting place.

Chapter 14 describes some of the things that investigators, fraud fighters, supervisors, leaders, and organizations can do to ensure all team members are performing at their highest levels.

Chapter 14

Personal and Professional Growth

"Compared to what we ought to be, we are only half awake. We are making use of only a small part of our physical and mental resources."
—William James, American philosopher and psychologist

Two of my favorite quotations are included in this chapter, one at the beginning and one at the end. I've had copies of these two quotes tacked on the wall next to my desk for as long as I can remember. Regardless of your profession, personal and professional growth is vital to becoming the best you can be. (Financial growth is often a by-product of the two types of growth combined.) This chapter touches on some areas in which all who serve as investigators and fraud fighters should seek to improve throughout their careers.

Training

Training does not always have to be completed in formal classroom environments. Numerous useful books, seminars, Webinars, and videos are available, sometimes at little or no cost. Many professional trade publications provide useful current information and professional insight that can be invaluable to fraud fighters and investigators.

Many useful classes and programs have been developed to provide the minimal basic and/or advanced knowledge needed to perform the jobs or to better perform the jobs. Passing and completing some of these (e.g., investigative academies) are often a prerequisite to getting or keeping some jobs. College degrees are also useful and sometimes also a prerequisite to employment with many agencies.

Many who serve in the fraud-fighting profession have also attained designations, such as certified fraud examiner (CFE), certified public accountant (CPA), accredited healthcare fraud investigator (AHFI), certified internal auditor (CIA), and others. All of these are well-recognized and prestigious credentials. (This is not an all-inclusive listing.)

In the interview and interrogation specialty, some professionals earn the CRT credential (certified in Reid Technique of Interview and Interrogation) or the CFI (certified forensic interviewer) credential.

The majority of sponsoring or licensing organizations/agencies also require credential holders to continue their professional training in order to maintain their certifications. Some states do not require a PI to be licensed to perform investigations in their states. However, most states that do require PIs to be licensed also require that those investigators complete approved additional training each year. Many organizations also require at least one hour of annual ethics training. Certified state law enforcement officers are also required to participate in a certain number of hours of approved annual training to maintain their peace officer certifications.

TIP: Create and maintain your own professional training history in an organized format. Do not rely on your agency alone to maintain and update this information. Include the name of the course, the sponsor, the dates attended, and the number of hours completed. Keep a copy of the certificates or diplomas earned as a result of completing the courses. This list will come in handy later when applying for other jobs, promotions, or accreditations from professional organizations listed above.

NOTE: Be cautious of some of the alphabet soup credential warehouses and diploma mills that offer less recognized or less prestigious designations or certificates of completion. These certificates or credentials may not really improve your credentials or employment prospects and may just reduce the money in your bank account.

Networking

For many years I was guilty of not taking the time to perform liaison with outside agencies and others. I've always been focused on doing my job and maximizing the use of my time. Sitting down to have a cup of coffee with someone or bringing doughnuts when stopping by to say hello always seemed like a complete waste of time. As I've mentioned, most of the time my Type A personality doesn't even allow me to go out to lunch. However, even in younger years, I noticed that the few people who did take time to perform liaison regularly were often very well liked. Even I liked most of them—especially when they brought doughnuts!

War Story 14.1

One day while sitting at my desk as a Military Police investigator, a local city detective whom I had immense respect for stopped by our office. He made his rounds to everyone's desk one at a time smiling and telling jokes. He was one of the funniest, hardestworking, and results-oriented cops I ever met. One day I asked him why he came by our office. He said, "Ya know, I break my rear nine days out of ten. But I take one day every two weeks and shoot the bull with the people I like and work with."

Frankly, I don't think the detective thought of what he was doing as performing liaison or networking. He was just being him. I think he genuinely liked all of us and felt he deserved to take a little break once in a while. But what he was doing also paid dividends—not just for him but for all of us. Very often during his visits we'd talk about cases, and very often we were able to help each other solve cases or make referrals to others in the profession who could help. That's really what networking is all about.

War Story 14.2

As a federal agent in Las Vegas, Nevada, I worked in a one-agent office, as did several other local federal agents from other agencies. All of our small office resources were limited. Very often, crooks who were defrauding our individual organizations were also defrauding others. I decided to create a local federal fraud investigative working group comprised of all the local agents from the small agency organizations. I arranged for us to have quarterly meetings at a facility that didn't charge us a fee for using their meeting space.

By ensuring we all got to know each other, we suddenly had access to combined resources that we didn't have before. If one of us needed a federal agent witness for an interview, all we had to do is pick up the phone. There was no longer a need to call our larger out-of-state offices and ask for an agent to travel (and incur travel costs) to our offices to provide minor assistance. By taking the initiative and thinking outside the box, you might be able to increase your resources and help each other accomplish mutual goals of stopping or reducing crime and providing for each other's safety.

I didn't fully realize just how valuable networking was until I retired from federal law enforcement and started looking for a job to make up for dollar loss incurred by collecting a pension instead of my full-time pay. Because I moved to a new city after retiring, I had to start over and didn't know anyone. I found out very quickly that I needed to get out there and meet people. I joined a few local professional groups, like the local chapter of the Association of Certified Fraud Examiners (ACFE) and a local private investigative association. Both charge small membership fees, but they offer training opportunities and I've made some good friends.

Social media groups like LinkedIn are invaluable for networking. Numerous other local, national, and international groups and organizations are comprised of like-minded professionals, including, in addition to the ACFE, the National Health Care Anti-Fraud Association, ASIS International, the Reid Institute, and the International Association of

Interviewers. I'm personally also a member of the Federal Law Enforcement Officers Association (FLEOA), the Memphis Bar Association, the Tennessee Association of Investigators, and others.

In short, take time to maintain and improve your list of professional contacts. It's a two-way street; you end up helping each other. Generally speaking, we are all in this together.

Physical Fitness

We all know the mental and physical benefits of performing regular physical exercise. We also all know it's not always easy to find the time to perform it. As a federal agent, I was allowed up to four hours every week to devote to physical fitness (in one-hour increments). But we also had to participate in semiannual physical fitness tests (1.5 mile run, push-ups, sit-ups, sprinting, and a flexibility test). Since we were allowed to use duty time (or off-duty time) to perform this activity, it was easy to take advantage of. Before you get jealous of the federal agents, keep in mind that we were also required to work a minimum of 10 hours overtime per week. As I described earlier, some weeks I worked up to 70 to 80 hours each week with no additional compensation.

In law enforcement, it's imperative that officers and investigators exercise regularly. Their lives and the lives of fellow officers and others could very well depend on it. My own personal opinion is that, barring some posthiring injury or illness, physically unfit law enforcement officers should be required to participate in remedial training until they can at least meet the minimally acceptable physical standards. I recognize it's not always easy to get started or get started again in a regular physical fitness routine, but in law enforcement, being physically fit is part of the job and is expected by the general public.

In writing the above, I don't want to come across as "Joe Super Jock." I know firsthand that it doesn't take any time at all to get out of shape and sometimes it's an uphill battle trying to keep excess weight off especially when work and family demands so much of our time.

TIP: If you are just starting out or getting back into the physical fitness mode, just remember that consistency is the key. Gradually try to improve or increase your efforts (assuming your doctor cleared you to do such exercise). One push-up leads to two; two leads to three; and so on. If you just keep doing the same thing, you're not progressing. My philosophy now that I'm older is to concentrate on what I can do; not what I can't do. If you are in doubt as to what you are capable of, see the quotation at the beginning of this chapter.

Morale

The job should be fun most of the time, or it should at least be tolerable 90 percent of the time.

All too often, morale in offices is in the pits. It should not be that way. Very often morale is low because of supervisory attitudes, decisions, or unnecessary requirements. Sometimes morale is low because of staff shortages, lack of resources, and/or being overtasked or overextended. Low or inadequate pay and lack of other benefits can also greatly affect morale.

I've found the secret to increasing morale is to ensure that the efforts, contributions, and accomplishments of individuals are recognized and rewarded regularly and frequently. Fair treatment of all employees and workers is also mandatory. Having reasonable expectations and requirements is a must. Empathizing with others will also go a long way to having a happy or at least a content workforce.

As much as those of us in this profession are alike, we are also unique. Each of us brings something to the table that another lacks, but we all should try to improve. Just as important as knowing what increases morale is recognizing what decreases it and then trying to avoid those tendencies, behaviors, and conditions.

Morale Killers
- Chronic complaining
- Backstabbing
- Gossiping
- Spreading rumors
- Favoritism
- Sexual harassment
- Other harassment

- Poor working conditions
- Excessive work hours
- Inadequate pay
- Inadequate benefits
- Incompetent leadership
- Authoritarian leadership
- Lack of training opportunities
- Lack of recognition for performance
- Lack of promotion opportunities

War Story 14.3

I worked in one large office where each and every weekday morning the veteran investigators came in, grabbed a cup of coffee, and gathered in the most senior investigator's office. It was like a zombie shop in there. All they did was whine and complain about everything and backstab others. It went on for at least one hour, and eventually the gathering would trickle away as the investigators slowly walked back to their own offices (often to read newspapers).

When I was new to the office, I used to go in there just to be social. But after a few minutes, I felt like the energy was being sucked out of me. They made me feel depressed and totally unmotivated. Since they were the majority, sometimes I thought there was something wrong with me because I hated being around that type of atmosphere.

After a couple of days of this, I decided I'd walk right by the depressing office group every morning and just wave and smile. I'm sure since I wasn't there that I became the subject of many of their discussions.

One day we were all attending a larger training conference and an investigator I had a lot of respect for from another office said to me, "How can you stand working there? It's so depressing. Everybody just sits around and complains all the time."

A few months later, a more senior investigator reported to our large office. Not knowing about the morning routine, he grabbed a cup of coffee and entered the dungeon full of slow-moving and complaining investigators. He politely listened to all the whining and backstabbing for a few minutes and then said, "I don't know anything about any of that." Then he took a sip of his coffee and walked away. Like me, that senior investigator quickly realized that group was like an infectious disease that could easily spread.

Factually, in that office, we were financially compensated very well, were not understaffed or overworked, and had very good working conditions. Other than some of our bosses making idiotic decisions, we had nothing to complain about. But those investigators got in a habit of doing the wrong thing over and over again every single morning.

I suggested earlier that when trying to improve physically, consistency is the key. Those investigators were consistently complaining, whining, and backstabbing, and it became a bad habit. In my mind, that negativity must have affected them throughout their day and probably throughout their lives.

TIP: Get rid of the negativity wherever possible, surround yourself with positive minded individuals and keep moving forward. Consistency is the key.

Insurance and Representation

As a federal agent, I paid for professional liability insurance. I was also (and still am) a dues-paying member of FLEOA. As a PI and business owner, I have liability insurance and error and omissions insurance. While serving as an investigator, law enforcement officer, and/or fraud fighter, there's always a chance that someone is going to make a complaint against you. Some might even file lawsuits against you.

President John F. Kennedy once said, "Victory has a thousand fathers but defeat is an orphan." When someone files a complaint against you, your agency or organization might very well kick you under the bus. Regardless of all the great work you've done in the past, sacrifices you've made, and people you've helped, a complaint can hurt you. Depending on the type of complaint, the complainant's position in society, the political climate at the time, any media coverage, and the attitude of the decision makers, a complaint has the potential to devastate your career. It may even affect the financial security of your family.

When I was a city cop, I not only wore a bulletproof vest to work, I also wore a sports protective cup. (After you get kicked where it counts a couple times, you learn to take precautionary measures.) Don't assume that just because you've chosen a profession to do right and help others that you can't get hurt in more ways than one. Make sure you have insurance and immediate access to representation that will help protect your interests.

When complainers go after your company, agency, organization, or senior leaders, you can expect that many within your organization might start circling the wagons. If you are also involved, you could be the scapegoat or sacrificial lamb. So if you have not already secured your fortress, put it on your to-do list.

Preparing for the Future

TIP: I'm not including a section on financial planning in this chapter. But believe it or not, one day that Superman cape will come off and you will start getting old. Guess what? Those little kids you have today or might have in the future are going to grow up in the blink of an eye—and you'll be on the hook for their college education (and room and board). Many older folks have expensive medical and prescription drug bills that insurance and social programs don't cover. Make sure you maximize your retirement contributions as well as your children's college education savings. Save for retirement and keep adding to your rainy day fund. Pay your house off as soon as you can, and don't live beyond your means. If you do all that, you won't need a lot of (expensive premium) life insurance when in your 50s, 60s, or 70s. Plus, you might actually be later able to enjoy your golden years.

NOTE: My uncle, who was a World War II veteran and former police officer, and had all kinds of medical problems when he was in his late 70s but maintained his incredible sense of humor. He said, "If I could get my hands around the neck of the guy who called these 'golden years,' I'd strangle him!"

Teddy Roosevelt

In addition to being the twenty-sixth President of the United States from 1901 to 1909, Teddy Roosevelt also served as president of the Board of the New York City Police Commissioners in the mid-1890s. Described as "an iron-willed leader of impeachable honesty," Roosevelt made radical changes in the city police department. He implemented policies for police officers that included annual physical examinations and regular inspections of firearms. He also established meritorious service medals and had telephones installed in police stations. Roosevelt created a bicycle squad to enforce traffic violations, established new disciplinary rules, and cracked down on police corruption.

Wouldn't we all enjoy the opportunity to work with and for someone like Teddy Roosevelt today? In my early days in law enforcement, my older brother, who previously enlisted in the U.S. Army during the Vietnam War and later served as a metropolitan police officer, provided me with a small sheet of paper with a copied quotation from Teddy Roosevelt. I carried it in my wallet or law enforcement credentials case for many years. As I mentioned, I also tacked a copy of it on my wall by my desk. (In fact, it's in front of my computer as I type these words.)

In closing this writing, I can think of no better way to end it than by providing one of President Roosevelt's most inspiring quotations:

> It is not the critic who counts; not the man who points out how the strong man stumbles, or where the doer of deeds could have done them better. The credit belongs to the man who is actually in the arena, whose face is marred by dust and sweat and blood; who strives valiantly; who errs, who comes short again and again, because there is no effort without error and shortcoming; but who does actually strive to do the deeds; who knows great enthusiasms, the great devotions; who spends himself in a worthy cause; who at the best knows in the end the triumph of high achievement, and who at the worst, if he fails, at least fails while daring greatly, so that his place shall never be with those cold and timid souls who neither know victory nor defeat.

Conclusion

The previous pages have provided guidance on how to plan and conduct thorough and complete investigations drawn from my own 30-plus years of professional investigative experience. I recognize that every investigation cannot be initiated or conducted with the intent of immediately expanding the investigative effort. However, after reading and absorbing the information provided, you will at least now be able to think along those lines most of the time. Even time-sensitive investigations can be expanded on later when time and resources permit.

Exhibit C.1 outlines the, "Piper Method" of conducting thorough and complete investigations. It can serve as a guide for your future investigative efforts.

Application of the methodologies, techniques, and/or guidance described in this book, combined with other experience and training, should greatly benefit not only investigators and fraud fighters but also their agencies and organizations as well as the individuals and assets being protected.

Whenever possible, investigators and fraud fighters should strive to kill two birds with one stone and avoid reinventing the wheel. By maximizing the use of resources and minimizing expenditures, you'll

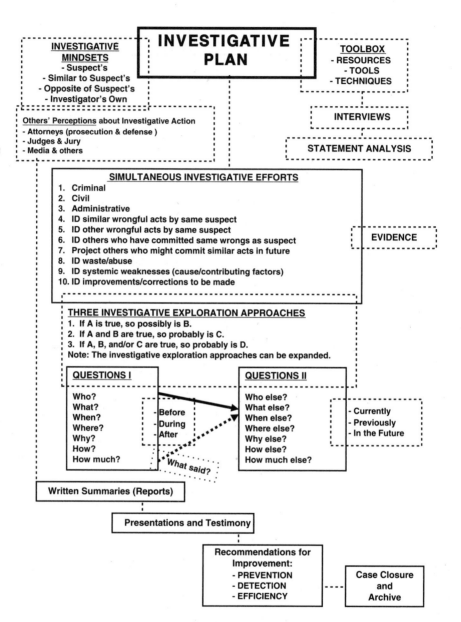

Exhibit C.1   Piper Method of Conducting Thorough and Complete Investigations

be able to get more bang for your buck. By conducting investigations with strong ethics and a commitment to the cause, you'll be able to walk the walk and talk the talk. Remember: "A good investigator can connect the dots, but a great investigator can find the dots to connect."

When you set out to conduct investigations with passion, integrity, and grit you'll undoubtedly end up with enough war stories to fill a book. I hope you've enjoyed and learned from some of mine. Trust me, there's many more to be told.

Appendix
Samples of Case
Presentation Visual Aids

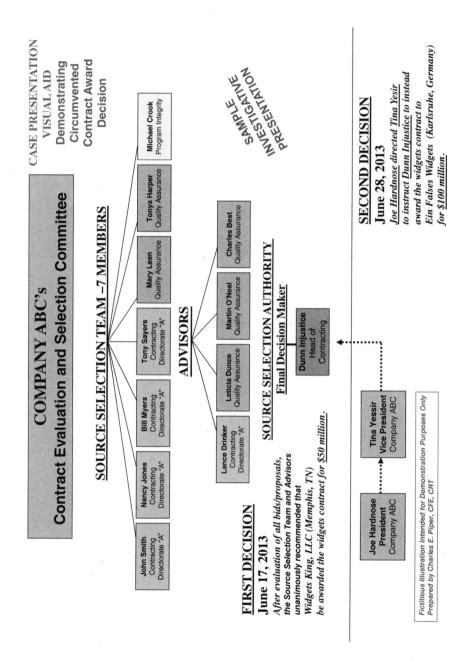

CASE PRESENTATION
VISUAL AID
Demonstrating
Circumvented
Contract Award
Decision

COMPANY ABC's
Contract Evaluation and Selection Committee

SOURCE SELECTION TEAM –7 MEMBERS

| John Smith Contracting Directorate "A" | Nancy Jones Contracting Directorate "A" | Bill Myers Contracting Directorate "A" | Tony Sayers Contracting Directorate "A" | Mary Lean Quality Assurance | Tonya Harper Quality Assurance | Michael Crook Program Integrity |

ADVISORS

| Lance Drinker Contracting Directorate "A" | Leticia Dunce Quality Assurance | Martin O'Neal Quality Assurance | Charles Best Quality Assurance |

SOURCE SELECTION AUTHORITY
Final Decision Maker

Dunn Injustice
Head of Contracting

SAMPLE
INVESTIGATIVE
PRESENTATION

FIRST DECISION
June 17, 2013

After evaluation of all bids/proposals,
the Source Selection Team and Advisors
unanimously recommended that
Widgets King, LLC (Memphis, TN)
be awarded the widgets contract for $50 million.

SECOND DECISION
June 28, 2013

Joe Hardnose directed Tina Yesir
to instruct Dunn Injustice to instead
award the widgets contract to
Ein Falses Widgets (Karlsruhe, Germany)
for $100 million.

Joe Hardnose
President
Company ABC

Tina Yessir
Vice President
Company ABC

Fictitious Illustration Intended for Demonstration Purposes Only
Prepared by Charles E. Piper, CFE, CRT

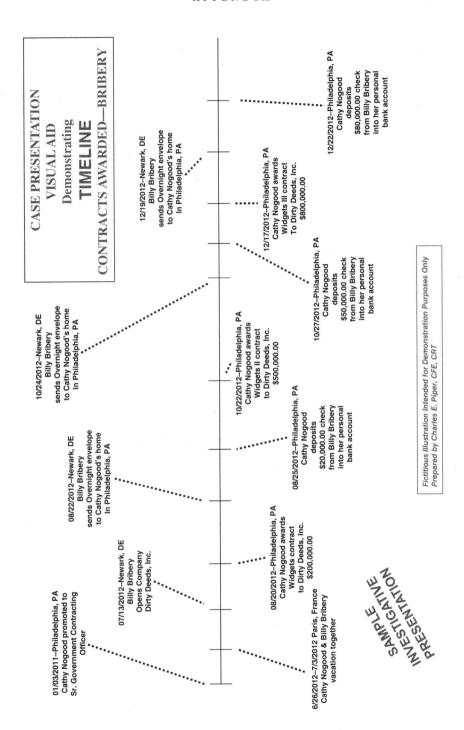

CASE PRESENTATION
VISUAL AID
Demonstrating
TIMELINE
CONTRACTS AWARDED—BRIBERY

*Fictitious Illustration Intended for Demonstration Purposes Only
Prepared by Charles E. Piper, CFE, CRT*

SAMPLE
INVESTIGATIVE
PRESENTATION

01/03/2011–Philadelphia, PA
Cathy Nogood promoted to
Sr. Government Contracting
Officer

07/13/2012–Newark, DE
Billy Bribery
Opens Company
Dirty Deeds, Inc.

08/22/2012–Newark, DE
Billy Bribery
sends Overnight envelope
to Cathy Nogood's home
In Philadelphia, PA

10/24/2012–Newark, DE
Billy Bribery
sends Overnight envelope
to Cathy Nogood's home
In Philadelphia, PA

12/19/2012–Newark, DE
Billy Bribery
sends Overnight envelope
to Cathy Nogood's home
In Philadelphia, PA

6/26/2012–7/3/2012 Paris, France
Cathy Nogood & Billy Bribery
vacation together

08/20/2012–Philadelphia, PA
Cathy Nogood awards
Widgets contract
to Dirty Deeds, Inc.
$200,000.00

08/25/2012–Philadelphia, PA
Cathy Nogood
deposits
$20,000.00 check
from Billy Bribery
into her personal
bank account

10/22/2012–Philadelphia, PA
Cathy Nogood awards
Widgets II contract
to Dirty Deeds, Inc.
$500,000.00

10/27/2012–Philadelphia, PA
Cathy Nogood
deposits
$50,000.00 check
from Billy Bribery
into her personal
bank account

12/17/2012–Philadelphia, PA
Cathy Nogood awards
Widgets III contract
To Dirty Deeds, Inc.
$800,000.00

12/22/2012–Philadelphia, PA
Cathy Nogood
deposits
$80,000.00 check
from Billy Bribery
into her personal
bank account

CASE PRESENTATION
VISUAL AID
Demonstrating
No Supportive Documents
for Healthcare Billings

**DOCTOR I. DONTCARE'S
MEDICAL TREATMENT CENTER
MIAMI, FL**

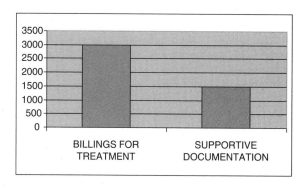

SAMPLE HEALTHCARE FRAUD INVESTIGATIVE PRESENTATION

**TIME PERIOD:
January 1, 2012
through
December 31, 2012**

3,000 Claims Submitted
1,500 Supportive Documentation

Fictitious Illustration Intended for Demonstration Purposes Only Prepared by Charles E. Piper, CFE, CRT

SAMPLE INVESTIGATIVE PRESENTATION

**1234 Liar Circle
Nashville, Tennessee 12345**

CASE PRESENTATION
VISUAL AID
Demonstrating
Three Businesses
Using One Address

Bad Parts, Inc.
Incorporated in TN: 1/3/2011
Pres & Sect & Treas: Bubba Boozer
Reg Agent: C. Ya Later
ACTIVE
Corp #:XXXXX-2011

Bubba Boozer Widgets, Inc.
Incorporated in TN: 12/5/2011
Pres & Reg Agent: Bubba Boozer
Sect & Treas: Mrs. Bubbet Boozer
ACTIVE
Corp #:XXXXX-2011

Nashy Electronics, LLC
Incorporated in TN: 8/8/12
Pres: Bubba Boozer
Sect: Mrs. Bubbet Boozer
Reg Agent: C. Ya Later
ACTIVE
Corp #: XXXXX-2012

THREE BUSINESSES AT ONE ADDRESS

Fictitious Illustration Intended for Demonstration Purposes Only Prepared by Charles E. Piper, CFE, CRT

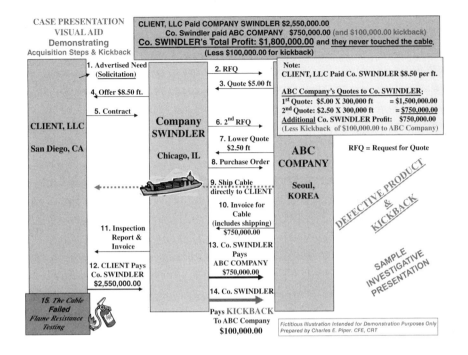

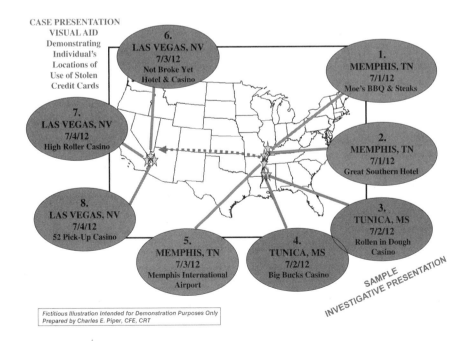

1. **2/25/2013**: Cash from "Company A" in New York deposited into bank account in Switzerland.
2. **3/1/2013**: Money wire transferred from bank account in Switzerland to bank account in Cayman Islands.

CASE PRESENTATION
VISUAL AID
Demonstrating
International
Movement of Funds

Fictitious Illustration Intended for Demonstration Purposes Only
Prepared by Charles E. Piper, CFE, CRT

CASE PRESENTATION
VISUAL AID
Demonstrating
Sudden Increased Laboratory Testing at Lot # 10

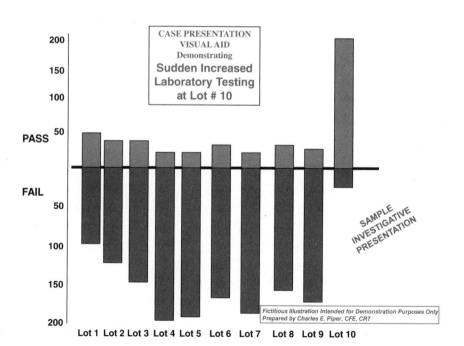

Fictitious Illustration Intended for Demonstration Purposes Only
Prepared by Charles E. Piper, CFE, CRT

ASSOCIATION OF CRIMINALS' ACTIVITY

Tom Tie   Joe Cool   Mark May   Richard Roe   Danny Dark   Billy Beard

SAMPLE INVESTIGATIVE PRESENTATION

Tokyo, Japan
3/3/2012
Cool & May Arrested
Counterfeit Credit Cards

Seattle, WA
6/3/2012
Tie & Dark Arrested
Bank Fraud

New York, NY
6/3/2012
Roe & Beard Arrested
Drug Sales

Los Angeles, CA
1/2/2013
Tie & Cool Arrested
Bank Fraud

Dallas, TX
1/2/2013
May & Roe Arrested
Drug Sales

New Orleans, LA
1/2/2012
Dark & Beard Arrested
Armed Robbery

CASE PRESENTATION
VISUAL AID
Demonstrating
Suspects'
Association
&
Previous Arrests

Fictitious Illustration Intended for Demonstration Purposes Only
Prepared by Charles E. Piper, CFE, CRT

About the Author

Charles Piper is a certified fraud examiner (CFE), private investigator (PI), consultant, trainer, and retired federal agent. He has over 35 years of successful investigative experience in the public and private sectors. Piper has conducted investigations from coast to coast and in Europe resulting in criminal and civil prosecutions of wrongdoers and the recovery of millions of dollars. As a federal agent, Piper conducted numerous large-scale and high-profile investigations. Several of these investigations received repeated national media coverage. Piper also provided investigative assistance into the September 11, 2001 terrorist attacks on America.

Prior to operating as a PI and consultant, Piper served for several decades in law enforcement. He got his start in the U.S. Army in the Military Police Corps and was promoted to the rank of sergeant, where he served as a patrol supervisor and Military Police investigator. His seven years of military service included two-and-a-half years in Germany. Piper next served as a metropolitan police officer, supervisory detective, and for over 20 years as a federal agent, where his office assignments included: Memphis, Tennessee; Orlando, Florida; and Las Vegas, Nevada.

Piper has led federal investigative taskforces and participated in joint investigations with numerous federal, state, local, and private industry investigative agencies. Those federal agencies included: the Federal Bureau of Investigation; the U.S. Immigration and Customs Enforcement; the Bureau of Alcohol, Tobacco, Firearms and Explosives; the Central Intelligence Agency; the U.S. Postal Inspection Service; U.S. Army Criminal Investigation Command; Air Force Office of Special Investigations; Naval Criminal Investigative Service; U.S. Secret Service; and others. He has also worked with federal agents from numerous Offices of Inspector General, including the Department of Defense, National Aeronautics and Space Administration, Health and Human Services, Department of Labor, Office of Personnel Management, Social Security Administration, and Veterans Administration.

Piper has received numerous awards and other recognition for investigative excellence, including Special Agent of the Year, Teamwork Award, Military Policeman of the Year (Runner-up), and the U.S. Army Commendation Medal. He also received special recognition for successfully investigating defective critical products utilized by the Department of Defense and the recovery of millions of dollars in fraud against the government. Currently serving as a PI and consultant with an office in West Tennessee, he provides investigative assistance to attorneys, business entities, and individuals in the United States and occasionally abroad.

As well as being a CFE, Piper is a graduate of three law enforcement/investigative academies (military, state, and federal) and is certified in the Reid Technique of Interview and Interrogation. He has provided training to law enforcement officers, investigators, fraud examiners, government employees, contractors, private sector employees, business owners, attorneys, and college students. As a business owner, Piper also provides anti-fraud and other types of training to various groups and professional associations and has even provided ethics training to law enforcement officers and fraud examiners.

Piper has authored several articles regarding fraud and investigations that have been published in trade journals, such as *Fraud Magazine*

(Association of Certified Fraud Examiners) and *Professional Investigator Magazine.* He is a member of these associations:

- Association of Certified Fraud Examiners
- Association of Certified Fraud Specialists
- Federal Law Enforcement Officers Association
- The Reid Institute
- The Tennessee Association of Investigators
- Memphis Bar Association

For more information, visit: www.piper-pi.com

Index